FIRST
FREEDOM

"Baptists have always been at the forefront in the fight for religious liberty, noting the high stakes involved in the battle. The very able stable of scholars in this volume continue the fight with biblical fidelity, historical awareness, and cultural sensitivity. What they ask for themselves they would ask for all. I hold out hope that their just cry still might be heard."

—**Daniel L. Akin**, president, Southeastern Baptist Theological Seminary

"Nearly every week, the news informs us of new threats to religious liberty at home and abroad. In America, many fear this first freedom is becoming an endangered species as our culture's idols of sex, money, and power converge increasingly against the free exercise of religion. For this reason, I'm grateful for this new edition of *First Freedom*. This second edition includes several timely new essays that strategically update an already helpful book. The result is a 'tract for the times' for Baptists and others who champion a free church in a free state and advocate for the religious liberty of Christians and other groups who suffer under foreign regimes that persecute religious outliers. I will be returning to some of the chapters frequently as I think through what it means to defend religious freedom until that day when every knee bows and every tongue confesses that Jesus Christ is Lord, to the glory of God the Father."

—**Nathan A. Finn**, dean of the School of Theology and Missions and
professor of Christian thought and tradition, Union University

"Historically, Americans have embraced freedom of religion, not merely freedom of worship. The former fosters freedom to practice one's religion in the church and the culture. The latter restricts the practice of religion to the confines of the church. As religious liberties erode in America, *First Freedom* is a refreshing resource presenting pertinent information for all to consider regarding this seminal topic."

—**Steve Gaines**, president, Southern Baptist Convention,
and senior pastor, Bellevue Baptist Church

"Religious liberty has been a foundational component since the formative years of our country. However, many Christians are ill informed about the assault upon their freedom as American citizens. This updated edition of *First Freedom* is a timely work that exposes the areas in which our religious freedoms are being threatened. In it, a number of well-respected Southern Baptist leaders help us better comprehend the biblical foundation and history of religious liberty, identify the current challenges we face, and provide ways to move forward in today's culture. After reading this book, you will feel confident to stand firm in the face of adversity and defend the religious freedoms our country was founded upon."

—**Robby Gallaty**, senior pastor, Long Hollow Baptist Church, and author, *Growing Up* and *Rediscovering Discipleship*

"It is difficult to exaggerate the historical importance of the Baptist witness to religious liberty. This immensely valuable collection of essays carries that witness forward, addressing new challenges to the rights of conscience presented by early twenty-first-century liberal secularism. The spiritual ancestors of the contributors to the volume would be as proud of them as I am grateful to them for placing their impressive intellectual gifts at the service of our first freedom."

—**Robert P. George**, McCormick Professor of Jurisprudence, Princeton University

"It is rare that a book and a moment perfectly meet, but that is what I believe has happened with the publication of *First Freedom: The Beginning and End of Religious Liberty*. Historically, Baptists have championed religious liberty for all citizens, believing that religious liberty is not a majoritarian right or a gift of government, but an inalienable right for all citizens. Presently in America, religious freedom is increasingly threatened as governmental authorities steadily attempt to compel people of all faiths to compromise their beliefs or face legal consequences. It is past time for the American Christian church in general, and Baptists in particular, to reclaim our theological and historical commitment to religious liberty in order to face the unique challenges of our day. This excellent collection of essays should be in the hands of every pastor, informed layman, and public servant in our nation."

—**David E. Prince**, pastor of preaching and vision, Ashland Avenue Baptist Church, and assistant professor of Christian preaching, The Southern Baptist Theological Seminary

"Religious liberty in America faces an uncertain and imperiled future. The great battles for religious liberty in the past continue today in the courtrooms and public square as we contend for the right to live and speak our faith freely. This book is an excellent resource for believers to be informed about religious liberty so they can take their place in helping to defend it both now and for future generations."

—**Erik W. Stanley**, senior counsel and director of the Center for Christian Ministries, Alliance Defending Freedom

Jason G. Duesing, Thomas White,
and Malcolm B. Yarnell III

FIRST FREEDOM

✝ ✝ ✝ ✝

THE BEGINNING AND END OF
RELIGIOUS LIBERTY

SECOND EDITION

ACADEMIC

Nashville, Tennessee

This volume is dedicated
to the saints of God
who gave their lives
to gain the religious liberty
that we enjoy and defend today.

The blood of the martyrs is the seed of the church.
—Tertullian

CONTENTS

ACKNOWLEDGMENTS

The original edition of *First Freedom* (2007) was born out of the first Baptist Distinctives conference held at Southwestern Baptist Theological Seminary in September 2005. Since that time, a decade has passed, and issues of religious liberty have only increased as matters of concern. National conversations have arisen from recent clashes between sexual freedom and religious freedom as well as from the 2016 presidential election debates. The time has come for an updated edition.

This volume would not exist were it not for the effort of Southwestern Baptist Theological Seminary and its leadership, which had the foresight to address this issue back in 2005. The editors wish to express their deep appreciation to the administration of Southwestern Seminary and those involved in the initial conference as well as the support for Malcolm Yarnell to again participate in this revised edition.

For the time and support to work on this project, we extend a thank-you to Midwestern Baptist Theological Seminary, where Jason Duesing serves as provost and associate professor of historical theology, and to Cedarville University, where Thomas White serves as president and professor of theology.

This project represents something amazing. It represents what occurs when Baptists come together to focus on a common cause and present a unified front. Three seminaries, one university, the Ethics and Religious Liberty Commission, and a Baptist publishing house have joined forces to present information on one of the most important issues of our time, and we appreciate the support from leaders who serve at these institutions.

We are especially thankful to B&H Academic for its investment in the second edition of this project. Audrey Greeson continuously helped overextended and well-intentioned leaders to stay on track with this project.

Finally, we want to express our appreciation to countless believers who have given their lives throughout history, leading to the freedom that we enjoy that allows us to craft such a volume. We stand on their shoulders and continue the witness of many who paid the ultimate price for King Jesus. We wish to do our part to maintain and defend the freedom to spread the Good News that Jesus Christ is Lord and this gospel is available for all who will repent and believe in him.

INTRODUCTION

The Beginning of Religious Liberty

Jason G. Duesing

When Thomas Jefferson replied in 1802 to a letter from the Danbury Baptist Association on the topic of the freedom of religion, he likely did not realize the weight that its most well-known phrase would carry. The phrase was a "wall of separation between church and state"—and if Jefferson did not have a full grasp of his intended meaning, the subsequent generations have labored to supply it for him—but without unanimity.[1]

A Wall Built

Whether or not Jefferson foresaw the impact his words would have, he clearly meant to protect the free practice of religion and to counteract the continued establishment of state churches. In that sense, Jefferson's

---

[1] Thomas Jefferson, "To the Danbury Baptist Association," January 1, 1802, in *The Papers of Thomas Jefferson* (Princeton: Princeton University Press, 2009), 36:258, https://jeffersonpapers.princeton.edu/selected-documents/danbury-baptist-association-0.

wall has served as a foundation of the history of religious freedom in the United States.[2]

The building of the wall has origins in the sixteenth-century Reformation and the expansion of the Reformation among English dissenting believers—some of whom traveled to the New World in the seventeenth century.[3] The state-church system extended to the colonies as well, and thus the building of the wall endured many stoppages. With the dawn of the eighteenth century and the Great Awakening of the 1730s, the connection between the state and church grew wider, making way for new ideas about religious liberty.

The conclusion of the French and Indian War in 1763 brought further economic and political tensions between the British motherland and the colonists that resulted in a tea party in Boston and the forming of the First Continental Congress. The colonists declared and won their independence, and, among many new ideas for this nation, the ground was cleared for the wall of separation to arise.

As Thomas Kidd and Matthew Harris note, "The two most celebrated confrontations over religious establishment and religious liberty took place in Massachusetts and Virginia."[4] Key building blocks in the formation of the wall of separation followed. In Massachusetts, a Baptist pastor and mobilizer for disestablishment, Isaac Backus, wrote *An Appeal to the Public for Religious Liberty* in 1773. Following the war, in 1786, Thomas

---

[2] For the following brief overview, I was helped immensely by editors Matthew L. Harris and Thomas S. Kidd, *The Founding Fathers and the Debate over Religion in Revolutionary America* (Oxford: Oxford University Press, 2012). See also Thomas S. Kidd, *God of Liberty: A Religious History of the American Revolution* (New York: Basic Books, 2010); William G. McLoughlin, *New England Dissent, 1630–1833: The Baptists and the Separation of Church and State* (Cambridge, MA: Harvard University Press, 1971); Philip Hamburger, *Separation of Church and State* (Cambridge, MA: Harvard University Press, 2002); and Nicholas P. Miller, *The Religious Roots of the First Amendment* (Oxford: Oxford University Press, 2012).

[3] For more on the role of Anabaptist and Baptist leaders like Balthasar Hubmaier, Thomas Helwys, and Roger Williams, see Thomas White's first chapter in this volume. See also E. B. Underhill, *Struggles and Triumphs of Religious Liberty* (New York: Lewis Colby, 1851).

[4] Harris and Kidd, *Founding Fathers*, 12. For the significant role played by Baptists in South Carolina such as William Screven, Oliver Hart, and Richard Furman, see Malcolm Yarnell's chapter in this volume.

Jefferson introduced his bill, the *Act for Establishing Religious Freedom*, that brought an end to the state-established church in Virginia.

Once the Constitution was ratified, its first amendment, adopted in 1791, ensured the free exercise of religion on the national level. Still, states like Connecticut and Massachusetts refused to fully adopt the disestablishment partition. Enter John Leland, friend of Thomas Jefferson and James Madison and another Baptist pastor and spokesman for religious liberty. In that same year, Leland published his influential *The Rights of Conscience Inalienable*. As Kidd and Harris note, "Although Leland and Jefferson held very different personal religious beliefs, they both agreed that full religious freedom was an essential component of American liberty."[5]

Upon Jefferson's election as president in 1801, the Baptists in Danbury, Connecticut, wrote him sharing that "they hoped that Jefferson's victory might signal a rising tide of religious liberty that would ultimately transform the New England states into bastions of freedom."[6] In reply, Jefferson famously reflected that, with the approval of the First Amendment, the American people built "a wall of separation between church and state."[7] By 1821, Connecticut no longer held to state-established religion. Massachusetts was the last state to recognize the wall but did so on November 11, 1833.

The Baptist Mr. Underhill

Earl Grey, the cost of turnips, and the early crowds milling about the shops of High Street were probably the only things on Edward Bean Underhill's mind on that November morning in 1833. Unbeknownst to Mr. Underhill, the conclusion of these significant strides forward in the struggle for religious freedom had taken place an ocean away.[8] Underhill,

---

[5] Harris and Kidd, *Founding Fathers*, 20.

[6] "From the Danbury Baptist Association," after October 7, 1801, in *The Papers of Thomas Jefferson*, 36:407–9, https://jeffersonpapers.princeton.edu/selected-documents/danbury-baptist-association.

[7] Jefferson, "To the Danbury Baptist Association," *Papers*, 36:258, https://jeffersonpapers.princeton.edu/selected-documents/danbury-baptist-association-0.

[8] Not to be confused with another Mr. Underhill from Britain famously invented by J. R. R. Tolkien as the pseudonym given to protect his protagonist at the start of his journey (see *The Fellowship of the Ring*, "The Shadow of the Past").

a grocer in Oxford, England, like his father before him, had yet to leave his imprint on the heritage of Baptists and religious liberty at this time when Baptists in America were celebrating. Soon thereafter, however, his wife's health-related issues caused Underhill to leave his occupation as well as the city of spires to devote "himself to the study of the history of the Baptist denomination."[9] Underhill would learn well of the beginnings and ongoing Baptist struggle for religious liberty.

The produce of Underhill's new labors culminated in his chief contribution to Baptist heritage, the founding of the Hanserd Knollys Society.[10] This society published early works of significant Baptist writers, focusing on the advancement of religious liberty. At the beginning of several of the ten total volumes published between 1846 and 1854, Underhill penned a continuous historical survey, later published in one volume as *Struggles and Triumphs of Religious Liberty*, which chronicled the advocates of the "rights of conscience," many of whom were Baptists, from the time of Henry VIII to the settlement of New England.[11]

Underhill saw these Baptists, and rightly so, as heroes worthy of honor because they "sounded the note of freedom for conscience as man's birthright" even while paying the ultimate price with "holy tears and the martyr's blood."[12] Underhill's survey of Baptists' role in the advance of religious

---

[9] W. B. Owen, "Underhill, Edward Bean (1813–1901)," rev. Brian Stanley, *Oxford Dictionary of National Biography* (Oxford: Oxford University Press, 2004).

[10] In addition to these early historical studies, Underhill would have a significant career as secretary of the Baptist Missionary Society and later president of the Baptist Union in England.

[11] The Hanserd Knollys Society published ten volumes from 1846 to 1854, including *Tracts on Liberty of Conscience*, vol. 1, and Roger Williams's *The Bloudy Tenet of Persecution*, vol. 3 (London: Hanserd Knollys Society), Archives, A. W. Roberts Library of Southwestern Baptist Theological Seminary (Fort Worth, TX). In 1851, Lewis Colby Publishers in New York reprinted Underhill's introductions to volumes 1, 2, and 4 under the title *Struggles and Triumphs of Religious Liberty. An Historical Survey of Controversies Pertaining to the Rights of Conscience, from the English Reformation to the Settlement of New England*. Citing Underhill's introductions as works of "great historical value," Lewis Colby explained in the preface that "it is to be regretted, that they have attained no wider circulation in this country."

[12] Underhill, *Struggles and Triumphs*, 201.

liberty served to remind his readers of the price that was paid for their freedom and to challenge them in the ongoing protecting and promoting of the freedom of religion for all.

First Freedom

Following the example of Underhill, the editors of this volume have sought in this new edition to revise and gather anew a collection of essays from current Baptist authors of note for the purpose of edifying and encouraging local churches, their pastors, and citizens at large in their understanding of the gift of religious liberty. Before interacting with current religious liberty concerns in America and beyond, this volume first presents the biblical and historical foundations for religious liberty.

Paige Patterson provides this volume with a biblical foundation as he seeks to answer the question of whether the positions of religious liberty and the exclusivity of salvation in Jesus Christ are coterminous or paradoxical. With a characteristically clever style, Patterson vividly displays his penchant for making the Scriptures come alive. Interacting with the Anabaptists of the Radical Reformation, Patterson gives a clear and biblical answer to the question of supposed paradox.

Thomas White follows Patterson's biblical introduction with the second of the three historical treatments. White lays the historical foundation for religious liberty by portraying the advancement of the doctrine from the Swiss and South German Anabaptists to the early Baptists in England and America. Of special significance is the contribution White makes by outlining six areas of agreement among these early Baptists on the freedom of religion, each offered in its respective context.

Malcolm Yarnell continues the historical inquiry by giving a sweeping yet thorough look at the traditions that shaped the expressions of the relationships between religious liberty and political involvement among Southern Baptists. He distinguishes between the Virginia tradition and the South Carolina tradition of political theology. Yarnell's chapter specifically serves the twenty-first-century reader as he clarifies the multifaceted religio-political concerns competing among Baptists in America that often confuse rather than instruct.

The second set of three chapters provides a "Religious Liberty 101"–style introduction. First, Barrett Duke's chapter on the Christian doctrine of religious liberty carefully argues that the doctrine of religious liberty is, in essence, a biblical articulation of a fundamental human right. Duke sets the stage for the chapters that follow by providing several definitions of religious liberty, including the entire article from the Baptist Faith and Message 2000.

Evan Lenow's chapter on the relationship of religious liberty to the gospel introduces the biblical and historical foundations and concludes by helping the reader think through practical implications for present-day living, including the way religious liberty should motivate people to share the gospel.

Andrew T. Walker concludes this section with a solid introduction to the relationship of religious liberty and the public square. Asking and answering how religion should interact with the institutions of culture, Walker examines the challenges to religious liberty and then provides constructive proposals for how to strengthen the cause of religious liberty.

The final section includes four chapters that survey current challenges to religious liberty. Russell Moore reminds the reader that the struggle for religious liberty can be reduced to a simple matter of priority: Christ before culture. His chapter combines alacrity, wit, and a truth-telling edge as no stone in our contemporary garden of Conservative Christianity is left unturned.

R. Albert Mohler Jr. contributes an incisive look at how religious freedom relates to the constantly evolving sexual revolution. With the legislation of same-sex marriage and the inevitable conflict between erotic and religious liberty, Mohler inspires and summons readers to action.

Thomas White addresses the unique religious liberty concerns facing Christian institutions of higher education. Discussing tax-exempt status, Title VII, Title IX, sexual orientation and transgender identity, accreditation concerns, and athletics, White provides an extensive overview of the many challenges facing these schools. He concludes with practical steps schools should take to protect and defend religious liberty on their campuses.

Travis Wussow, uniquely equipped in both training and vocation, opens a window for Americans to view the wider threats to religious freedom around the globe, especially in majority-Muslim countries. Specifically, he helps believers in the United States understand what they can do to help brothers and sisters in Christ suffering in countries where religious liberty is threatened or nonexistent.

The book's conclusion reminds readers that, regardless of the current threats and uncertainties regarding the state of religious liberty, the citizens of earth will one day see opportunities for religious freedom come to an end, and this should inform how they live in the present.

The purpose of this collection of essays, therefore, is first to provide an introductory look at the biblical and historical beginnings of religious liberty, and then also at several instances of its contemporary expression and defense. Second, however, both the editors and the contributors wish to play the role of Edward Bean Underhill—and many other historians like him—by reminding believers in the twenty-first century of the price that was paid by their Baptist brothers and sisters for the establishment and defense of religious liberty. To be sure, Providence used people of various religious and denominational preferences to implement the religious freedoms now enjoyed by all, but it would be a travesty for Baptists to overlook the contribution of their own. Underhill said it well:

> Thus the [B]aptists became the first and only propounders of "absolute liberty, just and true liberty, equal and impartial liberty."[13] For this they suffered and died. They proclaimed it by their deeds, they propagated it in their writings. In almost every country of Europe, amid tempests of wrath, stirred up by their faith, and their manly adherence to truth, they were the indefatigable, consistent primal apostles of liberty in this latter age. We honor them.[14]

---

[13] Underhill notes that a portion of this sentence is from "Locke on Toleration, p. 31, 4 to. ed.," *Struggles and Triumphs*, 201. The location of Underhill's inset quotation marks here are of significant historical significance, as many later historians and Baptists regrettably failed to notice this distinction and claimed the entire sentence as Locke's. However, as Conrad Henry Moehlman reveals, nothing could be further from the sentiments of the mind of Locke, who apparently did not hold Baptists and other dissenters in high regard. See Moehlman, "The Baptists Revise John Locke," *The Journal of Religion* 18:2 (April 1938): 174–82.

[14] Underhill, *Struggles and Triumphs*, 201.

May those who read this volume not only honor those who defended religious liberty from the beginning but also the Creator who made them and redeemed them. May this volume also stir many into a similar service of enthusiastic proclamation and defense of this freedom until our Creator and Redeemer returns in the day when religious liberty comes to an end.

Jason G. Duesing
May 2016

PART 1

RELIGIOUS LIBERTY IN HISTORY

CHAPTER 1

MUTUALLY EXCLUSIVE OR BIBLICALLY HARMONIOUS?

Religious Liberty and Exclusivity
of Salvation in Jesus Christ

Paige Patterson

Is it possible for one to hold to an exclusive view of salvation—i.e., Jesus and Jesus alone can save, and no one can be saved outside of conscious faith in Jesus, the Christ—and still be a proponent of religious liberty? Or is the possibility of religious liberty nullified or imperiled once one takes such an exclusivist position? This chapter attempts to answer that question. To set the stage, I begin with an illustration from personal experience.

Some years ago I appeared regularly on a nationwide program called *The American Religious Town Hall Meeting.* On this occasion a Roman Catholic priest; a Jewish rabbi; a Methodist bishop; an Episcopalian priest; a Seventh-day Adventist, who was the moderator of the meeting; and I

11

were participants. Usually I found the whole group pitted against me. What frustrated my colleagues endlessly was my insistence that salvation comes only through explicit faith in Jesus Christ.

What really made things interesting on this day occurred when the discussion turned to the question of exclusivism. The Roman Catholic priest looked at me and pointed to the Jewish rabbi and said, "You admit that he is a good man?"

I replied, "Absolutely, I do."

"You admit that he is your friend?"

"Absolutely, he is my friend."

"You admit that he is a faithful shepherd of his flock?"

"Well, I have not had the opportunity to observe that, but I would be shocked if it were any other way."

"But you will say that if he does not come to Christ and accept him as Messiah and as Lord he will go to hell?"

I knew that with the way things were staged I was going to be in trouble no matter what I did. So I replied, "Well, you need to understand that he is hardly the only one on this panel about whom I am concerned." When I said that, the place virtually exploded, and the three-ring circus was underway. After the show, one of the questions the panel continued to ask was, "How can you claim to be an advocate of religious liberty and hold the position that all who are outside of Christ are lost?"

This legitimate question is one I intend to answer in two ways. First, I will look at the biblical witness. Admittedly I will be carrying coals to Newcastle since most of those likely to read this book know the Scriptures. Why, then, carry coals to Newcastle? Is it because Newcastle hasn't enough coal? No, but our Southern Baptist "Newcastle" may in recent times have forgotten to stoke the fires found in God's Word with regard to these questions. Therefore, carrying the coals again to Newcastle serves to stoke those fires and get them burning once again concerning this issue of exclusivity and religious liberty. Second, I will present some incidents from the sixteenth-century Anabaptists who prominently held to Christ alone for salvation but who were at the same time the strongest possible advocates of religious liberty.

The Biblical Witness

Jesus and Exclusivism

The biblical witness can be divided into two areas: the witness of Jesus and the witness of the remainder of the New Testament. In the context of the Fourth Gospel, was our Lord an exclusivist? Did he believe that all other religious claims contrary to his own were false, and did he believe that his own position was true and indeed the only way of salvation?

In the meeting of Jesus with the woman of Samaria, she asked serious questions about the appropriate location of worship, juxtaposing the view of the Samaritans over against the view of the Jews. Jesus responded, "Believe Me, woman, an hour is coming when you will worship the Father neither on this mountain nor in Jerusalem" (John 4:21). And then he said, provocatively, "You Samaritans worship what you do not know. We worship what we do know, because salvation is from the Jews" (v. 22).

Regardless of the context in which you might express this idea in a postmodern society, the understanding conveyed by that simple statement would certainly be a great source of irritation for any inclusivist or pluralist listener. Clearly Jesus was not attempting to follow modern, conventional wisdom because in essence he plainly said, "You are mistaken in what you are believing." And then he continued, "We know what we worship. Salvation is of the Jews."

A discussion occurred between Jesus and the Pharisees, and Jesus responded to their questions:

> "Even if I testify about Myself," Jesus replied, "My testimony is valid, because I know where I came from and where I'm going. But you don't know where I come from or where I'm going. You judge by human standards. I judge no one. And if I do judge, My judgment is true, because I am not alone, but I and the Father who sent Me judge together. Even in your law it is written that the witness of two men is valid. I am the One who testifies about Myself, and the Father who sent Me testifies about Me."
>
> Then they asked Him, "Where is Your Father?"

"You know neither Me nor My Father," Jesus answered. "If you knew Me, you would also know My Father." (John 8:14–19)

That is an exclusive claim, but the Pharisees answered, "Our father is Abraham!" (v. 39).

"If you were Abraham's children," Jesus told them, "you would do what Abraham did. But now you are trying to kill Me, a man who has told you the truth that I heard from God. Abraham did not do this! You're doing what your father does."

"We weren't born of sexual immorality," they said. "We have one Father—God."

Jesus said to them, "If God were your Father, you would love Me, because I came from God and I am here. For I didn't come on My own, but He sent Me. Why don't you understand what I say? Because you cannot listen to My word. You are of your father the Devil, and you want to carry out your father's desires." (vv. 39–44)

Obviously, Jesus was running no popularity contest, then or now. Indeed, what he was saying is clear. Either you know the Father through Jesus, or you do not know the Father. Either you love God through Jesus, or you do not love God. That was a powerful and exclusive declaration then as now.

The man who was blind from birth got into trouble when he was healed by Jesus. At the end of John 9, when Jesus had heard that the Pharisees had cast the man out of the synagogue, Jesus found him and asked, "Do you believe in the Son of Man?"

"Who is He, Sir, that I may believe in Him?" he asked.

Jesus answered, "You have seen Him; in fact, He is the One speaking with you."

"I believe, Lord!" he said, and he worshiped Him.

Jesus said, "I came into this world for judgment, in order that those who do not see will see and those who do see will become blind."

Some of the Pharisees who were with Him heard these things and asked Him, "We aren't blind too, are we?"

"If you were blind," Jesus told them, "you wouldn't have sin. But now that you say, 'We see'—your sin remains." (John 9:35–41)

This language is tough. It clearly establishes Jesus as the only way to the Father. The Pharisees' rejection of Jesus was a rejection of the Father.

This brief study is concluded by a look into the Upper Room Discourse recorded in John 14 where Jesus presented most definitively the exclusivity of the faith that he was inaugurating, in response to a question from Thomas. Jesus told him, "I am the way, the truth, and the life. No one comes to the Father except through Me. If you know Me, you will also know My Father. From now on you do know Him and have seen Him" (vv. 6–7).

How did the disciples see the Father? They saw him revealed in Jesus. Now, when Jesus says, "No one comes to the Father except through Me," all who are Hindu and do not repent and place their faith in Christ alone are excluded. The same is true for Muslims, Buddhists, or anybody who is excluded from salvation because he has not explicitly exercised faith in Jesus. Jesus is making an exclusivist statement.

Jesus and Religious Liberty

However, did Jesus also trumpet the cause of religious liberty? If one could be so exclusive in his view of salvation, could he have also been an advocate of religious liberty? Barrett Duke says in his chapter that there is no clear exclusive declaration of religious liberty in the Bible. I concur with that; but I also believe, and know that he would agree, that the concept is implicit on almost every page of Scripture.

John said to him, "Teacher, we saw someone driving out demons in Your name, and we tried to stop him because he wasn't following us."

"Don't stop him," said Jesus, "because there is no one who will perform a miracle in My name who can soon afterward speak evil of Me. For whoever is not against us is for us. And whoever gives you a cup of water to drink because of My name, since you belong to the Messiah—I assure you: He will never lose his reward." (Mark 9:38–41)

Conceivably one might say that Jesus was talking here about others who are actually his followers though John did not realize they were Jesus' followers. That may well be the case, but, nevertheless, the attitude of the Lord is that one should not interrupt a person's religious practice in a coercive manner. You may confront him with the truth, but you dare not prevent him from his practice.

The favorite Anabaptist passage for defending religious liberty was Jesus' parable in Matthew 13:24–30:

> "The kingdom of heaven may be compared to a man who sowed good seed in his field. But while people were sleeping, his enemy came, sowed weeds among the wheat, and left. When the plants sprouted and produced grain, then the weeds also appeared. The landowner's slaves came to him and said, 'Master, didn't you sow good seed in your field? Then where did the weeds come from?'
>
> "'An enemy did this!' he told them.
>
> "'So, do you want us to go and gather them up?' the slaves asked him.
>
> "'No,' he said. 'When you gather up the weeds, you might also uproot the wheat with them. Let both grow together until the harvest. At harvest time I'll tell the reapers: Gather the weeds first and tie them in bundles to burn them, but store the wheat in my barn.'"

The Anabaptists never tired of pointing out that Jesus said to let the weeds and wheat grow together. Our business is not to remove by coercion that which was sown by the enemy. One may, however, warn them of an impending judgment. A day is coming when there is going to be a call for the reapers to come, and those reapers will take the weeds and burn them in fervent heat, but the wheat will be gathered into the Master's barn. Again, Jesus was apparently taking a position against coercion in matters of religious conscience. Discernment is the responsibility of the church, but judgment belongs only to God.

Another text that supports the New Testament idea of religious liberty is John 18:10–11. The soldiers and officers from the chief priests and Pharisees came to arrest Jesus, and Simon Peter was typically over-reactive. Forgetting that he was outnumbered, he drew his sword and cut off Malchus's ear, though that was doubtless not the object for which he was aiming. Jesus restored the severed ear and said to Peter in verse 11, "Sheathe your sword! Am I not to drink the cup the Father has given Me?" Jesus argued against coercion in matters of religion and forbade Peter's use of coercive means. Jesus consistently resisted the use of force.

Someone might raise a question regarding Jesus' cleansing of the temple (Matthew 21; John 2). The passage is a difficult one for those who advocate pacifism because obviously not only did Jesus make a whip, but he also evidently connected with it. In fact, since I believe Jesus to have been perfect God, I believe he connected perfectly. In sharp distinction to Simon Peter, he had excellent aim. He undoubtedly landed blows, and surely one of the reasons the money changers left with such alacrity was in order to avoid future blows. Therefore, what about Jesus' action in light of the argument for religious liberty?

In the temple, Jesus defended his Father's house as a house of prayer for all nations. He did not forbid those selling from practicing their nefarious trades. He simply said that they were not to do it in his Father's house. Therefore, Jesus did not violate any principle of religious liberty because again, as Peter later made clear, when Jesus was reviled, he did not revile in return. He made no effort to reply. He certainly could have, but he chose not to because he did not exercise coercion in religious matters but rather accepted the sweet providences of God.

The New Testament and Exclusivism

With regard to the rest of the New Testament, the doctrine of the exclusivity of Christ is well represented. Perhaps the clearest statement is found in Peter's address to the Sanhedrin: "There is salvation in no one else, for there is no other name under heaven given to people, and we must be saved by it" (Acts 4:12). When one looks at this passage in conjunction with John 14:6, there is not only a soteriological question but also a Christological question. If Jesus were deceived or deceiving in this claim, he would be unworthy of our worship. If, on the other hand, he is Lord, then we must affirm what he affirms. Was Jesus lying, or was he telling the truth? Peter believed Jesus was telling the truth to the degree that he was willing to say so before the religious officials. If you are really a follower of Jesus Christ, you no longer have an option. You are a religious exclusivist. By definition you have decided that Jesus is the only way of salvation.

Elsewhere we have the account of what happened on Mars Hill: "While Paul was waiting for them in Athens, his spirit was troubled within him when he saw that the city was full of idols. So he reasoned in the synagogue with the Jews and with those who worshiped God and in the marketplace every day with those who happened to be there" (Acts 17:16–17). "Reasoned" (Gk. *dielegeto*) will appear in several other contexts. If one is following Jesus, that is what he will do also. All believers have an evangelistic mandate and imperative to follow Jesus—i.e., the Great Commission. Therefore, daily we should be reasoning with people about Christ.

Picking up again in Acts 17, the Epicureans and the Stoic philosophers encountered Paul.

> Some said, "What is this pseudo-intellectual trying to say?"
>
> Others replied, "He seems to be a preacher of foreign deities"—because he was telling the good news about Jesus and the Resurrection.
>
> They took him and brought him to the Areopagus, and said, "May we learn about this new teaching you're speaking of? For what you say sounds strange to us, and we want to know what these ideas mean." Now all the Athenians and the foreigners residing there spent their time on nothing else but telling or hearing something new.
>
> Then Paul stood in the middle of the Areopagus and said: "Men of Athens! I see that you are extremely religious [Gk. *deisidaimonesterous*] in every respect." For as I was passing through and observing the objects of your worship, I even found an altar on which was inscribed: TO AN UNKNOWN GOD. Therefore, what you worship in ignorance, this I proclaim to you. The God who made the world and everything in it—He is Lord of heaven and earth and does not live in shrines made by hands. Neither is He served by human hands, as though He needed anything, since He Himself gives everyone life and breath and all things." (vv. 18–25)

Finally, Paul concluded:

"Being God's offspring then, we shouldn't think that the divine nature is like gold or silver or stone, an image fashioned by human art and imagination.

"Therefore, having overlooked the times of ignorance, God now commands all people everywhere to repent, because He has set a day when He is going to judge the world in righteousness by the Man He has appointed. He has provided proof of this to everyone by raising Him from the dead." (vv. 29–31)

There were diverse reactions to this event, but at least two trusted the Lord and followed him that day. Paul's claim was an exclusivistic claim, but you will note, however, that there is no hint of any coercive effort on his part. He was reasoning (Gk. *dialegomai*) with them.

In Galatians 1:6–9, Paul says:

I am amazed that you are so quickly turning away from Him who called you by the grace of Christ and are turning to a different gospel—not that there is another gospel, but there are some who are troubling you and want to change the good news about the Messiah. But even if we or an angel from heaven should preach to you a gospel other than what we have preached to you, a curse be on him! As we have said before, I now say again: If anyone preaches to you a gospel contrary to what you received, a curse be on him!

What friendship award did Paul seek? What a statement of the exclusive nature of the gospel! I do believe Paul here used a deliberate play on words. I know that to take words like *different* or *other* in verse 6 and *another* in verse 7 and say one word always means this and another word always means that is dangerous. Clearly that is not the case. But here I think Paul made an intentional selection when he said, "Who has turned from the grace of Christ to a *heteron* gospel." This is *another* gospel of a different kind which in fact is not an *allo* (same kind of) gospel. Paul said that if someone preaches anything else other than the true gospel, let him be accursed.

The same phenomenon is observable in the book of Hebrews. In the great chapter on the atonement, Hebrews 9, the author concluded that according to the law, almost all things are purified with blood, and without the shedding of blood (clearly the blood of Christ, in light of the context of the rest of the chapter) there is no remission (Heb 9:22). That is exclusivism.

The New Testament and Religious Liberty

Does the rest of the New Testament also speak of religious liberty or lack of coercion in the gospel other than that of appealing to people? What you find in the New Testament is not a direct statement but rather a discovery of the constant language of appeal.

In 2 Corinthians 5:20, we read, "Therefore, we are ambassadors for Christ, certain that God is appealing through us. We plead on Christ's behalf, 'Be reconciled to God.'" Paul said, "We plead [Gk. *parakalountos,* lit. 'calling beside']. We call you to our side in Christ's behalf and ask you to be reconciled to God." No coercion here! We plead. We beg you in Christ's stead to be reconciled to God.

Acts 20:21 records that the disciples, especially the apostle Paul, were "testifying" (Gk. *diamarturomenos*) to both the Jews and the Greeks of repentance toward God through the Lord Jesus Christ. "Testify" is the language of personal experience, not of coercion.

"Then Paul, as his custom was, went in to them, and for three Sabbaths reasoned [Gk. *dielexato,* the same word again] with them from the Scriptures" (Acts 17:2 NKJV). He opened the Scriptures to them. In Acts 18:4, the same word is used again: "He reasoned [Gk. *dielegeto*] in the synagogue every Sabbath, and persuaded [Gk. *epeithen*] both Jews and Greeks" (NKJV).

In Acts 19:8–9, we read, "And he went into the synagogue and spoke boldly for three months, reasoning [Gk. *dialegomenos*] and persuading [Gk. *peithoun*] concerning the things of the kingdom of God. But when some were hardened and did not believe, but spoke evil of the Way before the multitude, he departed from them and withdrew the disciples, reasoning daily in the school of Tyrannus" (NKJV). He did not force them but simply withdrew when they would not hear.

There is still a different word in 1 Peter 3:15: "But set apart the Messiah as Lord in your hearts, and always be ready to give a defense

[Gk. *apologian,* lit. an 'apology'] to anyone who asks you for a reason for the hope that is in you." You cannot have coercion with meekness and fear. Those two words are never a part of coercion. In fact, "defense" suggests the exact opposite. The word *apologia* is anglicized as "apology," having evolved in an odd way into being used today as a way of expressing regret.

For example, if I were in a weaving way as I preached and I accidentally stepped on someone's toe, his intense agony would probably yield some verbal objection. I would say, "I am sorry." But how do we get "I am sorry" out of a word that really means a defense? I would seldom say, "I am sorry. I was clumsy." I would probably say, "I am so sorry. You see, I was moving around and did not notice where your foot was. I did not realize I was moving that way." All of this explanation is how we got the word *apology* in English. Originally, the word referred to a defense or an organized presentation and defense of one's position: "To everyone who asks you for a reason for the hope that is in you with meekness in fear."

Acts 28:23 combines three different words, some of which we have already observed in other texts. "After arranging a day with him [Paul], many came to him at his lodging. From dawn to dusk he expounded [Gk. *exetitheto,* lit. 'placing out before them, exposing in the sense of explaining'] and witnessed [Gk. *diamarturomenos,* with the preposition *dia* enhancing the sense of the word, meaning that he witnessed through the thing with them; he walked through the whole thing with them (see Acts 20:21)] about the kingdom of God. He tried to persuade [Gk. *peithoun*] them concerning Jesus from both the Law of Moses and the Prophets."

In light of this text and others, the Bible does present a case for the proposition that there is only one way to be saved. And yet, never did New Testament witnesses resort to coercion, and always they attempted to persuade the wills and the hearts of those who listened. I believe the testimony of Scripture rests.

The Historical Witness

What about the historical witness? While one could invoke the story of English Baptists, American Baptists, and others, for the purpose of this chapter to focus alone on the Anabaptists of the Radical Reformation is sufficient. The name *Anabaptist* was used by the opponents of the Radical

Reformation as a descriptive term because of the radicals' insistence on believer's baptism. Since almost all had been "baptized" as infants, from the perspective of both the Roman Catholics and the Magisterial Reformers, this act of believer's baptism constituted "rebaptism" or *anabaptism*. However, the name notwithstanding, the essence of Anabaptism was the idea of a regenerate church witnessed by believer's baptism as a public profession of faith and the living of one's life with self-discipline so as to remain a holy and sanctified body.

My favorite Anabaptist theologian, Balthasar Hubmaier, was a remarkable individual. He was the only Anabaptist ever to attain a terminal degree. Hubmaier had a doctorate from the University of Ingolstadt under one of the keenest theological debaters of the era, John Eck. And Eck, who interacted prominently with Luther in the Leipzig Disputation, not only was adroit in debate, but he also made the mistake of teaching Balthasar Hubmaier everything he knew about debate. Once Hubmaier read his Greek New Testament, he came to conversion through Christ and he became an Anabaptist. And so he began to preach an exclusive Christ— Christ as the only way to salvation.

For example, in his book *On the Christian Baptism of Believers* in 1525, Hubmaier said, "Therefore, it is not sufficient to point one to Christ, he must actually call upon Him and hear and believe [the gospel] for the remission of sins."[1] That is exclusivism. The same exclusivism is observable in the hymn Hubmaier wrote.

> Rejoice, rejoice, ye Christians all and break forth into singing!
> Since far and wide on every side the word of God is ringing,
> And well we know no human foe our souls from Christ can sever,
> For to the base, and men of grace, God's word stands sure for ever.
>
> And, Peter, Jude, and James all three do follow in this teaching;
> Repentance and confession they through Christ our Lord are
>   preaching.
> In him men must put all their trust, or they shall see God never.

---

[1] Balthasar Hubmaier, "On the Christian Baptism of Believers," in *Anabaptist Beginnings (1523–1533)*, ed. William R. Estep (Nieuwkoop: B. De Graaf, 1976), 77.

The wolf may tear, the lion, the bear—God's word stands sure for
ever.

For our purposes, I want to highlight that one line, "In him men must
put all their trust or they shall see God never." Hubmaier was an exclusivist
preaching Christ as the only way of salvation. Then he concluded:

Ah, man, blind man, now hear the word, make sure your state and
calling;
Believe the Scripture is the power, by which we're kept from falling.
Your valued lore at once give o'er, renounce your vain endeavor;
This shows the way, no longer stray, God's word stands sure for
ever.

O Jesus Christ, thou Son of God, Let us not lack thy favor,
For what shall be our just reward, if the salt shall lose its savor?
With angry flame to efface thy name in vain shall men endeavor;
Not for a day, the same for aye, God's word stands sure for ever.[2]

Hubmaier had perceived the Scriptures correctly. Based on the epis-
temological truthfulness of God's Word, it is known that Jesus is the only
way of salvation.

Hubmaier could be rough in argumentation. His argumentation
made use of logic, exegesis of Scripture, irony, and even "gentle" sarcasm.
Would he then be an opponent of absolute religious freedom? The following is from a book he wrote in 1524 entitled *Concerning Heretics and
Those Who Burn Them*.[3] A series of articles developed Hubmaier's logical position.

Article 1 states, "Heretics are those who deceitfully undermine the
Holy Scriptures, the first of whom was the Devil, when he spoke to Eve.
You shall not surely die." The second article states, "The same are also
heretics who conceal the Scriptures and interpret them other than the
Holy Spirit demands, such as, those that everywhere proclaim a wife as a

---

[2] Hubmaier, "God's Word Stands Sure Forever," in Estep, *Anabaptist Beginnings
(1523–1533)*, 169–72.

[3] Hubmaier, "Concerning Heretics and Those Who Burn Them," in Estep,
Anabaptist Beginnings (1523–1533), 47–53.

benefice; ruling for pastoring; stones for the rock; Rome for the Church, and compelling us to believe this prattle."

However, article 3 says, "One should overcome such people with holy artifice, not with wrangling but softly, although the Holy Scriptures also contain wrath." Our approach should not be one of coercion but of holy artifice. Hubmaier continued in the fifth article, "If they will not learn with strong proofs or evangelical reasons then leave them alone, and permit them to rage and be furious, that those who are now filthy will become more filthy still." There is no coercion there at all. It is an articulate statement in favor of religious liberty.

The sixteenth article says, "But a Turk or heretic will not be convinced by our act either with sword or yet by fire but alone with patience and witness and so we, with those who are patient, await the judgment of God."

The twenty-second article says, "Therefore, it is well and good that the secular authority puts to death the criminals who do physical harm to the defenseless (Rom. 13). But no one may injure the atheist who wishes nothing for himself other than to forsake the gospel." We are not to coerce even the atheist. We are to help him see the truth, but we are not to coerce him.

The twenty-ninth article states, "Since it is such a disgrace to kill a heretic, how much greater the offense to burn to ashes the faithful preachers of the Word of God without a conviction or arraignment by the truth."

Article 36 reads, "Now it is apparent to everyone, even the blind, that the law which demands the burning of heretics is an invention of the Devil."

Balthasar Hubmaier was not alone. The other Anabaptists also vigorously held to religious liberty even though they held to the absolute necessity of Christ as the only way of salvation. Conrad Grebel and others sent a letter in 1524 to Thomas Müntzer, who was beginning to advocate a much more determinedly coercive form of the faith. Grebel wrote, making clear that he favored religious toleration:

> Press forward with the Word and create a Christian church with the help of Christ and His Rule as we find it instituted in Matthew 18 and practiced in the epistles. *Apply it with earnestness and common prayer and fasting, in line with faith and love, and without law and compulsion.* Then God will bring you and your lambs

to full soundness, and the singing and tablets will be abolished. There is more than enough wisdom and counsel in the Scripture, how all classes and all men shall be taught, governed, instructed, and made God-fearing. Whoever will not repent and believe, but resists the Word and moving of God, and so persists [in sin], after Christ and His Word and Rule have been preached to him, and he has been admonished in the company of the three witnesses and the congregation, *such a man, we declare, on the basis of God's Word, shall not be killed, but regarded as a heathen and a publican, and let alone.* One should also not protect the gospel and its adherents with the sword, nor themselves. We learn from our brother that this is also what you believe and hold to. True believing Christians are sheep among wolves, sheep for the slaughter. They must be baptized in anxiety, distress, affliction, persecution, suffering, and death. They must pass through the probation of fire, and reach the Fatherland of eternal rest, not by slaying their bodily [enemies] but by mortifying their spiritual enemies. They employ neither worldly sword nor war, since with them killing is absolutely renounced.[4]

In the 1520s, when Felix Manz was on trial, there were several different hearings at which he appeared, and Harold Bender notes that "the Zurich court records show that twice . . . [Manz] admitted that he taught that those of other faiths are to be left undisturbed in their practice."[5] That is absolute religious liberty.

Hans Denck, the Hebraist of the Anabaptists, said:

But with those who may not hear me and still will not remain silent regarding matters which are in dispute, I cannot have much fellowship. For I do not perceive in such the spirit of Christ, but a perverted one that would drag me from my faith by force and

---

[4] "Letters to Thomas Müntzer from the Swiss Brethren, Conrad Grebel and Others, Zurich, September 5, 1524," in Estep, *Anabaptist Beginnings (1523–1533)*, 35.

[5] Harold S. Bender, *The Anabaptists and Religious Liberty in the Sixteenth Century* (Philadelphia: Fortress, 1970), 7. See also Bender, *Conrad Grebel, c. 1498–1526: The Leader of the Swiss Brethren* (Scottdale, PA: Herald, 1950), 158–59.

compel me to do his will. . . . Then he should know that in the matters of faith all should be left free and uncoerced. . . . Concerning another who has subjected me to persecution and through the same kind of fear, ostracized me, but my heart has not separated itself from him and, above all, from no God-fearing man.[6]

Whatever the case and however stinging may have been the attempts to suppress the Anabaptist idea of religious liberty, the Anabaptist legacy was released in the sixteenth century like a tiger from its cage. The biblical ideas discovered by these courageous men and women will never be caged again. If we ever begin to faint in the way beneath the satanically induced onslaught of the state or state-sponsored ecclesiastical religion, then let us be invigorated afresh by the superlative examples of these Anabaptists who taught us how to advocate both the exclusivity of Jesus Christ and absolute religious liberty while debating, standing, and dying for our Lord.

Conclusions

As a result of the study of the Word of God and a brief look at the march of the free church through the ages, I will present my conclusions. To sound perfectly biblical, I need to have seven, and they follow:

First, exclusivism in religion carries two potential dangers: (1) The passions generated by the confidence that one is correct in his devotion and conviction lead to condescension and ultimately to coercion of others. This is evident in Islam. (2) The strategy employed to communicate those views can be such that the evangelist appears tyrannical or threatening. Either is unfortunate. Our method of presentation is important along with the content of the gospel message itself. If someone refuses Christ because of the offense of the gospel, his rejection needs to be because of the offense of the gospel and not the offense of the evangelist.

---

[6] "Hans Denck's Recantation, 1527," in Estep, *Anabaptist Beginnings (1523–1533)*, 135.

Second, exclusivism in religion does not necessarily lend itself to either of these unfortunate possibilities. Exclusivism may be maintained in nonthreatening ways.

Third, Christians embracing the exclusivity of Christ as the only saving and accurate expression of the true and living God are properly the most effective advocates of absolute religious liberty. Why is this the case?

- Because of their quiet confidence that truth will eventually triumph, which gives them the assurance and the ability to continue on without coercion.
- God himself is the only ultimate and adequate judge.
- The free marketplace of ideas favors the truth of Christ and will inevitably result in many people embracing that truth.
- The powerful presence of the Holy Spirit witnessing to the truth of Christ presented with both passion and compassion provides the most effective weapon in the appeal to the human mind, heart, and will.

Fourth, religious liberty, properly understood, is not only the right of an individual to remain in the faith context of his birth, but also he has to consider any and all perspectives and, if informed by conscience, the prerogative to change his position and worship.

Fifth, for freedom of religion to exist in more than theory or name, a free marketplace of ideas must be guaranteed by civil governments and authorities. Individuals must be guaranteed the right to hear, contemplate, and accept or reject the truth claims and values of any religion as long as the public airing of these views does not endanger the physical well-being of anyone.

Sixth, to become a consistent advocate of freedom for all, the government of the United States must be constantly exhorted to formulate foreign as well as domestic policy with a view toward establishing religious liberty around the globe. The words *constantly* and *exhorted* have been carefully chosen. Congress as a whole does not understand this concept. Unfortunately, the vast majority of senators and members of congress, and even most members of the Supreme Court, think that religious liberty means basically the right to continue in whatever context you were born. They do not tend to understand what a free marketplace of ideas is all about and the fact that pressure needs to be put on other governments to grant freedom.

Seventh, Baptists and other evangelicals who embrace the concept of religious liberty—especially those who insist on the exclusivity of Christ in salvation—must develop greater courage and determination in the advocacy of this idea.

In 1415, when Jerome of Prague was about to be burned at the stake, his tormenters asked if he had any final words. He was a preacher. What would you expect him to do? Jerome was not about to miss this opportunity, so he launched into a sermon about the sufficiency of Christ and how people could come to the Lord and be saved, totally oblivious to what was about to happen to him. In the midst of his sermon, the executioner grew weary of listening and thought he would get on with the execution. So he slipped around behind him with the torch and was about to ignite the flames.

Jerome caught sight of him out of the corner of his eye and put a comma right there in his sermon. He stopped and said, "Don't light the fire behind me. If I feared it, I would not have come here. Light it in front of me where all can see."[7] He was a man of genuine courage. May God help us be courageous advocates of absolute religious liberty, defined as the free marketplace of ideas. We never have to fear such liberty because with the truthfulness of Scripture and the witness of the Holy Spirit of God empowering that message, truth will always ultimately carry the day. May God help us to do so until he returns.

---

[7] For this account of Jerome of Prague's death, see William Gilpin, *The Lives of John Wicliff, and of the Most Eminent of His Disciples: Lord Cobham, John Huss, Jerome of Prague, and Zisca* (n.p.: John Mein, 1814), 214.

CHAPTER 2

The Defense of Religious Liberty by the Anabaptists and the English Baptists

Thomas White

The Baptist defense of religious liberty did not begin in a vacuum, nor did it begin in America. Years before the first Europeans set foot on American soil, the foundation for religious liberty had been laid by the Anabaptists and the English Baptists. These predecessors of modern Baptists fought vehemently for religious liberty, and discussion of this topic would not be complete without acknowledging those who paved the way with martyrdom or imprisonment. Thus, this chapter will discuss and summarize the defense of religious liberty as presented by the Anabaptists and the English Baptists.[1]

---

[1] Although the movement known as Anabaptism had a polygenesis beginning with diverse groups, the term *Anabaptist* in this chapter will describe primarily the group that arose in 1521 in Germany who baptized over again "as a due performance of

A lack of religious toleration cost many Anabaptists their lives. From 1520 to 1560 approximately three thousand legally sanctioned executions for heresy occurred. About two-thirds of those executed belonged to the Anabaptist movement.[2] Two of the earliest works arguing for complete religious liberty were *On Heretics and Those Who Burn Them*, written by Balthasar Hubmaier and *Concerning Heretics: Whether They Are to Be Persecuted and How They Are to Be Treated*, by Sébastien Castellion.[3] Strong support for religious liberty continued through the Anabaptist movement, which included the Waterland Mennonite Church. This church influenced John Smyth's beliefs about religious liberty and thus impacted the English Baptists. The English Baptists under Thomas Helwys and others fought for religious liberty in England, partially achieving their goal. This story of their defense of religious liberty will make up the content of this essay.

To trace the defense of religious liberty, this chapter will examine the most important written works of the Anabaptists and the English Baptists on the topic of religious liberty. The arguments presented by various members of these groups contain several areas of agreement. These areas of agreement continue to form the foundation for the Baptist defense of religious liberty. This chapter will demonstrate the use of six common beliefs supporting complete religious liberty. Those areas of agreement are (1) that under God's ultimate authority there exist two

---

what has been ineffectually performed previously." Found in J. A. Simpson and E. S. C. Weiner, eds., *The Oxford English Dictionary*, 2nd ed. (Oxford: Clarendon Press, 1989), 1:425. This chapter does not intend to answer the issue of when Baptists originated; however, this chapter will give the Anabaptists due recognition for supporting the Baptist distinctive of religious liberty.

[2] William Monter, "Heresy Executions in Reformation Europe, 1520–1565," in *Tolerance and Intolerance in the European Reformation*, ed. Ole Peter Grell and Bob Scribner (Cambridge: Cambridge University Press, 1996), 49.

[3] Balthasar Hubmaier, *On Heretics and Those Who Burn Them*, in *Balthasar Hubmaier: Theologian of Anabaptism*, trans. and ed. H. Wayne Pipkin and John H. Yoder (Scottdale, PA: Herald, 1989). Hubmaier wrote his work in 1524. Sébastien Castellion, *Concerning Heretics: Whether They Are to Be Persecuted and How They Are to Be Treated*, trans. Roland Bainton (New York: Columbia University Press, 1935). Castellion wrote his work after the death of Michael Servetus, who died October 23, 1553. This work was published in 1554.

separate kingdoms—the worldly and the spiritual,[4] (2) that civil government has no authority over the soul, (3) that spiritual discipline should
be handled by the church, (4) that voluntary faith cannot be coerced, (5)
that killing a heretic ends any evangelistic opportunity for that person,
and (6) that complete religious liberty should be extended to all groups—
even heretics.

In order to systematically prove this position, this chapter will discuss
the Anabaptist position as represented in Hubmaier, Castellion, and others
before tracing the Waterlander influence on John Smyth that resulted in
his defense of religious liberty, progressing to Thomas Helwys and other
English Baptists' defenses of religious liberty, and concluding with Roger
Williams. From the beginning it becomes obvious that the writers discussed
in this chapter felt it necessary to speak prophetically to the government.

The Anabaptist Defense of Religious Liberty

The various groups of people referred to as Anabaptists held to varying
opinions on whether a Christian could participate in the state; however,
the vast majority disagreed with a coercive state establishing religion.[5]
The main area of departure came from their unique understanding of the
church. Timothy George claimed, "Menno and the Anabaptists denied the
legitimacy of the *corpus christianum,* whereby church and society formed
an organic unity and religion was undergirded by the coercive power of the
state. This attitude was truly revolutionary in the 16th century and led to
violent reprisals against the nonconforming Anabaptists."[6]

---

[4] One may object that two kingdoms do not exist but that God controls all. The
belief in two kingdoms recognized God's ultimate authority over both kingdoms but
interpreted the parable of the Wheat and the Tares in Matthew 13 as stating that
sinners and saints would coexist until Christ's return. As a result, God in Romans 13
established the state to rule over the unregenerate (worldly kingdom) and the church
to enforce the laws of Christ through church discipline on the regenerate. Christ alone
rules the spiritual kingdom. Further evidence is found in John 18:36, where Jesus told
Pilate that his kingdom was not of this world.

[5] For more information on the Anabaptists, see George Huntston Williams, *The
Radical Reformation,* 3rd ed. (Kirksville, MO: Truman State University Press, 2000).

[6] Timothy George, *Theology of the Reformers* (Nashville: Broadman, 1988), 286.

Harold Bender wrote:

> Here the Anabaptists and the Reformers parted. For the latter, the state was to be the *Defensor fidei*, with the power and duty to maintain religious and ecclesiastical uniformity and suppress dissent. The Anabaptists broke completely with the state-church system with its *corpus christianum*, which the Reformers retained. Hence the Anabaptist concept of religious liberty and religious pluralism, advanced far beyond its time, was in direct clash with both the Catholic and Protestant concept.[7]

Finally, William Estep said, "It was clear that while the Anabaptists rejected the sacral society of medieval creation, they did not reject the state but rather redefined its role according to their understanding of the church."[8] The focus on the church as separate from the worldly kingdom controlled by the state quintessentially prepared the way for achieving complete religious liberty while challenging the hegemony of the Catholic Church.

Balthasar Hubmaier

Perhaps Balthasar Hubmaier presented the clearest and most formally educated Anabaptist voice on the issue of religious liberty. He served as the cathedral preacher at Regensburg and with John Eck on the faculty of the University of Ingolstadt. Sometime around September 1524, Hubmaier fled Waldshut for refuge in Schaffhausen. Hubmaier remained in the monastery there for about two months, writing *On Heretics*. On March 10, 1528, Hubmaier experienced firsthand the rejection of his arguments when he was burned to death for heresy in Vienna. His wife, Elizabeth Hugline, was drowned for the same reason three days later.[9]

Hubmaier did not believe the Bible supported state-sanctioned persecution of heretics. In *On Heretics and Those Who Burn Them*, he stated in article 6, "The law which condemns heretics to [execution by] fire is

---

[7] Harold S. Bender and Henry Smith, eds., *The Mennonite Encyclopedia* (Scottdale, PA: Mennonite Publishing House, 1955), s.v. "Anabaptist-Mennonite Attitude Toward the State," 612.

[8] William R. Estep, *Revolution within the Revolution: The First Amendment in Historical Context, 1612–1789* (Grand Rapids: Eerdmans, 1990), 27.

[9] Ibid., 31.

based upon Zion in blood and Jerusalem in wickedness."[10] He continued in articles 21 and 22, "Every Christian has a sword [to use] against the godless, namely the [sword of the] Word of God (Eph. 6:17ff), but not a sword against the evildoers. . . . It is fitting that secular authority puts to death the wicked (Rom. 13:4) who cause bodily harm to the defenseless. But the unbeliever should be harmed by no one should he not be willing to change and should he forsake the gospel."[11]

Hubmaier believed that one should correct true heretics and then leave the heretics alone so that in due time perhaps they might change their minds. To execute heretics instead of praying for their redemption sealed their fate. In article 13 he stated, "It follows now that the inquisitors are the greatest heretics of all, because counter to the teaching and example of Jesus they condemn heretics to fire; and before it is time they pull up the wheat together with the tares."[12] Additionally, he supported complete religious liberty for all by stating, "But a Turk or a heretic cannot be overcome by our doing, neither by sword nor by fire, but alone with patience and supplication, whereby we patiently await divine judgment."[13]

Hubmaier felt that an open marketplace of ideas would provide the opportunity to solve disagreements, and he criticized the state for not hearing and properly correcting the accused. He stated, "If to burn heretics is such a great evil, how much greater will be the evil, to burn to ashes the genuine proclaimers of the Word of God, without having convinced them, without having debated the truth with them."[14] Thus, Hubmaier defended religious liberty by supporting two kingdoms in which the state has no authority over the soul and by extending religious liberty to all, including heretics, acknowledging that in due time they could change their minds to make the necessary voluntary decision to follow Christ.

---

[10] Hubmaier, *On Heretics and Those Who Burn Them*, in Pipkin and Yoder, *Balthasar Hubmaier*, 60.

[11] Ibid., 63.

[12] Ibid., 62.

[13] Ibid.

[14] Ibid., 64.

Sébastien Castellion

Sébastien Castellion was a layman for most of his life. At times he identified with John Calvin, and at others he criticized Anabaptists who denied
the right of Christians to serve as magistrates.[15] However, his criticism of
the October 23, 1553, execution of Michael Servetus, which included a
defense of religious liberty, resulted in his identification as an Anabaptist.
Castellion wrote under the names Martin Bellius, Basil Montfort, and
George Kleinberg.[16] While writing *Concerning Heretics* under the name
Martin Bellius, he founded the movement known as Bellianism, which
denoted advocates of religious liberty such as David Joris and Bernardino
Ochino.[17]

In *Concerning Heretics,* Castellion specifically addressed the persecution and death of Michael Servetus. He stated concerning the persecution
of Christians by Christians, "We rather degenerate into Turks and Jews
than convert them into Christians. Who would wish to be a Christian,
when he saw that those who confessed the name of Christ were destroyed
by Christians themselves with fire, water, and the sword without mercy
and more cruelly treated than brigands and murderers?"[18]

Castellion began his argument by stating that current rulers should
follow the example of Christ. He wrote, "When I consider the life and
teaching of Christ who, though innocent Himself, yet always pardoned
the guilty and told us to pardon until seventy times seven, I do not see how
we can retain the name of Christian if we do not imitate His clemency and
mercy."[19] The primary argument of Castellion came by dividing the world

---

[15] For more information on Sébastien Castellion, see Roland Bainton, *The Travail of Religious Liberty* (New York: Harper & Brothers, 1951), 97–124; Roland Bainton et al., *Castellioniana: Quatre études sur Sébastien Castellion et l'idée de la tolérance* (Leiden: Brill, 1951); Ferdinand Buisson, *Sébástien Castellion: Sa vie et son oeuvre (1515–63): étude sur les origines du protestantisme liberal françis,* 2 vols. (Paris: Hachette, 1892); and Williams, *The Radical Reformation,* 959–62.

[16] Bainton, *The Travail of Religious Liberty,* 108.

[17] For more information on David Joris, see Bainton, *The Travail of Religious Liberty,* 125–48. David Joris was a Hollander and an Anabaptist. For information on Bernardino Ochino, see Bainton, *The Travail of Religious Liberty,* 149–76.

[18] Castellion, *Concerning Heretics,* 133. A brigand was a person who lived by plundering, a bandit.

[19] Ibid., 125.

into two separate kingdoms, both ultimately established by God. The civil authorities possess authority over the kingdom of the world but not over the kingdom of Christ. He stated:

> First of all we must observe that the children of Adam fall into two groups, the one in the kingdom of God under Christ, the other in the kingdom of the world under the magistrate. . . . Civil government has laws which extend only to bodies and goods on earth. God, who alone has jurisdiction and authority over the soul, will not suffer it to be subject to mundane laws. When civil government undertakes to legislate for souls, then it encroaches upon the province of God and merely perverts and corrupts souls.[20]

When addressing the work of Martin Luther, Castellion used stronger language: "Yet, consummate fools though they be, they must confess that they have no authority over souls. No man can kill the soul or make it alive, lead it to heaven or to hell. Christ makes this plain in the tenth chapter of Matthew."[21] He added, "The heart they cannot compel, though they burst themselves in the attempt."[22]

He pointed out two great dangers about the term *heretic.* First, the person being held as a heretic was not really a heretic.[23] Second, the real heretic would be punished in a manner more severe than that required by Christian discipline.[24] Castellion gave as the common definition of a heretic those "with whom we disagree."[25] He then sought to redefine heretic as one who has ignored proper church discipline and correction. He concluded that religions of all beliefs had various actions that were considered wrong and worthy of punishment; however, such consensus could not be found among religious beliefs. He concluded, "Let not the Jews or Turks condemn the Christians, nor let the Christians condemn the Jews or

---

[20] Ibid., 141–42.

[21] Ibid., 143. Matthew 10:28, "Fear not them which kill the body, but are not able to kill the soul: but rather fear him which is able to destroy both soul and body in hell" (KJV).

[22] Castellion, *Concerning Heretics,* 145.

[23] Ibid., 126.

[24] Ibid.

[25] Ibid., 129.

Turks, but rather teach and win them by true religion and justice, and let us, who are Christians, not condemn one another, but, if we are wiser than they, let us also be better and more merciful."[26]

Other Anabaptist Defenses of Religious Liberty

Some, such as Dirk Philips, argued that true Christians should expect persecution but should not themselves persecute. He wrote, "Thus, the true Christian must be persecuted here for the sake of the truth and of righteousness, but they persecute no one because of their faith."[27] Philips believed religious persecution jeopardizes a true church's status, stating, "They can never more exist or be considered a congregation of the Lord who persecute others on account of their faith. For, first of all, God the heavenly Father has thus given all judgment to Christ Jesus, that he should be a judge over the souls and consciences of people."[28] The congregation possessed no authority to forcefully compel unbelievers. He continued:

> Here [Matt. 13:29ff] is revealed that no congregation of the Lord may have domination over the consciences of people with an external sword, nor compel the unbeliever to faith with violence, nor kill the false prophets with sword and fire. But they must judge and exclude with the Lord's Word all who are within the congregation and found to be evil. Anything more than this that happens is neither Christian, evangelical, nor apostolic. And if someone wants to say that the authorities have not received the sword in vain, Rom. 13:1[ff], and that God through Moses has commanded to kill the false prophets, Deut. [15], to that I answer briefly: The authority has not received the sword from God to judge over spiritual matters (for these must be judged by the spiritual only spiritually), 1 Cor. 2:13, but to keep its subjects in good order and to keep peace, protect the pious, and punish the evil.[29]

---

[26] Ibid., 133.

[27] Dirk Philips, "The Congregation of God," in *The Writings of Dirk Philips: 1504–1568,* trans. and ed. Cornelius J. Dyck, William E. Keeney, and Alvin J. Beachy (Scottdale, PA: Herald, 1992), 374.

[28] Ibid.

[29] Ibid., 375.

Thus, Philips upheld the belief in two separate kingdoms established by God with different purposes.

Hans Denck stated, "For he must know that in matters of faith everything must be free and uncoerced."[30] He said of those who persecuted others, "For I do not notice the mind of Christ in them but a perverted spirit that seeks to coerce me from my faith with violence and to convert me to another regardless of whether it is right or not."[31] Denck consistently applied this freedom to all, "be he Turk or heathen, believing what he will—through and in his land, not submitting to a magistrate in matters of faith. Is there anything more to be desired? . . . That is to say, no one shall deprive another—whether heathen or Jew or Christian—but rather allow everyone to move in all territories in the name of his God."[32]

One final document, the Schleitheim Confession of 1527, demonstrated again the support of two kingdoms and religious freedom. In article 6, the confession stated, "The sword is ordained of God outside the perfection of Christ. It punishes and puts to death the wicked, and guards and protects the good."[33] The articles continued, "In the perfection of Christ, however, only the ban is used for a warning and for the excommunication of the one who has sinned, without putting the flesh to death,—simply the warning and the command to sin no more."[34] This confession rigorously defended religious liberty by clearly acknowledging two kingdoms, with the magistrate governing one and the church the other.

Conclusion

Roland Bainton concluded, "The best things on religious liberty were said in the sixteenth century but not practiced until the nineteenth."[35] The Anabaptists' views were ahead of their time and not accepted during the heights of the movement in the sixteenth century. However, the truth of

---

[30] Hans Denck, "Recantation," in *Anabaptism in Outline*, ed. Walter Klaassen (Scottdale, PA: Herald, 1981), 305.

[31] Ibid.

[32] Denck, "Commentary on Micah," in Klaassen, *Anabaptism in Outline*, 292.

[33] William Lumpkin, *Baptist Confessions of Faith* (Valley Forge, PA: Judson, 1969), 27.

[34] Ibid.

[35] Bainton, *The Travail of Religious Liberty*, 253.

their arguments paved the road to the eventual acceptance of religious liberty. Current Baptists must remember the shed blood of the Anabaptists and forever appreciate their dedication to establishing religious freedom.

The Development of Religious Liberty in England

The English Baptist movement began in the winter of 1609 when John Smyth took water from a basin and poured it over his head in the name of the Father, the Son, and the Holy Ghost, by self-baptizing and then baptizing the entire congregation at Amsterdam.[36] Smyth and others who withdrew from the Anglican Church argued for religious liberty.[37] A brief survey of a few major figures in this movement will now occupy our attention.

John Smyth

Smyth failed to serve as a solid leader for any one movement. Continuously developing, Smyth's theology changed like leaves in the fall, moving from Anglican to Puritan to Separatist to Baptist and almost becoming an Anabaptist. His move from Baptist to seeking membership with the Waterland Mennonite Church occurred because he began to doubt his self-baptism. Smyth doubted the validity of his baptism when someone brought to his attention that not even Christ baptized himself. In addition to his changing views on self-baptism and other theological beliefs, Smyth's thinking shifted on the issue of religious liberty.[38] This chapter will now examine John Smyth's shifting views on religious liberty.

Early on, Smyth believed the state should coerce everyone to worship God. He stated that "the Magistrates should cause all men to worship the true God, or else punish them with imprisonment, confiscation of goods,

---

[36] For more information on John Smyth, see Walter H. Burgess, *John Smyth the Se-Baptist, Thomas Helwys, and the First Baptist Church in England* (London: James Clarke, 1911), and Jason Lee, *The Theology of John Smyth* (Macon, GA: Mercer University Press, 2003).

[37] For a complete discussion of English Baptist literature on religious liberty, see Leon McBeth, *English Baptist Literature on Religious Liberty to 1689* (New York: Arno, 1980).

[38] For more information on the shifting theology of John Smyth, see Lee, *The Theology of John Smyth.*

or death as the qualitie of the cause requireth."[39] Even though Smyth himself was threatened by King James, he continued to support the role of the magistrate. In his first publication as a Separatist, he encouraged princes to erect churches and command their subjects to enter them.[40]

By 1609, Smyth began to doubt this view of the role of government because of Anabaptist influence. Timothy George stated, "Baptist historians have sometimes gone to great lengths to prove that Smyth's theological development was free from Anabaptist influence. Whatever may be said about his acceptance of believer's baptism and his break with Calvinistic theology, this case can hardly be made with reference to his view of church and state."[41] As already alluded, Smyth doubted his self-baptism and sought membership with the Waterland Mennonite Church. John Smyth and forty-two members of his congregation signed the confession written by Hans de Ries known as the Waterlander Confession of Faith.[42]

This confession, which Smyth defended, stated, "Worldly authority or magistry is a necessary ordinance of God, appointed and established for the reservation of the common estate. . . . This office of the worldly authority the Lord Jesus hath not ordained in his spiritual kingdom, the church of the New Testament, nor adjoined to the offices of his church."[43]

Shortly after Smyth's death in August 1612, a book containing one hundred propositions that Smyth had written was published. In articles 83–86, Smyth addressed the role of the magistrate. He affirmed it as part of the "permissive ordinance of God for the good of mankind," but also

---

[39] John Smyth, *The Works of John Smyth,* ed. W. T. Whitley (Cambridge: Cambridge University Press, 1936), 1:166.

[40] Ibid., 252.

[41] Timothy George, "Between Pacifism and Coercion: The English Baptist Doctrine of Religious Toleration," *Mennonite Quarterly Review* 58 (January 1984): 34–35. McBeth also alludes to this connection between Smyth and the Dutch Mennonites as being one source of the Baptist position. He does not limit it to this source but includes it as a "primary known factor" along with the English Bible. See McBeth, *English Baptist Literature on Religious Liberty to 1689,* 282–83.

[42] For more information, see Cornelius J. Dyck, "The First Waterlander Confession of Faith," *Mennonite Quarterly Review* 36 (1962): 5–13; and idem, "A Short Confession of Faith by Hans de Ries," *Mennonite Quarterly Review* 38 (1964): 5–19.

[43] Lumpkin, *Baptist Confessions of Faith,* 111. For Smyth's defense of the Waterlander Confession, see John Smyth, "Defence of Ries' Confession," in *The Works of John Smyth* (Cambridge: Cambridge University Press, 1915), 685–709.

cautioned that a Christian magistrate must not kill, punish, imprison, or banish his enemies but love them, practically accepting the Mennonite position.[44] However, the most important article was 84. McBeth commented on this article, "Article eighty-four is the clearest Baptist statement up to this time on religious liberty. It is properly regarded as the first major landmark among Baptists, and indeed among English speaking peoples, of the doctrine of absolute religious liberty."[45] Smyth wrote:

> That the magistrate is not by virtue of his office to meddle with religion, or matters of conscience, to force or compel men to this or that form of religion, or doctrine: but to leave Christian religion free, to every man's conscience, and to handle only civil transgressions (Rom. xiii), injuries and wrongs of man against man, in murder, adultery, theft, etc., for Christ only is the king, and lawgiver of the church and conscience (James iv. 12).[46]

This position put forth by Smyth came at the end of his life, when theoretically his thought should be mature. In addition, he did not simply affirm the work of another but with pen in hand formulated a succinct statement arguing for religious liberty. Although Smyth may have been the first of the English Baptists to argue for religious liberty, he was not the last.

Thomas Helwys

Thomas Helwys, born into a notable family in England, became a loyal follower of Smyth, even allowing Smyth to stay in his home during a lengthy illness.[47] In fact, Helwys was the leading advocate of the exile to Amsterdam, which brought the group in contact with the Waterland Mennonite Church. Because Helwys did not doubt the validity of his baptism, this partially led to his disagreement with Smyth's efforts to join with

---

[44] Lumpkin, *Baptist Confessions of Faith*, 139–40.

[45] McBeth, *English Baptist Literature on Religious Liberty to 1689*, 26.

[46] Lumpkin, *Baptist Confessions of Faith*, 140.

[47] For a discussion of Helwys family history, see Walter H. Burgess, "The Helwys Family, with Pedigree," *Transactions of the Baptist Historical Society* 3 (1912–13): 18–30; W. T. Whitley, *Thomas Helwys of Gray's Inn and Broxtowe Hall, Nottingham* (London: Kingsgate, n.d.).

the Waterland Mennonites. Furthermore, Helwys decided that fleeing to avoid persecution was not right, so he and others returned to England, establishing what has generally been regarded as the first Baptist church on English soil.[48] As a matter of survival as well as belief, Helwys pleaded with the king for religious liberty.

In 1612, Helwys submitted his appeal for complete religious liberty in the form of *A Short Declaration of the Mistery of Iniquity.*[49] McBeth and Robinson commented that Helwys likely wrote and published the book in Holland, distributing it immediately upon his return to England.[50] Unlike advocates of religious tolerance, Helwys's work supported complete religious liberty. Robinson wrote, "Helwys clearly was ready to give the liberty for which he asked to all those opponents, even the Roman Catholics—a fact which shows us how much ahead of his times he was."[51]

Helwys summarized his work on the flyleaf:

> Hear O King, and despise not the counsel of your poor, and let their complaints come before you. The King is a mortal man, and not God therefore hath no power over immortal souls of his subjects, to make laws and ordinances for them, and to set spiritual Lords over them. If the Kings have authority to make spiritual Lords and laws, then he is an immortal God and not mortal man. O King be not seduced by deceivers to sin so against God whom you should obey, nor against your poor subjects who should and will obey you in all things with body, life and goods, or let their lives be taken from the earth. God save the King.[52]

---

[48] For more information, consult E. A. Payne, *Thomas Helwys and the First Baptist Church in England* (London: Baptist Union of England and Ireland, 1962); George, "Between Pacifism and Coercion" 37.

[49] This author could not find publication data on this work, except for the date. In 1935, the Kingsgate Press published a facsimile copy with an introduction by H. Wheeler Robinson.

[50] McBeth, *English Baptist Literature on Religious Liberty to 1689,* 29. H. Wheeler Robinson, introduction to Thomas Helwys, *The Mystery of Iniquity* (London: Kingsgate Press, 1935), ix.

[51] Robinson, introduction to Helwys, *The Mystery of Iniquity,* xiv.

[52] Helwys, from the flyleaf of *The Mystery of Iniquity,* cited in McBeth, *English Baptist Literature on Religious Liberty to 1689,* 31.

The basic beliefs of Helwys mirror those already presented. Two kingdoms exist, and the magistrate must exercise power only in the kingdom of the world while the church of Christ must exercise authority in spiritual matters. Helwys wrote, "None ought to be punished either with death or bonds for transgressing against the spiritual ordinances of the New Testament, and that such offences ought to be punished only with spiritual sword and censures."[53]

Helwys believed that the magistrate held no power in the spiritual kingdom but simply functioned as a layman. He commented, "Far be it from the King to take from Christ Jesus any one part of that power and honor which belongs to Christ in his kingdom."[54] In addition to supporting the view of two separate kingdoms, Helwys also consistently supported complete religious liberty. Liberty should be extended to those of all faiths. He stated, "Let them be heretics, Turks, Jews, or whatsoever it appertains not to the earthly power to punish them in the least measure."[55]

Helwys, like the Anabaptists before him, felt that spiritual decisions were personal decisions that must be made through faith and that no amount of force could coerce a sincere decision. He believed that all should "choose their religion themselves seeing they only must stand themselves before the judgment seat of God to answer for themselves."[56] He added that since the secular kingdom held no power to create genuine decisions, any attempt to use such force marked a lack of faith in the power of the spiritual kingdom. Thus, people of faith should never resort to coercion with force.

Despite much common ground, Helwys differed with the Waterland Anabaptists by allowing for war and admitting magistrates to church membership. He wrote, "Our lord the king hath power to take our sons and daughters to do all his service of war, and of peace, yea all his servile service whatsoever."[57] In allowing for Christian magistrates, Helwys possessed similarities with Hubmaier, while Smyth and the Schleitheim

---

[53] Helwys, "The principal matters handled in the Booke," in *The Mystery of Iniquity*, no pagination.

[54] Helwys, *The Mystery of Iniquity*, 49.

[55] Ibid., 69.

[56] Ibid., 46.

[57] Ibid., 39–40.

Confession both opposed this position. Helwys furthered the case for religious liberty by holding to two separate kingdoms, supporting complete religious liberty for all groups, and denying the effectiveness of coercion in producing genuine spiritual decisions.

Other English Baptist Defenses of Religious Liberty

Leonard Busher. Little is known about Leonard Busher other than the fact that he contributed to the fight for religious freedom with his publication titled *Religions Peace: A Plea for Liberty of Conscience,* published in 1614.[58] Some believe this work was the earliest publication exclusively dedicated to the subject of religious liberty.[59]

Busher furthered arguments alluded to in earlier writings by focusing on evangelism to produce genuine spiritual decisions. He wrote:

> Also, if the believing should persecute the unbelieving to death, who should remain alive? Then none but the believing should live in the world, and the unbelieving should die in their unbelief, and so perish for ever. The Lord will not that the believing should live to the destruction of the unbelieving, but unto their conversion, edification, and salvation. And by persecuting of princes and people to death, because they will not hear and believe, is no gaining of souls unto God, but unto the devil.[60]

In addition to advancing the argument for evangelism, he continued previously used arguments. He held that new birth in Christ could only be achieved through the Word and Spirit of God and held to two kingdoms, specifically mentioning the "kingdom of Christ" and the "kingdom

---

[58] McBeth notes that "for years no copy of the original publication was thought to exist. There is, however, a copy in the Huntington Library Collection. The book was republished, with some changes, in 1646." See McBeth, *English Baptist Literature on Religious Liberty to 1689,* 39. This paper has used the edition of *Tracts on Liberty of Conscience and Persecution,* ed. Edward Bean Underhill (London: Haddon, 1846).

[59] Underhill calls it the "earliest treatise known to be extant on this great theme." See Underhill, *Tracts on Liberty of Conscience and Persecution,* 6. Earlier works addressed more than just religious liberty.

[60] Leonard Busher, "Religion's Peace: A Plea for Liberty of Conscience," in Underhill, *Tracts on Liberty of Conscience and Persecution,* 21.

of antichrist."[61] McBeth wrote of Busher's defense of religious liberty, "Perhaps Busher's most significant contribution is his attempt to justify religious liberty on the basis of spiritual necessity and abstract right. Liberty is no civil favor to be granted or withheld by the whim of the king; it is a God-given right of man and is essential because of the very nature of Christianity."[62]

John Murton. John Murton and his two works supporting religious liberty deserve mention. In 1615 and 1620 two documents were anonymously printed that apparently had the same author. Evidence since that time has indicated that John Murton was the author.[63] In Murton's work titled "The Epistle," one can clearly see the idea of two separate kingdoms. He wrote:

> We do unfeignedly acknowledge the authority of earthly magistrates, God's blessed ordinance, and that all earthly authority and command appertains unto them; let them command what they will, we must obey, either to do or suffer upon pain of God's displeasure, besides their punishment: but all men must let God alone with his right, which is to be lord and lawgiver to the soul, and not command obedience for God where he commandeth none.[64]

Additionally, he commented that "earthly authority belongeth to earthly kings; but spiritual authority belongeth to the one spiritual King who is KING OF KINGS."[65] Murton also argued that true conscious faith could not be coerced, devoting an entire section to defending this belief.[66]

The First London Confession. H. Leon McBeth commented in the work that resulted from his dissertation, "In volume, quality, and measurable influence, the 1640's must be accounted the great decade in English

---

[61] Ibid., 16–17.

[62] McBeth, *English Baptist Literature on Religious Liberty to 1689*, 47.

[63] Ibid.

[64] John Murton, "The Epistle," in Underhill, *Tracts on Liberty of Conscience and Persecution*, 100.

[65] Murton, "Persecution for Religion Judged and Condemned," in Underhill, *Tracts on Liberty of Conscience and Persecution*, 134.

[66] Murton, "A Humble Supplication to the King's Majesty," in Underhill, *Tracts on Liberty of Conscience and Persecution*, 225–31.

Baptist literature on religious liberty."[67] Among those documents was
the First London Confession of 1644. Signed by Baptist leaders such as
William Kiffin, John Spilsbury, and Samuel Richardson, the First London
Confession established a clear position in articles 48–52. In these articles the confession stated (1) that the civil magistrate is an ordinance of
God, (2) that believers should obey the laws of the king and parliament in
secular matters, (3) that there are two kingdoms (one of God and one of
Caesar), and (4) that we must obey God in spiritual matters.[68] This document represents the agreement of the Particular Baptists with what previous General Baptists and Anabaptists had been saying.

Roger Williams. Roger Williams spent most of his life in colonial
America, and the discussion of his defense of religious liberty primarily
belongs in a discussion of American development. However, Williams's
activity also played an integral part in English Baptist history, which war-
rants his mention in this essay. He grew up in London in the midst of an
Anglican tradition before graduating from Cambridge in 1627. In 1631,
Williams made the journey to Boston. He returned to England in 1643
to obtain a charter for Providence, Rhode Island, and while in England,
he wrote *The Bloudy Tenent of Persecution for Cause of Conscience.*[69] He
returned the next year to Providence.

Roger Williams's views as presented in *The Bloudy Tenent* were influenced by the previously discussed work of Murton. He began with twelve
statements that summarize the work. In those twelve statements, Williams
argued along the same lines as those before him. He stated that "civil states"
are "not judges, governors, or defenders of the spiritual, or Christian, state
and worship."[70] With this statement Williams supported the view of two
kingdoms—one secular and one spiritual. He also supported complete religious liberty when he wrote, "It is the will and command of God that, since
the coming of his Son the Lord Jesus, a permission of the most paganish,
Jewish, Turkish, or anti-Christian consciences and worships be granted to

---

[67] McBeth, *English Baptist Literature on Religious Liberty to 1689,* 275–76.
[68] Lumpkin, *Baptist Confessions of Faith,* 169–71.
[69] Ibid.
[70] Roger Williams, *The Bloudy Tenent of Persecution for Cause of Conscience* (London, 1644; reprint, Macon, GA: Mercer University Press, 2001), 1.

all men in all nations and countries, and they are only to be fought against
with that sword which is only, in soul matters, able to conquer, to wit, the
sword of God's Spirit, the word of God."[71] Williams took these beliefs to
the American continent and influenced the establishment of American religious liberty.

Unfortunately, this current discussion is bound by page limitations,
and many worthwhile authors cannot be discussed in detail. Solace can be
taken in the fact that many of these works repeat what has already been
stated; however, the scholar interested in further research should consult
the following authors: Edward Barber, Christopher Blackwood, Thomas
Collier, William Dell, Richard Laurence, Samuel Richardson, John Tombes,
John Clarke, Henry Denne, and John Sturgion, to name a few.

Conclusion

From this historical discussion, six statements summarize the defense of
religious liberty. First, God established two separate kingdoms with one
governing the worldly and the other the spiritual. Second, the civil government has authority in worldly matters but not over spiritual ones. Third,
the church should handle spiritual discipline. Fourth, none can influence
the soul to accept or reject Christ by force. Conversion must occur by a
voluntary decision of the individual in order to have validity. Fifth, killing
a person for improper spiritual beliefs does not allow that individual due
time to accept the proper beliefs, and ignores Christ's teaching of the parable of the Wheat and the Tares in Matthew 13. Sixth, complete religious
liberty must extend to all people, including heretics.

A blanket statement suggesting that all Baptists had consistently
advocated religious liberty as discussed in this chapter might be an
overstatement;[72] however, the majority of published authors have consistently supported religious liberty. McBeth wrote concerning the English
Baptists, "That Baptists alone in seventeenth-century England consistently

---

[71] Ibid.

[72] For instance, consider the Muenster Anabaptists and the English Fifth
Monarchists.

advocated complete religious liberty is to their credit."[73] Additionally, through publishing works on religious liberty, these authors believed it necessary to speak prophetically to the government. While Baptists must place their faith wholly and only in Christ and not in secular authorities, Baptists must also continue to speak prophetically to the government. This is religious freedom.

[73] McBeth, *English Baptist Literature on Religious Liberty to 1689*, 278.

CHAPTER 3

EARLY AMERICAN POLITICAL THEOLOGY

Malcolm B. Yarnell III

According to British ethicist Oliver O'Donovan, "Theology must be political if it is to be evangelical. Rule out the political questions and you cut short the proclamation of God's saving power; you leave people enslaved where they ought to be set free from sin—their own sin and others.'"[1] O'Donovan's thesis calls for us to reexamine the theological basis of American politics. The gospel, he suggests, is concerned with politics, the communal aspect of ethics. If that is true, then Christians, in their silence, forsake a dimension of the good news for their community. The gospel confession that "Jesus is Lord" entails the construction of not only a personal soteriology but also a political theology.[2]

---

[1] Oliver O'Donovan, *The Desire of the Nations: Rediscovering the Roots of Political Theory* (New York: Cambridge University Press, 1996), 3.

[2] Because it is rare for an American evangelical to present an essay on "political theology," a quick apology seems necessary. This may be one of the first American Baptist papers to treat political theology as a viable discipline. The very term

In another work I considered the historical development of political theology and religious liberty;[3] here I will focus upon the early United States. Opposing political theologies informed the legal foundations of the colonies that became the United States of America. The contours of Congregationalist theocracy promoted by the Puritan fathers who founded Massachusetts are fairly well known.[4] A counterpoint to this theocracy may be found in the toleration advocated in Pennsylvania's constitutional documents, which the great Quaker leader William Penn promulgated. According to the 1988 Williamsburg Charter, which prominently drew together the profound legacy of early American defenders of religious tolerance such as William Penn as well as Roger Williams and James Madison, "[The] right to religious liberty based upon freedom of conscience remains fundamental and inalienable."[5]

Among Baptists, however, the development of political theology is even more complex than the opposing extremes of Puritan theocracy and Quaker toleration.

-----

political theology seems like an oxymoron to the modern mind. The Enlightenment advocated separating politics and theology, and American scholars for the most part adopted that program as part and parcel of separating church and state. The religious contributions in history to the public square were thereby suppressed. Religion, for atheistic humanist and evangelical Christian alike, became a private matter, and any religio-political discourse brought dire proclamations regarding the betrayal of the Baptist tradition. For instance, with the rise of evangelical involvement in American politics, Bill Moyers decried a conspiracy that would lead to both "theocracy" (the rule of the state by the church) and "civil religion" (the rule of the church by the state). Bill Moyers, foreword to William R. Estep, *Revolution within the Revolution: The First Amendment in Historical Context, 1612–1789* (Grand Rapids: Eerdmans, 1990).

[3] Malcolm B. Yarnell III, "The Development of Religious Liberty: A Survey of Its Progress and Challenges in Christian History," *Journal for Baptist Theology and Ministry* 6.1 (2009): 119–38.

[4] McBeth summarizes the various challenges to religious liberty in New England, the middle colonies, and the southern colonies. H. Leon McBeth, *The Baptist Heritage* (Nashville: Broadman, 1987), 252–87.

[5] Arlin M. Adams and Charles J. Emmerich, "William Penn and the American Heritage of Religious Liberty," *Journal of Law and Religion* 8 (1990): 57–70. For the text of the 1988 document, along with a list of prominent signatories, see *Finding Common Ground: A First Amendment Guide to Religion and Public Schools*, ed. Charles C. Haynes and Oliver Thomas (Nashville: First Amendment Center, 2007), 283–308.

Two Baptist Traditions of Political Theology

At least two traditions in the American Baptist conversation concern church and state. They may be referred to as the "major tradition" and the "minor tradition," or the "Virginia tradition" and the "South Carolina tradition," respectively, taking those names from the geographic centers representing each tradition. The first tends toward the Quaker position, while the second tends toward the Puritan position. The first emphasizes individual freedom and the separation of church and state, while the second emphasizes divine providence, human constitutionalism, and social order in such a way that universal religious liberty might be moderated.

The Virginia tradition is identified with the rhetoric of John Leland, the agitation of the Danbury Baptist Association, and the subsequent separation doctrine in the federal judiciary. Its narrative rehearses the separation of church and state in English Baptist life, claims Roger Williams established Rhode Island with "complete religious liberty," and exults in an 1802 letter by Thomas Jefferson.[6] Jefferson's letter gained judicial force in 1878 when, in the case of a polygamist Mormon, US Supreme Court Justice Morrison Waite used Robert Baylor Semple's *A History of the Rise and Progress of the Baptists in Virginia* to interpret the Constitution's First Amendment in terms of "a wall of separation between the church and state." More significantly, Justice Hugo Black, in the 1947 case of *Everson v. Board of Education*, elevated separation to the status of a constitutional right.[7] The Virginia tradition has institutional advocates from the juridical perspective in the Supreme Court and the Americans United for the Separation of Church and State and from a Baptist perspective in the J. M. Dawson Institute of Church and State Studies at Baylor University.

---

[6] See Joseph Martin Dawson, *Baptists and the American Republic* (Nashville: Broadman, 1956); Robert A. Baker, "Baptist Heritage and Religious Liberty," in *Christianity and Religious Liberty: Messages from the Eighth Annual Christian Life Workshop* (Fort Worth: Texas Baptist Christian Life Commission, 1964), 8–19; Estep, *Revolution within the Revolution*; Bill J. Leonard, *Baptists in America* (New York: Columbia University Press, 2005), 157–61.

[7] See Philip Hamburger, *Separation of Church and State* (Cambridge, MA: Harvard University Press, 2002), 260, 454–78.

However, the Virginia tradition has not lacked theological and juridical critics. As early as 1937, Baptist scholars discovered inconveniences
in the narrative. For instance, the English Baptist confessions advocated
religious liberty but left separation unstated. English Baptist treatises
trumpeted liberty of conscience, the antithesis of persecution, but they
also proposed parliamentary laws that placed boundaries around religious
discourse.[8] Moreover, Williams's Rhode Island granted citizenship only to
Christians, discriminated against both blacks and Roman Catholics, and
utilized state funds to construct the First Baptist Church sanctuary ("A
degree of religious toleration existed from the beginning but there was no
complete separation of church and state"). Fortunately for the Virginia tradition, some have concluded that at least Virginia Baptists deserve a "merit
award" for "religious liberty."[9]

Alongside the Virginia tradition stands the South Carolina tradition.
Besides the obvious geographical difference, the traditions differ in their

---

[8] Leonard Busher wanted an open marketplace of religious discussion, but
discussions were to be limited by the authority of Scripture and were to refrain
from "reproach or slander." While king and Parliament should not intervene in the
church, they were to enforce the Bible's moral law. See *Religions Peace* (Amsterdam:
1614; reprint, London: 1646), 22, 31. "Busher was not entirely a utopian dreamer:
he believed that freedom of conscience would need some hedges round it if it were
to work." Barrie White, "Early Baptist Arguments for Religious Freedom: Their
Overlooked Agenda," *Baptist History and Heritage* 24 (1989): 7. For Busher's political
theology, see Malcolm B. Yarnell III, "Political Theology among the Earliest Baptists:
The Foundational Contribution of Leonard Busher, 1614–1646," in *Freedom and the
Powers: Perspectives from Baptist History Marking the 400th Anniversary of Thomas
Helwys'* The Mystery of Iniquity, ed. Anthony R. Cross and John H. Y. Briggs (Didcot:
Baptist Historical Society, 2014), 23–34.

[9] Conrad Henry Moehlman, "The Baptist View of the State," *Church History* 6
(1937): 24–49. Baptist concerns aside, from the juridical perspective, historians and
legal scholars have begun to cast doubt on the original intent of the founding fathers
of America. It has been argued that the judicial doctrine of separation may legally
protect the lone ranger while it restricts the freedoms of churchgoers. Indeed, there
is some doubt as to whether Jefferson really intended the establishment clause to
be understood in the modern metaphorical sense of a wall of separation between
church and state. In other words, the metaphor may be carrying more intellectual and
juridical weight than warranted. Questions of original intent have driven cultural and
legal scholars to reexamine the context and import of Jefferson's famous statement. Of
course, from a theological perspective, Jefferson's intent is germane only insofar as he
faithfully reflected broadly based Baptist beliefs.

class orientations and relationship to government. Virginia Baptists were of the "lower" and "middling" sorts[10] and fought a trenchant establishment foe in the aristocratic Church of England. Through persecution, they became convinced the state should never address religion. Upon returning to Connecticut from Virginia, John Leland wrote, "Let every man speak freely without fear, maintain the principles that he believes, worship according to his own faith, either one God, three Gods, no God, or twenty Gods; and let government protect him in so doing, i.e., see that he meets with no personal abuse, or loss of property, for his religious opinions."[11] The Virginia tradition bequeathed Baptists the doctrine of separation of church and state as a necessarily negative statement about political theology. The separation of church and state seeks to guarantee that no church be established by government or in any way privileged over any other church or religion.

The South Carolina tradition offers Baptists a more activist statement regarding political involvement. South Carolina Baptists arose from the first wave of British immigrants to what became the wealthiest American city in the eighteenth century, Charles Town or Charleston. These Baptists owned massive tracts of land and slaves, kept houses in the city and plantations in the country, advocated classical learning, and participated in colonial government. Their earliest members included aristocrats like Lady Elizabeth Axtell Blake.[12]

---

[10] Virginia Baptists were vividly described by a contemporary as "hare-lipped, blear-eyed, hump-backed, bow-legged, clump-footed; barely any of them looked like other people. But they were all strong for plunging" (Frank Lambert, *The Founding Fathers and the Place of Religion in America* [Princeton: Princeton University Press, 2003], 151); contemporary quoted in Moehlman, "Baptist View of the State," 41.

[11] *The Rights of Conscience Inalienable, and, Therefore, Religious Opinions Not Cognizable by Law (1791)*, in *The Writings of the Late Elder John Leland* (New York: G. W. Wood, 1845), 184.

[12] See Robert A. Baker and Paul J. Craven Jr., *Adventure in Faith: The First 300 Years of First Baptist Church, Charleston, South Carolina* (Nashville: Broadman, 1982), 24–26. Lady Blake was the wife of a governor of South Carolina, Landgrave Joseph Blake, and the descendant of a regicide. See M. Eugene Sirmans, "Politics in Colonial South Carolina: The Failure of Proprietary Reform, 1682–1694," *The William and Mary Quarterly* 23 (1966): 36. Concerning the South Carolina aristocracy composed of landgraves and cassiques, see ibid., n37.

In order to understand this lesser-known South Carolina tradition of political theology, this chapter will evaluate the thinking of three of its earliest and most prominent pastors: William Screven, Oliver Hart, and Richard Furman. Their pastorates at First Baptist Church of Charleston stretch from 1696 to 1825. These three theologians represent no mere historical sideline. Screven was the first Baptist pastor in the South. Hart established the first Baptist association in the South. And Furman founded the first national convention of Baptists and the first state convention. Moreover, their influence largely determined Baptist political thought in the southern United States into the Civil War period.

1. The Political Theology of William Screven

Dissenters from the Church of England, which included Presbyterians, Baptists, Quakers, and Huguenots, came to South Carolina with the promise of religious liberty. In 1663, shortly after "the era of the great persecution" began in England, Charles II granted a charter that guaranteed both religious liberty and limited self-government for those who would emigrate to Carolina.[13] In the advertisements published in 1664 and 1666 to entice settlers, religious liberty was prominent. "There is full and free Liberty of Conscience granted to all, so that no man is to be molested or called in question for matters of Religious Concern; but every one to be obedient to the Civil Government, worshiping God after their own way."[14]

In 1669, *The Fundamental Constitutions*, devised for the Carolina colony by Enlightenment philosopher and proponent of toleration John Locke, defined the structure of colonial self-governance and the extent of religious liberty. While restricting citizenship to theists and allowing the

---

[13] B. R. White, *The English Baptists of the Seventeenth Century* (Didcot: Baptist Historical Society, 1996), 95–133. The grant was reissued in 1665. Samuel Wilson, *An Account of the Province of Carolina in America. Together with an Abstract of the Patent* (London: 1682), 22, 25 (arts. 7, 19).

[14] *A Brief Description of the Province of Carolina on the Coasts of Floreda* (London: 1666), 6. See William Hilton, *A Relation of a Discovery lately made on the Coast of Florida . . . Together with Proposals made by the Commissioners of the Lords Proprietors, to all such persons as shall become the first Setlers on the Rivers, Harbors, and Creeks there* (London: 1664), 34 (art. 18).

colonial parliament to grant public maintenance to the Church of England, covenanted churches were allowed to form, set their own terms of communion, and expect protection from disturbance or molestation.[15] Revised in 1682, *The Fundamental Constitutions* retained their guarantees of religious liberty, furthering them in one important way: Dissenters could not be taxed to support the established church.[16]

One of the lords proprietor of the new colony, John Archdale, was active in both South Carolina and Maine as a governor. He was governor of Maine in 1691 and 1695, returning to Carolina each time. A moderate Quaker, Archdale was driven from Maine by the New England authorities. A Baptist from Maine followed Archdale on his final return to Carolina.[17]

That Baptist, William Screven, was the first Baptist pastor to settle among these Dissenters. Originally from Somerton in western England, Screven first surfaced as a disciple of the early Baptist leader Thomas Collier and signed the 1656 Somerset Confession drawn up by Collier.[18] Screven next appears in the governmental records of Maine and the church minutes of the Baptist church in Boston, Massachusetts. In 1676, he was named constable for lower Kittery, Maine, and served on the grand jury in 1678 and 1679. Also in 1679, he signed a petition asking the king to grant "liberty to tender consciences" against the theocracy of Massachusetts. In 1682, he was licensed by the Boston church and soon constituted a Baptist church by covenant at Kittery.[19]

---

[15] John Locke, *The Fundamental Constitutions of Carolina* (n.p.: n.d.), 20–23 (arts. 95–106).

[16] Sirmans, "Politics in Colonial South Carolina," 34–35.

[17] Peter H. Wood, "Archdale, John (1642–1717)," in *Oxford Dictionary of National Biography* (Oxford: Oxford University Press, 2004).

[18] Baker and Craven, *Adventure in Faith*, 33–40; Stephen Wright, s.v. "Collier, Thomas (d. 1691), *Oxford Dictionary of National Biography* (Oxford: Oxford University Press, 2004). Collier has been described by this most recent biographer as a "political preacher" who conceived authority as deriving from "the Agreement of the people." Collier engaged the religious politics of both Levellers and Fifth Monarchists. Although a Particular Baptist messenger, Collier mitigated against strict Calvinism. Collier's openness toward General Baptists may explain how Screven at first countenanced the fellowship of General Baptists with his own church.

[19] In line with the Collier tradition, the Kittery covenant affirmed the authority of Word and Spirit. They covenanted to keep the ordinances that are "Revealed to us in his sacred word of ye ould & new Testament and according to ye grace of God &

Screven was called before the colonial courts because "Infant Baptisms hee sayd was an ordinance of the Devil." After sentencing by three successive courts, he avoided punishment by agreeing to leave the province. However, he changed his mind, ignored the courts, grew the Kittery church, and raised a prosperous family. After the temporary weakening of the Massachusetts theocracy in 1684, he occupied several important civil offices. Over a decade later, Screven immigrated to South Carolina, along with several of his church members, purchasing a vast estate called Somerton. Screven's public weight, manifested in his ability to ignore the judgments of numerous courts, prompted Robert A. Baker, a meticulous historian, to conclude that "he and his church were not driven from Maine by Puritan persecution." Apparently, economic incentive and greater political influence compelled the move.[20]

Screven did not leave a corpus of extant writings, except for the occasional letter, covenant, or confession. However, in these fragments one can discern the rudiments of a political theology. In terms reminiscent of revolutionary English Baptist thought, he identified Jesus Christ as "the Lord . . . the King of saints."[21] He believed that "the ministry of civil justice is an ordinance of God, and that it is the duty of the saints to be subject thereunto not only for fear, but for conscience sake, and that for such, prayers and supplications are to be made by the saints."[22] His disobedience toward the Massachusetts magistrates is best explained by his belief that royal authority was superior to colonial authority. A scrupulous man motivated by the desire to obey "all [Christ's] most holy & blessed Commandments Ordinances Institutions or Appointments," he detected

---

light att present through his grace given us, or here after he shall please to discover & make knowne to us thro his Holy Spirit to ye same blessed word." Quoted in Baker and Craven, *Adventure in Faith*, 60–61.

[20] Robert A. Baker, "The Contributions of South Carolina Baptists to the Rise and Development of the Southern Baptist Convention," *Baptist History and Heritage* 17 (1982): 3.

[21] Screven to Thomas Skinner, September 13, 1682, quoted in Baker and Craven, *Adventure in Faith*, 58.

[22] *A Confession of the Faith of Several Churches of Christ in the County of Somerset, and of some Churches in the Counties neer adjacent* (London: 1656), art. 44, in William L. Lumpkin, ed., *Baptist Confessions of Faith*, rev. ed. (Valley Forge, PA: Judson, 1969), 215.

no conflict between holding ecclesiastical and civil offices simultaneously. Screven believed God intimately directs the affairs of men: his ministry and even his health were subject to being "cast" about "by providence."[23]

In a series of letters to the Boston church in 1708, Screven reaffirmed his belief in Providence and surmised that God was punishing theocratic Boston with sickness for committing "the sin of persecution."[24] Interestingly, two 1711 letters to the Euhaw church in South Carolina, which was closely affiliated with Screven's Charleston church, were sent from the South Moulton church in Devonshire, in response to the Euhaw church's query concerning slavery. (The Devonshire and Somersetshire churches associated with one another in the days of Screven's English residence.) The South Moulton church and the western association of churches approved the institution of slavery since it was legalized "by the Majestrate." Screven seems to have countenanced the institution.[25]

The above information is available in the modern literature; however, an important letter that Screven authored has not been recognized. Moreover, a seminal struggle for religious liberty in South Carolina has been misunderstood if not misrepresented.[26] The narrative of that struggle sheds light on the complex political theology of these southern colonial Baptists. The story begins in 1704, when a rogue governor and rump session of South Carolina's parliament tried to weaken their political opponents—many but

---

[23] Kittery Church Covenant; Baptist Church of Boston minutes, January 11, 1682; Screven to Skinner, September 13, 1682, quoted in Baker and Craven, *Adventure in Faith*, 53, 59, 60.

[24] Screven to Baptist Church of Boston, June 2, 1707; Screven to Ellis Callender, February 10, 1708; Screven to Ellis Callender, August 6, 1708; quoted in Baker and Craven, *Adventure in Faith*, 86–90.

[25] William G. McLoughlin and Winthrop D. Jordan, "Baptists Face the Barbarities of Slavery in 1710," *Journal of Southern History* 29 (1962): 495–501. B. R. White, ed., *Association Records of the Particular Baptists of England, Wales and Ireland to 1660*, part 2, *The West Country and Ireland* (London: Baptist Historical Society, 1973), 53. See also the western association's negative position in 1655 and 1656 on government maintenance of Baptist ministers (ibid., 62–66, 74–75). These associational meetings had representatives, including William Screven, from Somerton.

[26] Joe M. King, whose research is otherwise helpful, naively claims that the Establishment Act, which was "first passed in 1704, was again adopted in 1706." *History of South Carolina Baptists* (Columbia, SC: South Carolina Baptist Convention, 1964), 137.

not all of whom were Dissenters—by establishing the Church of England. They did this through the Establishment Act and the Preservation Act, both adopted amidst scenes of acrimony and violence.

The Establishment Act constituted six Berkeley county parishes. It funded their buildings through voluntary gifts first and then the public treasury. It made parochial charges payable by all inhabitants, and it established a commission to govern the Anglican clergy. The Preservation Act, which mirrored the occasional acts then seeking passage through England's Parliament, excluded from the colonial assembly those who would not receive the sacrament from or swear to the Church of England. This created a firestorm of protest in both South Carolina and London. In 1705, Daniel Defoe wrote a treatise on behalf of the Dissenters for presentation primarily to the House of Commons. Defoe identified "Party-Tyranny" with "High-Church-Tyranny" and asked the Commons to "Defend the English Subjects from all manner of Invasions of their Liberty."[27] Petitions and petitioners arrived in quick succession from South Carolina.

In 1706, a small book called *The Case of Protestant Dissenters* presented the Dissenters' logic and relevant documents not to the Commons but to the House of Lords. The anonymous writer warned that Dissenters, whom he characterized as "above two Thirds of the Inhabitants of Carolina, as well as the most sober, orderly, and the richest, that is, the most Landed and Trading Men in the Province," had been unconstitutionally persecuted. If their religious liberty was not to be protected, then civil liberty would also be lost, not only in the colony but in England.[28]

In a brilliant move, the Dissenters rejected the thesis that the establishment represented the views of the high church party in the Church of England. The Dissenters appealed to the travails of a Charleston Anglican

---

[27] "An Act for the Establishment of Religious Worship in this Province according to the Church of England," in *The Case of Protestant Dissenters in Carolina, Shewing How a Law to prevent Occasional Conformity There, has ended in the Total Subversion of the Constitution in Church and State* (London: 1706), addenda, 44–55; "An Act for the more effectual Preservation of the Government of this Province," in ibid., Addenda, 38–41; Daniel Defoe, *Party-Tyranny or, An Occasional Bill in Miniature; As now Practiced in Carolina (1705)*, in *Narratives of Early Carolina 1650–1708*, ed. Alexander S. Salley Jr. (New York: Scribner, 1911), 224.

[28] *Case of Protestant Dissenters*, 4, 16–17.

priest, Edward Marston, a Non-Juror, as proof of the subversive nature of the South Carolina acts. They heightened the emotional appeal with accounts of dissenting nobles, such as Landgrave Thomas Smith, whose family included Baptists, being accosted in the streets by government rabble; with an account of an Anglican minister being whipped by a government leader; and with an account of the rape and murder of a pregnant woman. They also printed a letter from Lady Elizabeth Blake concerning the tyranny of governance "by arbitrary power" as opposed to constitutional power.[29]

The Dissenters also presented an affidavit signed by a leading Presbyterian minister, Archibald Stobo, and Baptist minister William Screven. Screven, whose name is listed first, reviewed a recent sermon on the Fifth Commandment by Marston, the high church minister in Charleston. Screven concurred with Marston's assertion that a minister did not owe an accounting to the government for his actions, even if he received a government stipend. He also agreed that Marston was due a maintenance "by Divine Right" and that a minister is superior to the government, "his Authority being from Christ": "We (Ministers of the Gospel) do not arrogate too much to our selves, nor take too much upon us, when we affirm, That we are superior to the People, and have an Authority over them in Things Spiritual, and appertaining to God."[30]

Although the lead proprietor approved the new laws and defended them in print against the protests of the dissenting aristocracy, the Dissenters carried the day.[31] The House of Lords, upon reviewing the case, resolved that the Act of Establishment was "not warranted by the charter granted to the Proprietors" and that the Act of Preservation "is founded on falsity in matter of fact, is repugnant to the laws of England, contrary to the charter of the Proprietors, is an encouragement to atheism and irreligion, destructive to trade, and tends to the depopulation and ruin of the Province." The

---

[29] Ibid., addenda, 42–44.

[30] Bishop Ezekiel Hopkins's works are subsequently cited as authoritative in the matter (ibid., addenda, 55–56).

[31] *An Account of the Fair and Impartial Proceedings of the Lords Proprietors, Governour and Council of the Colony of South Carolina (1706).* A petition by Joseph Boone and others entitled *The Case of the Church of England in Carolina* is referenced, but the document is not extant.

House of Lords also asked Queen Anne to deliver South Carolina "from the arbitrary oppressions under which it now lies" because "the powers given by the crown have been abused by some of your subjects."

Queen Anne vowed to protect her Carolinian subjects "in their just rights," nullified the acts, and considered revoking the proprietary charter. The defeat of the conformists was complete. Even the Society for the Propagation of the Gospel in Foreign Parts, an Anglican missionary society formed to counter the influence of American Dissenters, passed a resolution against the Act of Establishment. A Presbyterian historian affirmed that "wise and religious men of all denominations" aided in breaking the colonial government.[32]

Subsequently, Governor Joseph Blake's 1697 Act for Granting Liberty of Conscience was recognized as authoritative. The Acts of Preservation and Establishment and similar acts were "Repealed, Annulled, Revoked and forever made void." A new Act of Establishment was adopted in 1706 but in a severely chastened form. The Church of England was indeed established and its parish system received parliamentary definition, but the dissenting churches, though not established, were protected. Moreover, the colony moved toward voluntary maintenance of the churches. An act from the sixth year of George II, which discussed the construction of St. George's parish church, mandated that the minister's stipend was to be funded by pew rents and by the expected gift of "any person or persons" of a glebe.[33] In 1712 the colony again recognized the charter's grant of religious liberty.

By 1720, Baptists were celebrating marriage ceremonies in spite of Anglican complaints. By 1744, the Anglican clergy reluctantly affirmed the rights of these Dissenters to "full Liberty of Conscience." When the General Baptists and Particular Baptists argued over the ownership of the Charleston church property in 1745, all parties appealed to the colonial assembly. The assembly judiciously rendered a split decision, seeking to

---

[32] Alexander Hewat, *An Historical Account of the Rise and Progress of the Colonies of South Carolina and Georgia* (London: 1779), 161–78. See John Oldmixon, *The British Empire in America, Containing the History of the Discovery, Settlement, Progress and State of the British Colonies on the Continent and Islands of America* (London: 1741), 1:473–91.

[33] Nicholas Trott, ed., *The Laws of the Province of South Carolina in Two Parts* (Charles-Town: 1736), 1:105–6, 127–44; 2:63.

satisfy the influential members of the First Baptist Church of Charleston. The only possible case of persecution after the 1704 debacle occurred shortly before 1772, when a Baptist preacher named Joseph Cates was publicly whipped. However, Cates was being punished for immorality— certainly not a cause célèbre for religious liberty. Moreover, at this very time, a visiting Anglican minister complained that Dissenters dominated the colonial government and nobility. By 1790, the parishes were still established, but the limited ministerial maintenances that the 1706 revision had provided for a few of the original parishes were simply absented from the public laws. The 1712 blue law requiring attendance at some religious assembly on Sunday and the 1722 poor law requiring parochial maintenance of public welfare remained but occasioned no comment. The oath of all public officers required the swearer to "maintain and defend the laws of God, the Protestant religion, and the liberties of America."[34] South Carolina Baptists appear not to have objected.

Eighteenth-century Baptists in South Carolina, under the leadership of Screven, who expired at an advanced age in 1713, rose to the top of society and prospered within the colonial government. When their religious liberty was threatened, they formed alliances with Presbyterians, Quakers, and even Non-Juror Anglicans to maintain a generally tolerable environment. Yet these Baptists were not fully committed to universal religious liberty, preferring a dalliance with a limited establishment.

2. The Political Theology of Oliver Hart

After Screven's death, the Charleston church entered a period of internecine struggle. The core of the church, composed of Particular Baptists, wanted their next pastor to subscribe to the Second London Confession, as Screven did. However, the Calvinist party vied both with a Unitarian-Arminian party and with a moderating party led by their next pastor,

---

[34] In 1730, the charter of the proprietors was revoked and the colony received royal protection. John Faucheraud Grimke, ed., *The Public Laws of the State of South-Carolina* (Philadelphia: 1790), 11–14, 17–21, 100, 117–18, 203, 297; Baker and Craven, *Adventure in Faith*, 107–21; Grimke, *Public Laws*, xxxv; King, *History of South Carolina Baptists*, 137–38.

Thomas Simmons. The parties split into separate fellowships, but the Arminian and moderate fellowships declined and ultimately disappeared. Subsequently, the only pastoral ministry in the Charleston church came from Isaac Chanler of the nearby Ashley River Church, and when he died in December 1749, the Baptists of the area despaired. Providentially, however, Oliver Hart, a Baptist minister from the Philadelphia Association, having heard of the needs in Charleston, arrived by ship on the same day as Chanler's funeral. Discerning divine mercy, the Charleston church immediately called Hart as their pastor.[35]

Hart was shaped religiously not only by the Particular or Regular Baptist ethos of the Philadelphia Association but also by the revivalistic fervor of the Great Awakening. Hart was especially affected by George Whitefield's preaching and later invited the grand itinerant to speak in his church. One of Hart's own disciples, Nicholas Bedgegood, later managed Whitefield's Savannah orphanage. It is widely believed that Whitefield's preaching, by violating parish boundaries, created a democratic impulse that helped foster the American revolution.[36] Hart may have supported the egalitarian impulses the Great Awakening set loose, but he also maintained a traditional view of "ranks and orders."

In stark contrast to the disparaging picture presented of the Virginia Baptists, Richard Furman, whom we will come to momentarily, said of this South Carolinian pastor, "In his person he was somewhat tall, well proportioned, and of a graceful appearance; of an active, vigorous constitution, before it had been impaired by close application to his studies, and by his abundant labours; his countenance was open and manly, his voice clear, harmonious and commanding; the powers of his mind were strong and capacious, and enriched by a fund of useful knowledge; his taste was elegant and refined." Similarly, the wider Charleston community highly respected Hart. On one occasion, for instance, Hart was robbed of 30

---

[35] Loulie Latimer Owens, "Oliver Hart, 1723–1795: A Brief Biography," *Baptist History and Heritage* 1 (1966): 21–25.

[36] Nancy Ruttenburg, "George Whitefield, Spectacular Conversion, and the Rise of Democratic Personality," *American Literary History* 5 (1993): 429–58; Nathan O. Hatch, *The Democratization of American Christianity* (New Haven: Yale University Press, 1989), 56–57; Lambert, *The Founding Fathers and the Place of Religion in America*, 127–49.

pounds in currency. Yet the townspeople, from all denominations, reimbursed Hart with 730 pounds, later Baptist pastor Basil Manley recounted. Manly also rehearsed how Hart left the Charleston church with a phenomenal endowment of 14,700 pounds. The cultured Hart developed irenic relations not only with Regular Baptists, General Baptists, Welsh Baptists, and Separate Baptists but also with Independents, Methodists, Presbyterians, and Anglicans. Hart was quite comfortable with wealthy citizens of all denominations in this premiere southern city. Being "elegant and refined" was obviously a prerequisite for the leading Baptist pastor in the high culture of late-colonial Charleston.[37]

Hart's influence reaped political as well as social and financial rewards for the Baptists. He organized the first association of Baptist churches in the southern United States in 1751. This association furnished the exemplar for all future southern associations and state conventions and gave southern Baptists a comprehensive model of denominational cooperation. The Charleston Association's powers were carefully restricted to that of "a Council of Advice," but this did not prevent the association from promoting missions, ministerial education, the adoption of a confession, the adoption of an official ecclesiology, and, most importantly for our purposes, the advocacy of religious liberty. In 1775, the association sought contributions for Massachusetts Baptists in their struggle for effective religious liberty. In 1777, the association encouraged Baptist churches to incorporate themselves with the government. In 1779, the association delegated authority to Hart and two other leading ministers to "treat with government on behalf of the churches" and monitor the ministers in the area.[38]

In 1776 and 1777, Hart joined the leading Independent minister, William Tennent, to promote a multidenominational petition for a constitution that would simultaneously seek to establish all Protestant churches and provide full liberty for all Protestants. The General Assembly of South

---

[37] Richard Furman, *Rewards of Grace Conferred on Christ's Faithful People: A Sermon, Occasioned by the Decease of the Rev. Oliver Hart, A.M.* (Charleston: 1796); Basil Manly, *Mercy and Judgment: A Discourse, Containing Some Fragments of the History of the Baptist Church in Charleston, S.C.* (Charleston: 1837), n34, 45–46; Baker and Craven, *Adventure in Faith*, 133–35.

[38] King, *History of South Carolina Baptists*, 62–68; Baker and Craven, *Adventure in Faith*, 149–54.

Carolina published a bill for the new constitution on February 3, 1777. Two days later, the Charleston Association issued a circular letter composed largely by Hart. He said the bill provided "universal religious liberty in this State" and included "reasonable and easy" terms that all churches should adopt. The bill detailed five beliefs that an established church must affirm in order to be "incorporated, and esteemed as a Church of the established religion of this state." All Protestant denominations were deemed equal; the clergy were given basic instructions on piety and performance; voluntary giving was recognized as the only means of support; and clergy were placed on the same level as laity, except that they were barred from government office. A week later, in a private letter to Richard Furman, Hart opined that Baptists should look to the state to grant "all our Privileges, civil and religious." His only fear was that some of the Separate Baptists might not "unite together in one band" in order to have more influence on the state. One Virginia scholar deemed this constitution "a definite limitation on liberty of conscience," but Hart, the leading Baptist in eighteenth-century South Carolina, was rather enthusiastic.[39]

Hart was a fervent advocate of the American Revolution. His cousin John Hart signed the Declaration of Independence for New Jersey. Hart himself scouted British military activities in New York and, upon his return to Charleston, was deputed by the Council of Safety for a special task. Along with William Tennent and William-Henry Drayton, subsequently president of the South Carolina Congress, Hart traveled to "the Back Country" to represent the revolutionary cause and to counter the influence of Tories and pacifists upon the Separate Baptists. Hart's commissioning document referred to him as a "lover of constitutional liberty." For his largely successful services, the provincial congress publicly recognized him in November

---

[39] *"First*, That there is one eternal God, and a future state of rewards and punishments. *Second*, That God is to be publickly worshiped. *Third*, the Christian Religion is the true religion. *Fourth*, That the Holy Scriptures of the Old and New Testament, are divinely inspired, and are the rule of faith and practice. *Fifth*, That it is lawful, and the duty of every man being thereunto called by those that govern, to bear witness to the truth." *A Bill for Establishing the Constitution of the State of South Carolina* (Charlestown: 1777), 14, 19–23; Hart to Furman, February 12, 1777; Baker and Craven, *Adventure in Faith*, 167–71. The primary source materials printed by Baker for this period are helpful, but his commentary reflects the Virginia tradition.

1775. Unfortunately, the British troops also recognized Hart's contributions and, when they occupied Charleston, appropriated the Baptist properties to store salt beef and forage. Hart fled from the city to the home of his daughter, who had married Captain Thomas Screven. He subsequently escaped northward from the advancing British troops and ended his days as pastor of a New Jersey church.[40]

Hart advocated the political theology of the South Carolina tradition, not only in deed but also in print. His diaries and letters are filled with references to the guidance of divine Providence over the affairs of individuals and of nations, in war and in peace. In the same paragraph, he could refer both to human constitutional deliberations and to their utter dependence on God: "After all, nothing can save us but the Interposition of the great Governor of the Universe; in Him may we place all our Confidence and may He mercifully condescend to help a sinful People." Hart not only correlated divine Providence with human politics; he also correlated the emergence of civil liberty with religious liberty. The "perfect form of Government" is that in which "the best of Rulers [are] chosen by ourselves." In the context of the expected establishment of civil liberty, religion, "encouraged and promoted, shall spread far and wide."[41]

In 1767, Hart led the Charleston Association to adopt the Philadelphia Confession of Faith, an expansion of the Second London Confession. The Charleston Confession defined divine Providence as God bounding, governing, and ordering creation "in a manifold dispensation." As the "first Cause," God uses "Means" or "second Causes, either necessarily, freely, or contingently," thereby preserving his holiness while advancing his will. Providence delivers judgment on the wicked and both mercy and judgment upon the elect "for their good." Christian liberty is spiritual in nature: "Freedom from the Guilt of Sin." Liberty of conscience means, "God alone is Lord of the Conscience, and hath left it free from the Doctrines and Commandments of Men which are in any Thing contrary to his Word, or

---

[40] *Extracts from the Journals of the Provincial Congress of South-Carolina* (Charlestown, SC: 1776), 164; Manly, *Mercy and Judgment*, 44; Owens, "Oliver Hart," 31–33; King, *History of South Carolina Baptists*, 91–95, 139–40.

[41] Oliver Hart to Joseph Hart, July 5, 1778; Oliver Hart to Joseph Hart, February 16, 1779, quoted in Baker and Craven, *Adventure in Faith*, 170–73.

not contained in it." As for the civil magistrates, God has ordained them to be "under him, over the People, for his own Glory, and the publick Good."[42]

In a fascinating sermon published by the Philadelphia Association, Hart envisioned the perfect religio-political society. The text was Haggai 2:4, and the central figures were "the King of Saints," followed by first, "a prince," second, "an high priest," and last, "the people." The ordering is not merely textual but theological. Repeatedly, Hart cites "the several ranks and orders of men in the christian church." First, he considered "the civil magistrate," whose office "is by no means incompatible with true piety and church-membership." Indeed, pious magistrates, like King David or King Solomon or Constantine the Great, are "nursing fathers" who believe the work of the church is "their main concern." The work of the civil magis- trate is to "protect and defend" the church, "attend" worship as an example to others, "contribute chearfully and liberally," and revere ministers of the church as "ambassadors of Christ."

However, magistrates also have limits with regard to the church. In general, they "have no power in, or over the church, by virtue of civil office." Specifically, "1. They have not authority to enact laws to bind the consciences of men," because "Christ is the sole Lord of conscience." "2. They have no coercive power to compel men to be of this, that, or the other religion; or to worship God in any way, contrary to their own free and voluntary consent." "3. Neither have magistrates any right to impose taxes on church members, or any others, for the support of religion." Hart next sketched the responsibilities of pastors and deacons and, finally, ordinary church members. His social ordering is reminiscent of the medieval great chain of being. The "Lord of Hosts" exceeds angels, who exceed rulers, who exceed other humans. Although he would not allow any man to "arro- gate the title of Head of the church, or vicar of Christ," Hart called rulers, "the vicegerents of Almighty God!"[43]

---

[42] *A Confession of Faith Put forth by the Elders and Brethren of many Congregations of Christians (Baptized upon Profession of their Faith) in London and the Country. Adopted by the Baptist Association met at Philadelphia, Sept. 25, 1742*, 6th ed. (Philadelphia: 1743), 26–30, 75–77, 86–87.

[43] Oliver Hart, *An Humble Attempt to Repair the Christian Temple* (Philadelphia: 1795), 3–5, 7–12, 40, 45.

What was the influence of Oliver Hart? The leading Southern Baptists of the next generation were extensive in their praise. Numerous ministers in the South and a few in the North were ordained and/or educated by this pastor. Edmund Botsford called him, "my honored Father." Basil Manly highly commended him: "While his great end in life was the glory of God, he viewed the salvation of sinners as a principal means of promoting it." Richard Furman honored the life and ministry of "that venerable and excellent man of God," noting the careful interconnections and distinctions of the relationship between politics and religion in Hart's teaching. On the one hand, Hart sought "to preserve his *political liberty*, with which he found his *religious* [liberty] intimately connected." He loved liberty and pursued the rights of his country "against the encroachments of arbitrary power." On the other hand, "Yet he did not mix politics with the gospel, nor desert the duties of his station to pursue them; but attending to each in its proper place, he gave weight to his political sentiments, by the propriety and uprightness of his conduct; and the influence of it was felt by many."[44]

Where William Screven brought South Carolina Baptists governmental influence, Oliver Hart taught Baptists how politics and religion might be "intimately connected," but without being improperly mixed on both the national and local levels.

3. The Political Theology of Richard Furman

After Oliver Hart's departure, the church looked to the Charleston Association to provide ministerial leadership. They offered the pulpit to Richard Furman, then pastor at High Hills of Santee, but he declined. Later, however, Furman changed his mind. Manly reckoned that Furman's pastorate represents "the most important period of the church's history."[45]

---

[44] Manly, *Mercy and Judgment*, 34; Furman, *Rewards of Grace*, 7, 22, 26–27; Baker and Craven, *Adventure in Faith*, 183; Owens, "Oliver Hart," 28–29.

[45] In 1787, the church petitioned the state legislature to grant the church property entirely to the Calvinist group that had incorporated it. The state granted the petition, and the city of Charleston, moreover, withdrew its claims to part of the property after Furman spoke to them. Furman then led his church to formally "frame constitutional rules and by-laws" insuring congregational governance. Manly, *Mercy and Judgment*, 52–54.

Furman's political theology had three major aspects. First, he considered all human events to be the outworking of divine Providence. Second, divine approval of human authority is granted only through a constitution based upon human consent. Third, God has providentially ordained the very structures of society, and it is a human duty to live within those structures.

First, in his sermon commemorating the life of George Washington, Furman asserted that God "speaks to man in afflicting dispensations" and exercises "special interposition in favor of the just and innocent." God is "the great Arbiter of heaven and earth," who directs "all events, both of the moral and natural world," with regard to individuals and to nations. Although some try, it is "impiety, folly, and madness" to oppose Providence. Rather, "let us learn sincere and humble resignation." Furman believed the American Revolution succeeded under "divine auspices" or "the patronage of Heaven." Indeed, "genuine and enlarged liberty, both civil and religious, brought about by the revolution, and . . . constitutionally established" are due to "God's moral government."

Therefore, the new nation can be called "our American Israel," and our "sacred duty" is to preserve her constitutional "rights and privileges." However, every nation is subject to judgment, and "the grand schemes of Providence" will be revealed only at the end of time. Although Furman warned against mistaking the human instrument for the divine Provider, he lauded Washington, who demonstrated both the classic virtue of justice and the Machiavellian virtue of magnanimity. The president's greatest virtue was his Christian piety. Although Washington may not have been as public with his faith, Furman believed he was "acquainted with the sublime doctrines of christianity, and their gracious, experimental influence on the heart."[46]

---

[46] Furman envisioned a dynamic interplay between divine sovereignty and human responsibility. Although he extols the surety of Providence, he also demanded human action: "What exertions should we not make, to obtain an interest in the justifying righteousness, atoning blood, and living intercession of the adorable Redeemer, who is the resurrection and the life; and to be found faithful in his service" (Furman, *Humble Submission to Divine Sovereignty the Due of a Bereaved Nation: A Sermon Occasioned by the Death of His Excellency General George Washington* [Charleston: 1800], passim). See Henry Holcombe, *A Sermon Occasioned by the Death of Lieutenant-General George Washington, Late President of the United States of America* (Savannah: 1800).

The second aspect of Furman's political theology states that the only legitimate authority is constitutional. General Richard Richardson printed and distributed a 1775 address by a young Furman advancing the revolutionary cause, wherein he defended the actions of the American Congress in opposing the unlawful authority of king and Parliament. If one does not object to another's exercise of unlawful authority, "I then submit to his unlimited power over me; and by my own consent, he has a right to lay upon me, what he pleases." Inaction itself results, therefore, in the grant of authority. In a unique reading of Romans 13, Furman subjects the king to the constitution. The "peace and happiness of the people" is guaranteed by the principles of the British "constitution," which is a "mixt monarchy, where the King and People make laws. The people do this by their representatives, whom they choose."

Representative law thus becomes binding upon the people. But through ignoring colonial representation, the British had "broken the principles of the constitution, by taking away the power of our Assemblies." In order to preserve the constitution, the American colonies opposed London's Parliament. Such rebellion is not rejection of the king's "lawful authority," for "what the King does, contrary to the constitution, is not the power, that is of God, spoken of in Scripture, and therefore ought not to be obeyed." In other words, legitimate authority is divinely granted through a popular constitution. Because America only seeks to preserve constitutional liberty, any who oppose her may incur "divine displeasure." Moreover, if they had submitted to the British, Americans would have bound themselves to "Arbitrary power." In the end, God will judge all human actions, but in the meanwhile, those who support the British "conspire against the liberty of Conscience, and would extinguish that precious jewel out of the constitution."[47]

Furman's regard for constitutionality, based upon popular consent and resulting in legitimate authority, reappeared throughout his writings and drove both his civil and his ecclesiastical politics. From 1784 to 1790,

---

[47] Furman, *An Address to the Residents Between the Broad and Saluda Rivers Concerning the American War for Independence (November 1775)*, printed in James A. Rogers, *Richard Furman: Life and Legacy* (Macon, GA: Mercer University Press, 2001), 268–73.

Furman tried to convince the Charleston Association to incorporate itself so that it might receive and disburse educational funds. Other associational leaders, at first, cautiously supported the idea. However, substantial opposition arose. Prominent pastors worried the advisory character of the association might be lost. Subsequently, Furman convinced them to support the incorporation of a General Committee affiliated with the association but with no authority over the independent churches. Jesse Mercer, the future leader of Georgia Baptists, was the first beneficiary of Furman's educational efforts.[48]

In 1790, Furman was elected to represent Charleston at the Constitutional Convention of South Carolina. The 1778 constitution, which Hart had supported, was considered temporary. When the convention assembled in May, Furman was asked to "perform divine services in the Convention Chamber," the performance of which garnered him accolades. However, when the convention discussions began, an objection was raised against the presence of Furman, four other Baptist ministers, and one Anglican priest among the delegates. The 1778 constitution had explicitly denied civil offices to the clergy. But Furman argued that ministers were qualified to serve in such roles, especially when elected by the people. As Furman's protégé and fellow Baptist leader William B. Johnson reported, "He repudiated the principle of disenfranchising a class of citizens on the ground of their consecration to holy office."

Furman's opponent disagreed, expressing concern that clerical influence might be too great. The opposition prevailed and ministers were barred from holding state offices. Hart's earlier victories in securing incorporation and "free exercise" for the churches were affirmed, but the language of establishment was dropped. Moreover, liberty of conscience was retained, but it was not to "be so construed as to excuse acts of licentiousness, or justify practices inconsistent with the peace or safety of this state." Charles Pinckney presided over the 1790 convention.[49]

---

[48] Rogers, *Richard Furman*, 118–23.

[49] *A Bill for Establishing the Constitution*, 14; *The Constitutions of the Sixteen States which Compose the Confederated Republic of America, According to the Latest Amendments* (Newburgh, NY: 1800), 219, 222, 224; William B. Johnson, "Biographical Sketch of Dr. Richard Furman," in *Annals of the American Baptist Pulpit* (New York, 1860), 163; Zaqueu Moreira de Oliveira, "Richard Furman, Father of the Southern

Furman believed the church could utilize state resources and should influence civil government. In his early days as a preacher, he attempted to preach in the Camden courthouse. The sheriff barred him from doing so, and some bystanders became irate; but Furman quietly drew the people to an open field. Impressed with his demeanor and delivery, "the most respectable persons" made certain he could preach from the courthouse in the future. During the war, he was such a proponent of the Revolution that Lord Cornwallis offered a large reward for "so notorious [a] rebel." In the 1800 presidential race, it will be recalled that the infidel Thomas Jefferson was the Republican candidate for religious liberty while John Adams and his running mate, Charles Pinckney, ran on the Federalist platform of religious orthodoxy. Furman and Pinckney had a longstanding relationship, and Furman publicly supported Pinckney's own subsequent candidacy for the presidency. Thus, the Danbury Baptists under John Leland and the Charleston Baptists under Furman found themselves political opposites.

In 1801, Furman led his association to petition the South Carolina House of Representatives to allow slaves a measure of religious liberty. In 1804, Furman preached before two civil societies concerning the death of Alexander Hamilton in a duel. "The address began as a sermon, continued as a eulogy, and concluded as an attack against dueling, with a call to abolish it by law." Again, Furman led the Charleston Association to petition the legislature to abolish dueling. Upon his return from an 1814 convention, Furman traveled through Washington, DC. After a conversation with James Monroe, he was invited to preach before the president, foreign ambassadors, and numerous other dignitaries. He boldly proclaimed from Acts 22:16 their need to "arise and be baptized." In 1822, he addressed the governor of South Carolina concerning the issue of slavery on behalf of the Baptist Convention of South Carolina. Simultaneously, the convention sought a government-approved "Day of Humiliation, Prayer, and Thanksgiving."[50]

Baptist Convention," in *The Lord's Free People in a Free Land: Essays in Baptist History in Honor of Robert A. Baker,* ed. William R. Estep (Fort Worth: Faculty of the School of Theology, 1976), 92; Rogers, *Richard Furman,* 69–70.

[50] De Oliveira, "Richard Furman," in Estep, *The Lord's Free People in a Free Land,* 92; Rogers, *Richard Furman,* 71–72, 163–64, 210–11; Furman *et ux* to South Carolina, Records of the General Assembly, 1801; Lambert, *Founding Fathers and the Place of*

Furman's constitutionalism also influenced the development of ecclesiastical polity. In 1814, Furman was elected the first president of the newly formed "General Missionary Convention of the Baptist Denomination in the United States of America for Foreign Missions," popularly known as the Triennial Convention. Furman and his protégé, Johnson, were elected to a fifteen-member constitutional committee during the first session of the convention. After an 1813 meeting with Luther Rice, the premier proponent of American Baptist missions, Johnson had prepared a constitution for the event. However, the committee began to debate and was reduced to five members. Furman was retained but Johnson was dropped. The constitutional debate concerned whether the new convention would follow the multidimensional, church-based associational model or the single-task, broader-membership society model. Furman advocated the associational model but temporarily acquiesced to the convention's adoption of a society model. The convention organized only for the foreign mission, but Furman wanted the convention to address the home mission and "deeply regretted" that more attention was not paid to ministerial education.[51]

A greater disappointment occurred, however, when Luther Rice and the Board of Foreign Missions tried to enact Furman's plans for a national seminary without constitutional authority. Concerned with Rice's "hasty" and unauthorized procedure, Furman led the Charleston Association to object. Ultimately, Furman's wisdom was vindicated, and Rice suffered severe criticism for his financial missteps with Columbian College. In 1821, Furman developed the constitutional principles of the first state convention of Baptists, that of South Carolina. In 1822, he and Johnson dominated the convention committee that drafted the new constitution. Against detractors, Furman, Johnson, and Manly successfully defended the polity of the new state convention with its comprehensive embrace

---

Religion in America, 274–85; James Pickett Wesberry, Baptists in South Carolina Before the War Between the States (Columbia, SC: Bryan, 1966), 46, 60–63.

[51] Address concerning the formation of the Triennial Convention, in Proceedings of the Baptist Convention for Missionary Purposes (Philadelphia: 1814), 38–43, cited in A Sourcebook for Baptist Heritage, ed. H. Leon McBeth (Nashville: Broadman, 1990), 209–10; Rogers, Richard Furman, 148–61; Robert Andrew Baker, Relations Between Northern and Southern Baptists (n.p.: 1948), 12–14; W. W. Barnes, The Southern Baptist Convention, 1845–1953 (Nashville: Broadman, 1954), 1–11.

of missions, education, and other endeavors. This constitution eventually formed the basis for the constitution of the Southern Baptist Convention.[52]

The third aspect of Furman's political theology concerns social order and personal duty. Furman believed that Providence compelled the definition of freedom in terms of constitutional power. Providence then required men to fulfill their duties according to their order. In an 1802 sermon entitled "America's Deliverance and Duty," Furman rehearsed his doctrines of Providence and of constitutionalism and began developing his doctrine of duty. The sermon enlarged two truths: "the American revolution was effected by the special agency of God," and certain "duties and obligations are incumbent on our citizens, in consequence of his kind interposition." The duties of the American citizenry include expressing gratitude to God, securing and improving his blessings, and relying on his Providence in the future.

The best means of securing the nation is "a strict attention to religion." This did not mean the establishment of a national religion by civil authority but personal attention to religion by the people. If the people reject Christ, then they will incur divine wrath and endanger the American Revolution. Religion leads to virtue, which in turn leads to "real happiness" for the individual and the body politic. In order to prevent national sin, Furman provided a litany of cures, including strict adherence to the constitution, respecting constitutional authorities, electing only virtuous leaders, and maintaining the love of liberty.[53]

In a circular letter, "On Religious and Civil Duties," Furman rehearsed a similar list of duties required of those who have received "civil and religious liberty." He also reviewed parental responsibilities in educating children and servants, a matter to which "much attention ... should be

---

[52] De Oliveira, "Furman Rogers," in Estep, *The Lord's Free People in a Free Land*, 94–95; Rogers, *Richard Furman*, 179–96, 231–43, 305–8; Hortense Woodson, *Giant in the Land: A Biography of William Bullein Johnson, First President of the Southern Baptist Convention* (Nashville: Broadman, 1950), 45–49.

[53] Furman, *America's Deliverance and Duty: A Sermon Preached at the Baptist Church* (Charleston: 1802), in *Life and Works of Dr. Richard Furman, D.D.* (Harrisonburg, VA: Sprinkle Publications, 2004), 389–408. Thanks to Tom Nettles for his assistance in acquiring this text. See also Thomas J. Nettles, "Richard Furman," in *Baptist Theologians*, ed. Timothy George and David S. Dockery (Nashville: Broadman, 1990), 140–64.

bestowed." Furman believed that Scripture clearly taught the "station and duties of servants." Because Providence "has placed them in that situation," servants must learn to obey "as to the Lord." Likewise, masters are obligated "to rule their servants with justice and moderation; to afford them a reasonable portion of the comforts, as well as necessaries of life; and to regard with seriousness their religious interests, as of persons who are placed by the Divine government under their care and direction."[54]

It is with this unique institution of slavery that Furman's political theology becomes troubling. Furman himself was ambivalent about the institution. Southern evangelicals went through several phases concerning slavery. Until around 1800, many criticized slavery. Between 1800 and 1820, they began to cooperate with it. Finally, between 1820 and 1845, they began to defend it.[55] Furman reflects this same transition. Early in the nineteenth century, Furman said slavery was "undoubtedly an evil." In 1821, Manly said it was introduced "from motives of avarice" and considered it "repugnant to the spirit of our republican institutions."[56] But after the Denmark Vesey uprising in the summer of 1822, South Carolina Baptists revised their position.

In a December 1822 communication to the governor of South Carolina, Furman's concept of order solidified. He reminded citizens of "the government of the Deity" that dispensed both "mercies" and the "chastening rod." He defended slavery from the Old and New Testaments, while affirming slaves are still human. "In things purely spiritual, they appear to have enjoyed equal privileges; but their relationship, as masters and slaves, were not dissolved." Indeed, Furman observed, the apostles enjoined obedience on the part of slaves. Although Christians live under the Golden Rule, "this rule is never to be urged against the order of things, which the Divine government has established." Moreover, slavery need not be cruel and unjust, Furman believed.

---

[54] Furman, "On Religious and Civil Duties" (1800), in ibid., 545–49.

[55] Marty G. Bell, "The Beginnings of the Southern Baptist Convention, 1845," *Baptist History and Heritage* 30 (1995): 18–19.

[56] Loulie Latimer Owens, *Saints of Clay: The Shaping of South Carolina Baptists* (Columbia, SC: Bryan, 1971), 70–71.

Furman said he treated his slaves as if he were their "father." The Africans, he argued, were enslaved under constitutional principles "by their own consent." By this, Furman meant they became enslaved through their own customs of war with other Africans. Freedom is not a permanent right "when that right is forfeited, or has been lost" in this way. (With this coercive definition of consent, Furman's system loses its coherence.) Furman was interested in the salvation of Africans and saw slavery as the means by which they were introduced to Christianity.[57]

This leading Baptist pastor and patriarch ruled many blacks in his church and in his family. Moreover, not only was he called "Father" by child and slave; he was entitled "Our Beloved Father" by his ecclesiological peers and has been named the "Father of the Southern Baptist Convention."[58] The constitutional political theology of Furman, as interesting as it may be, culminated in the peculiar institution of the south. Furman's patriarchal and patronizing attitude toward Africans, whom he yet recognized as his fellows in humanity and in the church, metastasized fatally in the perverse practice of chattel slavery.

4. Political Theology in the Early Southern Baptist Convention

Finally, we consider the political theology of two founding leaders of the Southern Baptist Convention. These two pastors represent the South Carolina tradition of political theology as it became institutionalized in a denomination: Basil Manly Sr., a successor of Furman and leader of Alabama Baptists, and William B. Johnson, a coworker of Furman and leader of South Carolina Baptists. Both considered themselves heirs of the aforementioned leaders. Johnson wrote a biography of Furman, and Manly detailed the contributions of Screven, Hart, and Furman in his

---

[57] Furman, *Exposition of the Views of the Baptists Relative to the Coloured Population of the United States (Charleston: 1822)*, in Rogers, *Richard Furman*, 274–86.

[58] De Oliveira, "Richard Furman," in Estep, *The Lord's Free People in a Free Land*, 87, 95.

monumental history of the Charleston church. Manly and Johnson, among many others, highly revered Richard Furman.

First, Basil Manly Sr. worked alongside Furman in associational endeavors until the latter's death. He was afterward called to pastor Furman's church. In his history of the First Baptist Church of Charleston, *Mercy and Judgment*, Manly reiterated Furman's doctrines of divine Providence and duty. In Psalm 101, David sang of God's mercy and judgment, which Manly took to be "very important principles of government." Mercy is God's "benevolence to sinners," while judgment concerns the "mysterious and afflictive" acts of the sovereign God. This dialectic of divine mercy and judgment provides a theology of history not only for churches but for states. Church history is the record "of those mysterious, but wise dispensations of Providence, in which mercy and judgment are blended." History encourages Christians to fulfill their "duty" and adjust their course "to the methods of his mercy and judgment." It also helps Baptists fulfill their duty by furnishing direction, imposing restraints, supplying powerful motive, and promoting perseverance. Manly apparently believed history was scaling new heights with "a call in providence for our churches . . . to send the gospel among the heathen" through the Baptist convention.[59]

Manly left the Charleston church to become a university president, plantation owner, and the leading figure among Alabama Baptists. Having been led to Christ by a slave, he encouraged his slaves to become Christians. He also encouraged them to submit to the design of Providence in establishing the social order into which they were providentially born. He helped found the Southern Baptist Convention in Augusta, Georgia, in 1845 after being publicly abused by a northern abolitionist. He could "agree to disagree" with the moderate northerner Francis Wayland and "by love to serve one another," but he believed the abolitionist movement intractably violated Baptist principles, forcing an undesirable separation.

---

[59] Manly, *Mercy and Judgment*, 3–7, 59. Manly developed a series of twenty-one "Sermons on Duty." See "Notes of a Sermon Delivered by Rev. Basil Manly, D.D. at Pleasant Grove Church, Fayette Co., Ala., April 8th, 1849," in Thomas J. Nettles, *Southern Baptist Sermons on Sovereignty and Responsibility* (Harrisonburg, VA: Sprinkle Publications, 1984), 7–32.

Manly authored the Alabama resolutions that prompted the acting board of the Triennial Convention to deny convention authority. The convention had repeatedly resolved that slavery should not be addressed, but the acting board finally admitted it could "never be a party to any arrangement which would imply approbation of slavery."[60] Manly later assisted in the foundation of the Southern Baptist Theological Seminary. On February 18, 1861, he attended the inauguration of Jefferson Davis as president of the Confederate States of America, symbolically consecrating Davis to his office. Manly supported the Confederate war effort wholeheartedly, even authoring patriotic tracts.[61]

Second, William Bullein Johnson's local ministry encompassed Georgia and South Carolina, and both ecclesiastical and educational institutions, but his greatest impact was on the national stage. Trained as a lawyer and possessing an organizational outlook, it has been said that Furman's "mantle fell squarely upon him." In 1809, he organized the First Baptist Church of Columbia, South Carolina. In 1813, he led the Savannah Baptist Society for Foreign Missions to adopt a constitution in which the denomination's terminology of "elicit, combine and direct" first appeared. Although a proponent of church independence, he also believed church union could occur without endangering freedom, to the point of even advocating the administration of baptism and the Lord's Supper at associational and convention meetings. He believed that churches could make a "judicious concentration" of their energies in "one sacred effort" to bring in the kingdom of God through missions and education.

From a political-theological perspective, Johnson provided pro forma constitutions to the Triennial, South Carolina, and Southern Baptist conventions and presided over each convention, most importantly as the first president of the Southern Baptist Convention. Johnson perpetuated

---

[60] G. Thomas Halbrooks, "Francis Wayland: Influential Mediator in the Baptist Controversy Over Slavery," *Baptist History and Heritage* 13 (1978): 21–35.

[61] A. James Fuller, *Chaplain to the Confederacy: Basil Manly and Baptist Life in the Old South* (Baton Rouge: Louisiana State University Press, 2000), 1, 292–97; Manly, *The Young Deserter* (ca. 1861–65; North Carolina Collection, University of North Carolina at Chapel Hill).

Furman's doctrine of constitutionalism in these conventions.[62] While Southern Baptists have been correctly taken to task for breaking with northern Baptists over the terrible doctrine of slavery, scholars have provided additional nuance. Although the cultural issue was indeed slavery, the crisis included polity, specifically the north's apparent violation of constitutional principles.[63]

Which Tradition of Political Theology?

The South Carolina tradition of political theology, which reached its apex in Richard Furman, impacted the development of Southern Baptist thought far more deeply than our review of these five leading pastors may imply.[64] Further soundings could be made into the lives and writings of Jesse Mercer of Georgia, Richard Fuller of South Carolina, James P. Boyce of South Carolina, Basil Manly Jr. of Alabama, Jeremiah B. Jeter of Virginia, and James B. Taylor of Virginia, all of whom were Christian leaders in the early American south. Each of these prominent churchmen give evidence of the South Carolina understanding of political theology with its three lenses of divine Providence, human constitutionality, and social orderliness.

---

[62] Wesberry, *Baptists in South Carolina Before the War Between the States*, 63–66; William B. Willis, "William Bullein Johnson," *Baptist History and Heritage* 1 (1965): 24–26; James M. Morton Jr., "Leadership of W. B. Johnson in the Formation of the Southern Baptist Convention, *Baptist History and Heritage* 5 (1970): 3–12, 55; Joe M. King, "William Bullein Johnson," *Baptist History and Heritage* 6 (1971): 76–79; Gregory A. Wills, *The First Baptist Church of Columbia, South Carolina, 1809 to 2002* (Nashville: Fields Publishing, 2003), 1–21, 26–37.

[63] Bell, "The Beginnings of the Southern Baptist Convention," 16–24; H. Leon McBeth, "The Broken Unity of 1845: A Reassessment," *Baptist History and Heritage* 24 (1989): 24–31, 48.

[64] The importance of the South Carolina tradition should not be understated. Robert A. Baker, a leading Southern Baptist church historian of yesteryear, cited approvingly the statement by W. W. Barnes, another leading Southern Baptist church historian, that the First Baptist Church of Charleston is "holy ground" for Southern Baptists. Baker, "The Contributions of South Carolina Baptists to the Rise and Development of the Southern Baptist Convention," *Baptist History and Heritage* 17 (1982): 2–9, 19. See J. Glen Clayton, "South Carolina Shapers of Southern Baptists," *Baptist History and Heritage* 17 (1982): 10–19.

So, which is the major tradition and which is the minor tradition in southern American political theology? Is the Virginia tradition a myth and the South Carolina tradition the reality, or vice versa? Is southern Baptist political theology best characterized by a wall of separation or by a limited intimacy between church and state? Perhaps the answer depends upon the particular historian or ideologue being asked.

Iconography speaks volumes about ideological presentations of history. Take two iconographic lists for example. On the one hand, of "The Ten Most Influential Baptists" identified by the Baptist History and Heritage Society, the first three icons represent the Virginia tradition, and the South Carolina tradition is not represented whatsoever. On the other hand, of the twenty-one Southern Baptists represented on the portico frieze of the central rotunda at Southwestern Baptist Theological Seminary, four directly represent the South Carolina tradition, and the Virginia tradition is not represented whatsoever. The only iconic figure represented in both places is Edgar Young Mullins.[65]

To understand the political theology of early American Christians, especially of Baptists in the south, we may remember positively both the Virginia tradition, with its emphasis on human freedom and the separation of church and state, and the South Carolina tradition, with its emphasis on providential constitutionalism. But, ominously, we must never forget the moral problems that handicap every human political philosophy. The solipsism that accompanies undue emphases on freedom and the tyranny that accompanies undue emphases on social order stand over American Christian political theology as warnings against any hope in purely human constitutions. Rather, we expectantly hope for the eschatological perfection that will only come with the gracious return of our King Jesus.

---

[65] Pamela R. Durso, "The Ten Most Influential Baptists," (accessed June 24, 2016) http://www.centerforbaptiststudies.org/resources/heritageseries/influential.htm (accessed June 24, 2016); W. W. Barnes, "Biographical Sketches of the Twenty One Southern Baptists Represented on the Portico Frieze," March 1950 (Fleming Library Paper, Southwestern Baptist Theological Seminary). For a critique of Mullins and the propagation of a solipsist individualism, see Malcolm B. Yarnell III, "Changing Baptist Concepts of Royal Priesthood: John Smyth and Edgar Young Mullins," in *The Rise of the Laity in Evangelical Protestantism*, ed. Deryck Lovegrove (London: Routledge, 2002), 236–52.

PART 2

RELIGIOUS LIBERTY 101

CHAPTER 4

THE CHRISTIAN DOCTRINE
OF RELIGIOUS LIBERTY

Barrett Duke

Recently, the United States government sought to prosecute the Hosanna-Tabor Evangelical Lutheran Church and School for firing one of its teachers. The church had determined she no longer adhered to all of its core beliefs. Before the US Supreme Court, therefore, the church presented theological as well as constitutional principles to argue for its right to conduct its affairs free of governmental interference. The government, on the other hand, argued that it had the authority to determine when a church could fire a minister for violating its core beliefs.[1]

In another example of the federal government interfering in matters of faith, the United States Department of Health and Human Services asserted it could require religious institutions to provide contraceptives and abortion-causing drugs and devices to their employees, contrary to

---

[1] Hosanna-Tabor Evangelical Lutheran Church and School v. EEOC, 132 S. Ct. 694 (2012).

the religious convictions of these organizations. In so doing, the government effectively claimed that it has the right and authority to dictate to these institutions the boundaries of the practices of their faith.[2]

Meanwhile, in the Middle East, a militant form of Islam is rising that persecutes and kills those it considers to be errant Muslims. It also engages in a genocidal rampage to eradicate Christians and other faith groups from the territory it is taking by force. Adherents to this form of Islam believe their goal to create a religiously pure state justifies such vicious behavior.

Challenges to Religious Liberty

This chapter's first three paragraphs are only a few examples of the animus people of faith are under today. In many areas around the world, persecution remains a serious and deadly problem for millions of people of faith, especially, but not limited to, Christians. Fortunately, in the United States, the demise of state-sponsored religion has significantly reduced these kinds of atrocities. However, an emerging fundamentalist secularism in the United States brings a new intolerance with it.

Clearly, it is time to revisit the issue of religious liberty and clarify its significance and meaning for a new generation. While many religious groups can claim the right to speak on the topic of religious liberty because of their experiences as persecuted people, Baptists approach this topic from their own uniquely qualified position. Baptists, as a distinct group, lived and died through more than two centuries of religious persecution. In fact, it was their earlier spiritual brethren the Anabaptists who were among the first to speak out against the Magisterial Reformers' use of state power to punish those whose religious practices were at odds with their own beliefs.[3]

---

[2] The Tenth Circuit Court of Appeals decision against these institutions provides insight into the government's erroneous claim that it is not substantially burdening their religious freedom. See http://caselaw.findlaw.com/us-10th-circuit/1707852.html.

[3] Harold Bender notes that the Anabaptist Balthasar Hubmaier's 1528 pamphlet, *Von ketzern und iren verbrennern,* "has been called the first Protestant declaration for religious freedom." *Anabaptists and Religious Liberty in the Sixteenth Century* (Philadelphia: Fortress, 1970), 9.

Religious and Secular Threats to Religious Liberty

Religious liberty is threatened on at least four fronts today. First, a new religious fundamentalism among Muslim, Hindu, and Buddhist groups began to grip many countries in the late twentieth century and the early decades of this century. Such groups use the power of the state to suppress other faiths, whether through the direct assistance, sympathy, or apathy of the civil powers. Second, religious liberty is threatened in other countries by Christ-confessing groups. They believe in the superior nature of their sect or regard other Christ-confessing groups as nuisances or threats to their dominance. This occurs in the former Soviet countries, for example.

Third, the world's remaining totalitarian states consider religious belief a threat to their dominance over every aspect of life. China still imprisons, tortures, and murders people who feel compelled to follow the dictates of their conscience in matters of faith. North Korea's attitude toward unsanctioned religious groups is even more brutal.[4]

Fourth, a fundamentalist type of secularism has emerged in many countries that considers the church's denouncement of certain sins to be bigotry. A growing movement is afoot to label certain kinds of religious speech, such as sermons that characterize homosexuality as sin, as hate speech.[5] The movement means to marshal the civil powers to restrict and to punish. In other quarters, a new militancy against the involvement of people of faith in political life is emerging, such that moral convictions are equated with religious beliefs and deemed unconstitutional intrusions of faith in the body politic.

As churches seek to speak to these new and old threats to religious liberty, they must also contend with a postmodern mind-set among Western intellectual elites who no longer believe in absolute moral truth. This abandonment of moral truth has led many to question whether any culture can

---

[4] The 2015 annual report from the US Commission on International Religious Freedom provides insight into the atrocities committed by these two countries (pp. 32–37; 50–54), http://www.uscirf.gov/sites/default/files/USCIRF%20Annual%20 Report%202015%20%282%29.pdf.

[5] Canada's Supreme Court ruled recently that some forms of religiously motivated speech can be treated as hate speech. Saskatchewan (Human Rights Commission) v. Whatcott, 2013 SCC 11 (2013) 1 S.C.R. 467.

demand certain behaviors of any other culture. After all, if one accepts the postmodern axiom that each community constructs its own reality, and that one community's construction of reality and its attendant moral rules are as valid as another, within certain humanitarian boundaries, then it becomes nearly impossible for someone from one community to insist that another community change.

Postmodernism creates significant challenges for those who attempt to promote religious freedom throughout the world. Gene Veith provides a superb summary of its tenets:

1. Social Constructivism. Meaning, morality, and truth do not exist objectively; rather, they are *constructed* by the society.
2. Cultural Determinism. Individuals are wholly shaped by cultural forces. Language in particular determines what we can think.
3. The Rejection of Individual Identity. People exist primarily as members of groups. Identity is primarily collective.
4. The Rejection of Humanism. Values that emphasize the creativity, autonomy, and priority of human beings are misplaced. There is no universal humanity since every culture constitutes its own reality.
5. The Denial of the Transcendent. There are no absolutes.
6. Power Reductionism. All institutions, all human relationships, all moral values, and all human creations—from works of art to religious ideologies—are expressions and masks of the primal will to power.
7. The Rejection of Reason. Reason and the impulse to objectify truth are illusory masks for cultural power. Authenticity and fulfillment come from submerging the self into a larger group.
8. Revolutionary Critique of the Existing Order. Modern society with its rationalism, order, and unitary view of truth needs to be replaced by a new world order.[6]

The implications of these tenets for religious liberty are obvious. If our concept of religious liberty is merely a construct of our community and not

---

[6] Gene Edward Veith Jr., *Postmodern Times: A Christian Guide to Contemporary Thought and Culture* (Wheaton: Crossway, 1994), 158.

universally valid for the myriad reasons suggested herein, postmodernists will argue that this is a relative value and not binding on all cultures. They will respond by attempting to hinder any effort to "impose" this value on other cultures.

Two Responses

This is the environment in which people of faith must contend today. As we relate to these various pressures, we can respond in one of two ways. We can accept the postmodern construct and write off people of faith being persecuted by other cultures, taking a Star Trekkian "prime directive" attitude toward them. Or we can reassert the universal nature of religious liberty and insist that all cultures, our own as well as others, respect the various faith groups in their midst. We can also protect them and their right to practice their faith as they choose, within reason, including their right to engage in religious speech and in the life of their community and nation.

The first option is hardly acceptable. To sit by idly while people are murdered, raped, imprisoned, dispossessed, displaced, and marginalized because of their faith is tantamount to the barbaric acts themselves. The second option is the only acceptable option for any civilized people.

Arguments for Religious Liberty

Given the general increase in religious persecution and intolerance for religious belief we are witnessing, it seems necessary to regain some lost ground in order to press the cause of religious liberty around the world, as well as in our own nation. Of foremost concern must be the ideological basis for advocacy on behalf of faith. One can argue that religious liberty is a universal right for all people from a number of perspectives.

Natural Law Arguments

First, one can take a naturalist approach and argue the case from Natural Law. Proponents of Natural Law theory argue that one can deduce universal moral absolutes by observing the created order or human behavior and social systems. While Natural Law theory has seen its share of triumph and defeat, it still provides a solid footing for many. The insightful work by J. Budziszewski, *What We Can't Not Know*, asserts the importance of this approach to moral values in general and, consequently, to the case for religious liberty in particular. Budziszewski does not argue that people know moral law inherently, as though they are born knowing it. He argues that a morality is inherent in the created order and that humans cannot prevent themselves from learning it. Four evidences or "witnesses" are at work in every human that "provide real moral knowledge." These "witnesses" are deep conscience, design as such, our own design, and natural consequences.

Budziszewski does an excellent job in a brief space demonstrating how these witnesses lead to the understanding of certain moral truths. However, he has not proven whether people discover these moral laws or produce them in response to these inner witnesses. He even admits this failing: "I have not proven that they do; I have only declared it. There is no way to prove the obvious."[7]

But even if one were to assume he does not need to prove that these moral laws are already present, there is another problem with Natural Law theory. Whether people discover certain moral truths or produce them, there is no guarantee they will come to the right moral conclusions as they respond to the "witnesses." Fortunately, they usually do, but left to their own faulty reasoning capacities, they also miss things—and sometimes draw the completely wrong conclusions.

Natural Law theory eventually succumbs to the same argument opposing postmodern formulations of moral values—it depends on the reasoning capacity of the individual. Unfortunately, pure objective reasoning is not easy to achieve or maintain. In most cases a person's cultural exposure affects his deductive reasoning. A perfect example can be found in a later section of Budziszewski's volume. He notes that people discount the credibility of Natural Law arguments because some of its proponents have been wrong about what they considered to be natural laws. For example, one of the greatest Natural Law proponents of all time, Aristotle, as well as many others, argued that slavery was natural. To this

---

[7] J. Budziszewski, *What We Can't Not Know: A Guide* (Dallas: Spence, 2003), 103.

Budziszewski retorts rather glibly, "They were wrong."[8] Yes, Aristotle and the others were wrong. They were preconditioned by their own experiences, cultures, and their own limitations to arrive at their conclusion, and they were not even aware of it.[9]

Yet the question this example raises for us is, why should we believe Budziszewski or anyone else is correct on every count? And when are they right, and when are they wrong? Carl F. H. Henry raised the same concerns. He noted,

> The sin-warped predicament of man in whom God's creation-image is now flawed raises questions also about a body of commonly or universally perceived ethical imperatives. It is not in question that humans are confronted in general divine revelation by the will of the Creator, and that such revelation contains both formal and material elements. What is in question is the ability of sinful humanity to translate the moral revelation into a universally shared body of ethical truth. If, as champions of natural morality insist, human nature is inherently structured with imperatives, how can humans know that these requirements are ethically legitimate? . . . The predicament of man in sin includes a propensity for perversion of religious reality. What humanity affirms solely on the basis of inherent instincts and philosophical reasoning lacks normative force; only what God says in Scripture and has disclosed in Christ is normative.[10]

---

[8] Ibid., 108.

[9] In his defense, I point out that Budziszewski admits humans may not know these moral truths "with unfailing perfect clarity, or that we have reasoned out their remotest implications: we don't, and we haven't." That is the point, however. How can we know when we have attained "perfect clarity" or the "remotest implications"? Future generations, or other cultures, can always argue that current moral formulations are either incomplete or mistaken (ibid., 19).

[10] Carl F. H. Henry, "Natural Law and Nihilistic Culture," *First Things* 49 (1995): 59. I am gratified that God's moral law is discernible, with great clarity at times, through careful, honest scrutiny of the natural order. Natural law arguments can be quite persuasive for many people, and that is good. But, in the end, only that which Scripture affirms can truly be considered certain.

Social Arguments

Second, one can take a utilitarian approach and argue for religious freedom as a social necessity. In this case, the issue isn't so much whether or not certain moral absolutes are part of the warp and woof of the natural world but whether or not humans must choose to adopt a certain universal morality in order to create an orderly society. The *Humanist Manifesto 2000* takes this approach.[11] The author of the *Manifesto* recognizes that postmodernism has destroyed the notion of universal absolutes. Consequently, a solid foundation no longer exists for arguing for certain shared moral values from natural law. However, because people must respect a certain moral code if they ever hope to live together in peace, the author appeals to his readers to adopt his proposed set of moral values as a reasonable approach to civil life together.

The question this approach raises, of course, is why should anyone accept this set of values? The values are based on the author's perception of the way things ought to be, but they have no authoritative basis beyond the strength of the arguments used to promote them. One can easily dismiss the author's proposal as a product of a particular culture and reject the *Manifesto*'s system as inferior to one's own.

Theological Arguments

The third approach is to argue for a theological basis for religious liberty. In this case religious liberty will rest on the foundation of deity itself. Given the severe weaknesses of the other two options, I believe the most dependable foundation for the promulgation of a doctrine of religious liberty is deity. If it can be established that religious liberty is a divinely granted right, we have the ideological foundation we need to insist that it be respected universally.

Of course, even this proposed foundation has some obvious shortcomings. First, not everyone accepts the same deity. Because I believe there is a God, and that he is a person who wills certain things for humans, does not make it so. Others can, and do, argue that I am mistaken. The second problem with this approach is the need for an authoritative source that reveals unerringly the thoughts and will of this deity.

---

[11] Paul Kurtz, *Humanist Manifesto 2000: A Call for a New Planetary Humanism* (Amherst, NY: Prometheus Books, 2000).

I resolve both of these problems for myself by appealing to the person of Jesus Christ as he is revealed in the Bible. First, I accept that Jesus is deity incarnate. His message, actions, miracles, and life satisfy my need for verification of his deity. Those who disagree must either show that he is not divine or that the deity they acknowledge is more credible. Otherwise, they must give serious consideration to the evidence for the deity of Jesus Christ.

I resolve the second issue of an authoritative source by accepting the Bible as an inerrant and authoritative record of the revealed will of God. I do not have the space to make the case for the trustworthiness and authority of the Bible. Others have done this quite effectively.[12] I will simply state here my belief that the Bible, Old and New Testament, is the revealed will and truth of God. As for the Old Testament, it is clear that Jesus accepted the Scriptures of his day, essentially the Christian Old Testament. His supreme confidence in the veracity and inerrancy of the Hebrew Scriptures instills confidence that I can trust those texts to reveal the mind of God. As for the New Testament, I believe it deserves the same level of confidence in its divine inspiration as Jesus placed in the Old Testament. It has withstood the scrutiny of the critics, bears the marks of men of integrity and veracity, and has the support of two millennia of church history such that it passes the authority test.

Scripture, then, is the ultimate authoritative source for discerning the divine will. As an objective, inerrant guide, it is the most reliable starting point available for developing a theological basis for religious liberty. The following, then, is a theological approach, rooted in Scripture, to the question of religious liberty.

A Theological Argument for Religious Liberty

Scripture reveals that religious liberty is a fundamental, universal right granted to every human by God himself. Unfortunately, arriving at this understanding is not as simple as providing chapter and verse. Nowhere

---

[12] E.g., Craig Blomberg, *Can We Still Believe the Bible? An Evangelical Engagement with Contemporary Questions* (Grand Rapids: Brazos Press, 2014), and Michael Kruger, *Canon Revisited: Establishing the Origins and Authority of the New Testament Books* (Wheaton: Crossway, 2012).

in Scripture does God say, "I want all people to be free to worship or
not to worship whatever they want." In fact, scholars are pretty much in
agreement that a doctrine of religious liberty such as I have described is
not immediately identifiable in Scripture. Luke Johnson comments, "The
Christian Scriptures, in short, do not in any direct or obvious way provide
support for the contemporary proposition that 'it is a human right to be
religious.'"[13]

While we cannot find direct references to religious liberty in such a
way that we can speak of a theology of religious liberty, sufficient implications are in the major theological doctrines of the Christian faith to argue
that God has granted humankind the freedom to choose who or what they
want to worship in the way that they please.[14] In other words, there is a
derived doctrine of religious liberty.[15]

Scripture is steeped in the medium of religious liberty. J. D. Hughey,
former president and professor of church history at the Baptist Theological
Seminary in Ruschlicon, Switzerland, agreed that "religious liberty is not
a truth explicitly revealed in Scripture." Nevertheless, he concluded, "religious liberty is implicit in Christian teaching," and he produced a succinct,

---

[13] Luke Johnson, "Religious Rights and Christian Texts," in *Religious Human
Rights in Global Perspective: Religious Perspectives,* ed. John Witte Jr. and Johan van
der Vyver (Boston: M. Nijhoff Publishers, 1996), 66.

[14] This recognition is not new. This article, in many ways, repeats what others have
said on this subject in fuller and more eloquent ways. Certainly one of the greatest statements on the foundations of religious liberty, natural and theological, is the Vatican's
"Declaration on Religious Freedom (*Dignitatis Humanae*)," adopted on December 7,
1965. While arguing for religious liberty principally from Natural Law, the declaration acknowledges that the doctrine "has its roots in divine revelation." It continues,
"Revelation does not indeed affirm in so many words the right of man to immunity
from external coercion in matters religious. It does, however, disclose the dignity of
the human person in its full dimensions. It gives evidence of the respect which Christ
showed toward the freedom with which man is to fulfill his duty of belief in the Word
of God." http://www.vatican.va/archive/hist_councils/ii_vatican_council/documents
/vat-ii_decl_19651207_dignitatis-humanae_en.html. Additionally, the statement "In
Defense of Religious Freedom," by Evangelicals and Catholics Together, affirms religious freedom for all "on the authority of the Bible." *First Things* 221 (March 2012), 31.

[15] William Brackney comments, "Christian theologians have derived from
Scripture the bases of religious freedom and organized and embellished that data to
form dogma" *Human Rights and the World's Major Religions* (Denver: ABC-CLIO,
2013), 113.

well-argued case for religious liberty from the doctrines of God, humankind, Christ, salvation, and the church. He followed that by developing an ethic of religious liberty built on humankind's creation in the image of God, the "fundamental Christian teaching of love," and the Golden Rule.[16] This chapter follows the same track. I am, of course, indebted to Professor Hughey, and others, for their careful work on this important topic.[17]

Theological-Anthropological Arguments for Religious Liberty

Humans as God's Image Bearers. Theological anthropology, or the biblical doctrine of the human species, provides a number of entry points for discerning the universal nature of religious liberty. For starters, religious liberty can be discerned in the Bible's account of humanity's creation. The book of Genesis declares that God created humankind in his image (Gen 1:27). Theologians have many opinions about what it means to be created in the image of God, many of which seem credible. One certainty, however, is meaningful for our purposes: Only humans possess this image. Nothing else in creation is created in God's image.

This image is fundamental to what it means to be human. It separates us from the rest of creation. Furthermore, all humans possess this image to the same degree. There are not greater and lesser image bearers. Consequently, there are no superior people in the eyes of the Lord. Scripture states, "There is no partiality with God" (Rom 2:11 NKJV). Given this truth, it would be inappropriate for someone to claim that he possesses an inherent spiritual superiority that entitles him to suppress another's spiritual freedom. All people bear the same image of the divine, to the same degree; therefore, all have equal spiritual status before God.[18]

---

[16] J. D. Hughey, "The Theological Frame of Religious Liberty," *Christian Century* 80, no. 45 (November 6, 1963): 1365–68.

[17] I am also indebted to the research assistance of Andrew Lewis and Marshall Griffin, interns in the Washington, DC, office of the Ethics and Religious Liberty Commission, whose efforts to gather relevant materials for this paper were invaluable.

[18] Pope Benedict XVI grounds religious freedom in "the very dignity of the human person," who is created in God's "image and likeness." "Religious Freedom: The Path to Peace," message, celebration of World Peace Day (January 1, 2011); http://w2.vatican.va/content/benedict-xvi/en/messages/peace/documents/hf_ben-xvi_mes_20101208_xliv-world-day-peace.html.

There are four areas where one might choose to disagree with this statement. First, one can argue that the scriptural offices of pastor and deacon involve the exercise of spiritual authority over others. This is true, but this authority is not inherent in the individuals holding these offices. It is the result of the calling of God. Furthermore, pastors and deacons are responsible to enforce God's spiritual standards, not their own. But even this exercise of authority has its limits. Pastors and deacons are not authorized to be dictators over their congregations, nor are they authorized to force spiritual conformity in others. Peter instructs elders, or pastors, to "shepherd God's flock among you, not overseeing out of compulsion but freely, according to God's will; not for the money but eagerly; not lording it over those entrusted to you, but being examples to the flock" (1 Pet 5:2–3).

Second, one can argue that if there is no such thing as a spiritually superior person, parents would not have the right to exercise spiritual authority over their children. To an extent this is true. God authorizes parents to guide their children spiritually not because they are spiritually superior but because he has tasked them to impart his spiritual values to their children (Deut 6:4–8; Prov 22:6). However, not even a parent can force a child to believe. Parents can coerce compliance and outward conformity to their religious beliefs and practices, but they cannot make the spirit of the child accept these things.

Third, one can argue that the state has authority over humans. This authority has been granted by God (Rom 13:1–7). But there is no evidence that this authority extends to spiritual matters. I will develop this more when I talk about the difference between Israel and all other political entities.

Fourth, some would argue that a husband exercises spiritual authority over his wife. But this is an incorrect view of spiritual headship. Headship entails responsibility for the physical, emotional, and spiritual well-being of the family, which of course includes the wife, but nowhere in Scripture is it said that the husband is the spiritual superior of the wife. Paul says that in matters relating to God, there is no Jew or Greek, slave or free, male or female (Gal 3:28). All people, including husbands and wives, enjoy religious liberty. The husband is responsible to see to it that his wife has opportunity for spiritual growth and worship, but he does not have the authority to force her to mature spiritually, to worship, or to believe.

Humans as Fallen Beings. We gain further insight about the doctrine of religious liberty from the fall. In Genesis 2:16–17, God told the man and the woman that they were free to eat from any tree in the garden except for the tree of the knowledge of good and evil. This instruction implies that God had given these first humans significant latitude in their choices. They were given a will capable of choosing whether or not to obey God. Their subsequent choice to disobey (Gen 3:1–7) reveals the reality of this liberty.

One can see in this event a significant freedom in religious matters granted to our original parents. God put them in the garden, surrounded them with all they needed, and then gave them the freedom to choose his way or their own. As we are well aware, they chose their own way. From that moment on, the biblical story depicts God's activity calling men and women back to himself and his plan to redeem them. Yet, not once do we find that God violates a person's freedom to choose between his or her own sinful ways and God. Granted, he confronts them dramatically, as in the flood or through the forty years of wilderness wandering. But people remained free to choose their spiritual path.

There is yet more to be learned about religious liberty from the fall. The prophet Jeremiah declared, "The heart is more deceitful than all else and is desperately sick" (Jer 17:9 NASB). Because they are fallen, people are incapable of fully interpreting the will of God in all matters for other people, and they are certainly incapable of properly enforcing spiritual standards. Fallen humanity's propensity for cruelty and merciless retribution too often in the name of just causes, including religious ones, provides a strong argument for religious liberty. Consider the example of Cain. He feared that his sin would be a cause of retribution from anyone who met him, which was evidently more than God required. In response God took the unusual step of providing assurance that no one would require more than God had already exacted (Gen 4:9–16).

In summary, theologian James Wood eloquently explains how the fall contributes to the doctrine of religious liberty. He comments, "The sinful nature of man negates the possibility of the absolutizing of human

authority, religious or political, and by limiting all human authority provides an important foundation for religious liberty."[19]

Humans as Free Moral Agents. God's respect for individual choice
carries over to the church as well. In the book of Revelation, Jesus chided
the church at Laodicea for their severe spiritual failings (3:14–22). He
declared them lukewarm (v. 16). Yet, in spite of his obvious disappointment, he did not forcefully compel them to change. Instead, he called them
to be zealous and repent, and then issued his amazing invitation: "Behold, I
stand at the door and knock; if anyone hears My voice and opens the door,
I will come in to him" (Rev 3:20 NASB). Jesus did not coerce; he appealed.

God's attitude toward human freedom of choice highlights an essential aspect of faith. Faith is an internal matter. Coercion can produce external compliance to a set of behavioral standards, but it cannot produce a
change in mind. Brainwashing can produce a desired response, but it does
not represent the true opinion of the individual. It is an overlay that turns
the victim into a mindless drone. Evidently, God did not desire this kind of
person, or he would have created people with the correct mind-set toward
him and made it impossible for them to hold a contrary opinion. Because
God so highly values individual choice, it seems unlikely that he would
designate any other individual or institution to exercise power over that
which he himself has chosen to honor.

Humans as Religious Beings. In his great sermon to the Areopagus
in Athens, the apostle Paul argued that God created humans with a capacity to seek him. He asserted that God wanted all people to seek him and
find him. He said that God "made from one man every nation of mankind
to live on all the face of the earth . . . that they would seek God, if perhaps
they might grope for Him and find Him" (Acts 17:26–27 NASB). It seems
reasonable to deduce from this passage that God intends for humans to
have the freedom to search for him. Unquestionably, they will reach false
formulations of faith, yet Paul's word "grope" intimates that this is part of
the search process. People have to search out questions of faith in order to
come to the end of their own efforts and be prepared to accept the truth
when it appears. Luke Johnson's reflections on this passage led him to

---

[19] James E. Wood Jr., "A Biblical View of Religious Liberty," *The Ecumenical Review*
30 (January 1978): 37.

conclude that Paul's statement is "remarkably positive toward the legiti-macy of Gentile religious longing."[20]

Humans and the Inviolability of Conscience. Ultimately, religious liberty is about the human conscience. The conscience is the crucial inter-nal guide to moral judgment in the New Testament. H. C. Hahn writes of the conscience, "Conscience appears—to put it graphically—as a court of appeal which is not able to promulgate any statutes (for only God him-self can do this) but is able to deliver judgment on the cases before it."[21] Paul characterized the conscience of the unbelieving Gentiles as capable of directing them to obey the law written on their hearts (Rom 2:14–15). He called it the judge of his own moral life (Rom 9:1). He trusted that the con-sciences of others would testify to the truthfulness of his message (2 Cor 4:2). Hahn concludes, "The conscience can be regarded as the place where the 'mystery of faith' is to be found (1 Tim. 3:9)."[22]

Conscience is the inviolable witness within each person that gives guidance about moral accountability. Some in the Corinthian church, for instance, were confused about whether or not eating meat sacrificed to idols or eating at pagan shrines was permissible (see 1 Cor 8–10). Paul referred them to the role of the individual conscience. What mattered most in these instances was whether or not a person violated his or her conscience. Luke Johnson notes that Paul's answer focused on the indi-vidual's perception of things, not on the objective facts of the case: "Proper behavior depended on the circumstances, and the discernment of the cir-cumstances in turn was the business of the individual's conscience."[23]

The conscience offers moral guidance for each person, and Paul taught that it was inviolable. A person either follows the lead of his or her con-science and experiences harmony within or fails to follow its guidance and experiences internal condemnation. No one is to create a situation that

---

[20] Johnson, "Religious Rights and Christian Texts," in Witte and van der Vyver, *Religious Human Rights in Global Perspective*, 87.

[21] H. C. Hahn, "Conscience," in *The New International Dictionary of New Testament Theology* (Grand Rapids: Zondervan, 1975), 1:350.

[22] Ibid., 351.

[23] Johnson, "Religious Rights and Christian Texts," in Witte and Van der Vyver, *Religious Human Rights in Global Perspective*, 89.

would offend or interfere with an individual's conscience.[24] Consequently, Johnson argues that human conscience "provides the fundamental ground for religious liberty."[25]

The centrality of conscience in matters of faith seems to have first appeared in official form in a 1612 confession of faith referred to as "Propositions and Conclusions concerning True Christian Religion, containing a Confession of Faith of certain English people, living at Amsterdam." W. L. Lumpkin suggests that the document may have been a modification of a confession written in Dutch by John Smyth, a principal leader in what would become the General Baptist Church.[26] This Confession states:

> That the magistrate is not by virtue of his office to meddle with religion, or matters of conscience, to force or compel men to this or that form of religion, or doctrine: but to leave Christian religion free, to every man's conscience, and to handle only civil transgressions (Rom. xiii), injuries and wrongs of man against man, in murder, adultery, theft, etc., for Christ only is king and lawgiver of the church and conscience (James iv. 12).[27]

Lumpkin credits the confession as "perhaps the first confession of faith of modern times to demand freedom of conscience and separation of church and state."[28]

Freedom of conscience was a key issue in Roger Williams's arguments for religious liberty. In his 1644 tractate "The Bloudy Tenent of Persecution," Williams made the matter of conscience a central theme. He stated:

---

[24] Wood comments, "Persons are to be free in matters of conscience and religion, without hindrance or coercion, first and foremost in order that God may be sovereign of their lives and that in turn they may freely respond to that sovereignty and bring about the ordering of their lives according to the will of God." "A Biblical View of Religious Liberty," 35.

[25] Johnson, "Religious Rights and Christian Texts," in Witte and van der Vyver, in *Religious Human Rights in Global Perspective*, 89.

[26] W. L. Lumpkin, *Baptist Confessions of Faith*, rev. ed. (Valley Forge, PA: Judson, 1969), 123. W. R. Estep speaks with more certainty about this. He says that Smyth "can be considered the author." *Religious Liberty: Heritage and Responsibility* (Newton, KS: Bethel College, 1988), 37.

[27] Lumpkin, *Baptist Confessions of Faith*, 140.

[28] Ibid., 124.

It is the will and command of God that, since the coming of His Son the Lord Jesus, a permission of the most paganish, Jewish, Turkish, or anti-christian consciences and worships be granted to all men in all nations and countries, and they are only to be fought against with that sword which is only, in soul matters, able to conquer, to wit, the sword of God's Spirit, the word of God.

He also avowed, "God requires not a uniformity of religion to be enacted and enforced in any civil state; which enforced uniformity, sooner or later, is the greatest occasion of civil war, ravishing of conscience, persecution of Christ Jesus in his servants, and of the hypocrisy and destruction of millions of souls."[29]

In 1773, Isaac Backus offered a similar opinion:

God alone is Lord of the conscience, and hath left it free from the doctrines and commandments of men, which are, in *any thing* contrary to his word; or *not contained in it*; so that to believe such doctrines, or to obey such commands, out of conscience, is to *betray* true liberty of conscience; and the requiring of an implicit faith, and an absolute blind obedience, is to destroy liberty of conscience and reason also.[30]

Christology and Religious Liberty

Additional confirmation of the God-given right of religious liberty is available in the doctrine of Christ. Jesus provides a perfect example of God's respect for religious liberty. Throughout his ministry, Jesus respected the right of every person to choose or reject him. He even came in the form of a servant rather than a king (Matt 20:25–28; Phil 2:5–8). As a servant,

---

[29] Roger Williams, *The Bloudy Tenent of Persecution for Cause of Conscience*, in *Roger Williams*, ed. Richard Groves (Macon, GA: Mercer University Press, 2001), 3. David Little provides a brief but helpful discussion of Williams's views about conscience in the context of four contemporary areas of interest: social regulation, duties of citizenship, human sexuality, and life and death issues. "Conscientious Individualism: A Christian Perspective on Ethical Pluralism," in *Christian Political Ethics*, ed. John Coleman (Princeton: Princeton University Press, 2008): 113–40.

[30] Isaac Backus, *An Appeal to the Public for Religious Liberty, Against the Oppressions of the Present Day* (Boston: John Boyle, 1773), 56.

he pointed people to God and faith, but he is never depicted as coercing faith. One can think of many examples of this attitude, but a prime example is Jesus' lament over the city of Jerusalem. He declares, "O Jerusalem, Jerusalem, the city that kills the prophets and stones those sent to her! How often I wanted to gather your children together, just as a hen gathers her brood under her wings, and you would not have it" (Luke 13:34 NASB). Here Jesus acknowledges his desire to see Jerusalem embrace him, yet he does not force the people to accept him. This is all the more significant when we recognize that, as God, he had the power to make people do anything. Nevertheless, he chose a different approach.

Jesus reveals that approach in his parable of the Wheat and Tares (Matt 13:24–30). In the parable the wheat symbolizes true believers, and the tares symbolize unbelievers. When the servants in the parable ask their master if they should go and uproot the tares, the master says, "Allow both to grow together until the harvest" (Matt 13:30 NASB). Jesus does not want humans to root out unbelievers for their lack of faith. God will do that in his own time and way.

Soteriology and Religious Liberty

The doctrine of salvation itself contributes to our understanding of God's design for religious liberty. Salvation is an individual, spiritual event. It is a matter of the will. Scripture shows the apostles preaching, even pleading with people to trust Christ as Savior, but it never shows them violating the right of the individual to choose or reject their message, and ultimately salvation. In fact, the individual nature of salvation requires religious liberty. People must be free to respond to the gospel. It is unlikely that God would have ordained an institution, secular or religious, designed to oppose the freedom of people to make decisions in matters of faith. Why would he design humans to seek and find him, and then give an institution the power of life and death (which the civil government possesses) to forbid them from this search? That would be equivalent to creating people with a need for water and then forbidding the search for water.[31]

---

[31] J. D. Hughey remarked concerning this that "no earthly power has the right to enforce obedience to God, since his authority over the spirit of man has not been delegated." "The Theological Frame of Religious Liberty," 1365.

Ecclesiology and Religious Liberty

The Three Social Spheres. The doctrine of the church holds additional keys for developing a biblical understanding of religious liberty. The church is not a political entity. It is a spiritual entity. It has not been given the means to exercise control over those outside the faith. Consequently, the church cannot dictate to others on matters of faith.

Scripture teaches that God established three social institutions—the family, the church, and the government. The family is the foundational social structure that nourishes its members physically, emotionally, mentally, and spiritually to provide a citizenry capable of fulfilling God's design for creation (Gen 2:18–25). Civil government is the institution charged with maintaining civil order. According to Paul it is God's minister to reward good behavior and punish evil behavior (Rom 13:1–5). The church is God's spiritual institution (Matt 16:15–20; 18:15–20). Its task is to provide a structure for Christian ministry and spiritual maturity. Each of these institutions has its distinct tasks. While the institutions share some responsibilities, none of them are designed to fulfill the God-given purposes of the other. For example, the family and the church share a common responsibility for the spiritual development of others, but the church is not a substitute for the family. The father is the one responsible for the spiritual development of the family. The church is there to assist him in that task. Similarly, the church is tasked with the responsibility to share the gospel throughout the world. In fulfilling this task, it depends on governments to protect the rights of its workers but not to do its work.[32]

This understanding of the separation of responsibility has not always been respected. In the past the church too often looked to civil government to enforce its vision of Christian beliefs and practices. Contrary to popular belief, this unbiblical union of the church and civil government has not been practiced only by the Roman Catholic Church. For example, leaders of the Reformation also used the power of the state to enforce

---

[32] Wayne Grudem argues that the doctrine of religious freedom is further supported by the fact that the state was not involved in choosing the church's leadership. He notes, "There was clearly no involvement by the civil government . . . in any selection of officers in the early church." *Politics According to the Bible* (Grand Rapids: Zondervan, 2010), 100.

church doctrine.[33] Today, a monument stands in Geneva as a testament to Michael Servetus, who was executed by the civil authorities for his heretical views. The great reformer John Calvin appears to have approved of the action, concerning himself only with the manner of the execution.[34]

An interdependence among the three God-ordained social spheres of family, church, and government does exist, but it has limits. In thinking about these limits in the current context, a question inevitably rises: Does the state possess legitimate authority—either by its own choice or by consent of the church—to rule over matters pertaining to the church? This, of course, is not an idle question. This was a serious issue well into the late eighteenth century in the United States. Baptists found themselves persecuted regularly by the state for refusing to follow the established church's practices, such as infant baptism, and for disturbing the peace, i.e., preaching the gospel. Understandably, it was a Baptist, John Leland, who led the charge to write an end to these practices into the United States Constitution, through the First Amendment. The question is, was he correct to insist on the separation of the state from the church? Scripture supports this position.

The Difference between the Church and Israel. The only possible way someone can argue from Scripture that the church, or any religious group, can rely on the civil authorities to enforce doctrine or to punish error is to believe that Old Testament teachings intended for Israel are normative for religious entities today. Obviously, Israel was a theocracy. She had judges,

---

[33] David Little tracks the development of the modern conception of separation of church and state in the Reformed tradition. He credits Calvin himself for much of the confusion of later Reformers on the relationship between the two. He notes that, while Calvin stipulated a clear separation between the two on matters of internal faith, he considered false doctrine and impious behavior a threat to the civil order, which the civil magistrate was responsible for. Consequently, the civil magistrate had a biblical mandate to secure the peace, which included jurisdiction over external faith practices that it considered dangerous to this peace. David Little, "Reformed Faith and Religious Liberty," *Church and Society* (May/June 1986): 9.

[34] Perez Zagorin credits Calvin's complicity in the execution of Servetus as the impetus for Sébastien Castellion's anonymously published 1553 work entitled *Concerning Heretics and Whether They Should Be Persecuted.* He calls it "one of the first great protests in the sixteenth century against the persecution of heresy and a landmark in the struggle for religious toleration." Zagorin, *How the Idea of Religious Toleration Came to the West* (Princeton: Princeton University Press, 2003), 103.

governors, a king, an army, and a prescribed faith. God had stipulated death for a number of errant beliefs and practices, some theological and others civil in nature, within this community. The Old Testament acknowledges that the sentence of death was carried out at times.

If the Old Testament depiction of Israel as a theocracy is normative for other entities, some could argue that religious entities can forge a union with civil authorities today as well. For example, if the church is the continuation of or replacement for the theocracy of Israel, then it is possible to argue that the church can employ the power of the state to enforce its views. However, there are a number of evidences that the church is not the replacement for the state of Israel. Here I will point out only a few.

First, Jesus intimated that the church was a new thing, not to be equated with Israel. In Matthew 16:17–19, he said he would build his church on Peter's confession. The church was not a continuation of the old but something entirely new. Second, Jesus discouraged the use of physical force to protect himself. He declared that his kingdom was not of "this world" (John 18:36). Therefore, it was inappropriate to use the powers of this world in its work. Third, the church has two offices, pastor and deacon. These offices are spiritual in nature, not civil. There is no army, no king, no civil magistrate within the church structure. Consequently, Scripture provides no structure for the use of physical force to advance the work of the church or to protect it from error. Israel was a one-of-a-kind entity, never to be duplicated.

It seems clear that there was only one theocracy: Israel. The church is an entirely new organism. Therefore, one cannot apply the religious-state model of Israel to the church or to the state.[35] The church and the state are separate entities, addressing different aspects of human life. Each supports the other but is not tasked with doing the other's work. Jesus put it very simply: "Render to Caesar the things that are Caesar's, and to God the things that are God's" (Matt 22:21; Mark 12:17; Luke 20:25 NASB).

---

[35] God's guidance in the government of ancient Israel isn't even normative for the modern state of Israel. All that God intended to accomplish through the theocratic state of Israel was accomplished when the Messiah, Jesus, came. That civil code is now void. Of course, this doesn't mean, in my opinion, that Israel as a people and a nation no longer factor into God's plan. They do. But modern-day Israel is not a continuation of the ancient theocratic state.

This central truth was a crucial component in the thinking of John Locke. Locke was strongly opposed to the union of the state and the church. He made the same argument I have made here—the civil magistrate and the church have different tasks, and they are not to be relegated to the other or assumed by the other. In considering how Israel factors into an understanding of the relationship between faith and the state, Locke commented:

> The laws established [in Israel] concerning the worship of One Invisible Deity were the civil laws of that people and a part of their political government, in which God Himself was the legislator. Now, if any one can show me where there is a commonwealth at this time, constituted upon that foundation, I will acknowledge that the ecclesiastical laws do there unavoidably become a part of the civil, and that the subjects of that government both may and ought to be kept in strict conformity with that church by the civil power. But there is absolutely no such thing under the Gospel as a Christian commonwealth.[36]

The Church and Religious Coercion. Today, much of the discussion of religious liberty takes place within the context of the Christian faith. This is because Christians are under extreme pressure at the current time to limit their activities in the United States and around the world. But religious liberty does not apply only to Christianity. Religious liberty extends to all people. Every person is to be free from coercion to believe or not to believe. If God has not empowered the church, which he himself created, to employ the power of the state to advance its work, then we can be assured that no religion possesses this right.

Jesus sent his disciples into all the world to make disciples, but their methodology was to make disciples by teaching others to observe all that he taught them (Matt 28:19–20). There is no hint in the Great Commission that Jesus expected his disciples to coerce true faith or to stop people from practicing false religion. The Vatican Declaration agrees: "From the very origins of the Church the disciples of Christ strove to convert men to faith

---

[36] John Locke, *A Letter Concerning Toleration* (New York: The Liberal Arts Press, 1950), 43.

in Christ as the Lord—not, however, by the use of coercion or by devices unworthy of the gospel, but by the power, above all, of the Word of God." The declaration cites both 1 Corinthians 2:3–5 and 1 Thessalonians 2:3–5 in support.[37]

If ever there was an opportunity to force true faith on others, it was during Israel's days as a kingdom, complete with a king and an army. Yet whenever God wanted to get the attention of the surrounding nations, he didn't call on the kings of Israel to send in their armies; he called prophets to go and preach repentance. Jonah is the perfect example of this. The Assyrians were a wicked people. They needed to repent. They certainly needed to believe in the true God. Yet, knowing what the stakes were— wrath or mercy—God sent Jonah to preach. The Assyrian people had to decide based on an appeal.

Some may object that God instructed the Israelites to wipe out all the pagans in Canaan when they took possession of the land. That is true, but we must remember first of all that this was the fulfillment of a judgment God had determined long before then (see Gen 15:16). Second, God was establishing a theocracy with Israel. It is entirely within the nature of a theocracy to use the power of the state to eradicate error if it chooses to do so. As I stated earlier, there is no scriptural evidence that God intended any other theocracies to exist.

Two Crucial Questions

Clearly, ample theological support exists for the doctrine of religious liberty; however, two questions remain.

Does religious liberty apply only to the freedom of people to believe certain things but not to express them in public or, possibly, even in private? The Bible does not present any theological model for the right of the state to restrict religious speech or public or private practice. The only instances where the Bible describes state-sanctioned efforts to regulate spiritual life, outside of the theocratic government of Israel, are negative. Jesus was executed under the auspices of the Roman government. The apostles were jailed and most were ultimately executed under the authority

---

[37] The Vatican, "Declaration on Religious Freedom."

of the state because of their religious practices. The book of Revelation describes a time in the future when people of faith will once again be persecuted under the auspices of the state for their beliefs and practices.

The early church recognized the power that the state possessed to punish evil and reward good (Rom 13:1–5), and the Bible calls on Christians to honor the civil authorities and obey them (1 Pet 2:13–17). The early church also recognized that the state had the power to punish them for their beliefs and practices, but they did not believe they were bound to obey the government, or that the government acted legitimately, when its dictates violated their spiritual calling. For example, when the apostles were brought before the civil authorities and told to stop preaching about Jesus, they responded famously, "We must obey God rather than men" (see Acts 5:27–29).

H. Richard Niebuhr answered the question of the state's ability to interfere in matters of faith. He stated, "Religion, so understood, lies beyond the provenance of the state not because it is a private, inconsequential, or other-worldly matter but because it concerns men's allegiance to a sovereignty and a community more immediate, more inclusive, and more fateful than those of the political commonwealth."[38]

A. F. Carillo de Albornoz actually reverses the argument of separation of church and state. He comments:

> Now, it seems that it would be extremely difficult to find in the Christian revelation the precise limits of civil authority concerning man *in virtue of the State's nature.* On the contrary, Christian revelation does show us that man, as he has been created, redeemed and called by God and as God intends to deal with him, is responsible solely to God and that, *therefore,* the State, which is subordinated to God's authority and laws, must respect this human responsibility before God. Consequently, in thinking this way, religious liberty would *not* be ultimately based on the limitation of political authority but, inversely, the latter would flow from the freedoms which God has given man.[39]

---

[38] H. Richard Niebuhr, *Radical Monotheism and Western Culture* (New York: Harper and Row, 1960), 70–71.

[39] A. F. Carillo de Albornoz, *The Basis of Religious Liberty* (New York: Association Press, 1963), 87.

If religious liberty applies also to public expressions, can legitimate limitations be placed on these freedoms by third parties, such as governments? Writers, dissidents, and scholars have addressed this question numerous times. Carillo de Albornoz noted that the Vatican Declaration usually referred to religious freedom in the singular, but in reality it was proclaiming "many religious freedoms: freedoms exercised by different classes of people—organizations, families, individuals—or involving different activities—preaching, teaching, witnessing, etc."[40] He argued that each of these contexts requires a separate treatment since they can infringe on other social conventions. At times, he argued, religious freedoms must give way to other rights within the community.

Philip Wogaman agrees with Carillo de Albornoz's categorization of religious freedoms, but he differs with him on the abridgement of those freedoms when they interfere with other rights. He provides three useful categories of religious freedom and then discusses briefly how the intersection of other rights might affect their exercise. "Absolute religious liberty" is the internal freedom to believe and worship as one pleases. "Qualified absolute religious liberty" is the freedom to profess or to express one's faith verbally through social communication. He calls this a qualified liberty because "a case must be made for limiting speech which is not designed as communication of faith, knowledge, or opinion but as malicious slander or incitement to action of an illegal sort." "Qualified religious liberty" is the freedom to act in accordance with one's religious insights and values. He says this kind of liberty "raises problems" when it is made into an absolute. Issues like withholding medication for religious reasons, education of children, and activities that harm other people require that this liberty be restricted in some manner.[41]

These are not only useful distinctions; they are reasonable. As we make our claims for religious liberty, and insist on them with zeal, we must keep in mind that humans are still fallen. Some people will abuse any liberty. When they do, government must step in to protect its citizens.

---

[40] A. F. Carillo de Albornoz, *Religious Liberty* (New York: Sheed and Ward, 1967), 13–14.

[41] Philip Wogaman, *Protestant Faith and Religious Liberty* (Nashville: Abingdon Press, 1967), 182–90.

That said, however, we must always be mindful of what is at stake
when we are dealing with religious liberty. Faith is the principal point of
connection between God and humanity. Through faith, people commune
with God, learn his will, and act in the world in response to him. What
one government may decide is inappropriate religious behavior because
it interferes with the life of the community may be a perfectly legitimate
behavior in the eyes of God. For example, China is currently engaged in a
brutal policy of repressing the house church movement. The government
believes that these groups pose a real threat to order. Yet we must do all
we can to assert the right of these Christians to engage in such legitimate
expressions of their faith as worshipping God free from governmental control. Whenever anyone claims a legitimate right to abridge the religious
liberty of another, that person must demonstrate greater interests than the
God-given right to believe and practice faith according to the dictates of
conscience.[42]

The Baptist Faith and Message on Religious Liberty

In conclusion, I reiterate that many men and women have contributed
in significant ways to our current understanding of religious liberty, too
often at the expense of their lives. Many have made their statements about
this topic in quite powerful and instructive ways. But I believe it would
be difficult to find a more succinct statement of the Christian doctrine of
religious liberty than that found in the Baptist Faith and Message. Article
XVII reads:

> God alone is Lord of the conscience, and He has left it free from
> the doctrines and commandments of men which are contrary to
> His Word or not contained in it. Church and state should be sepa-
> rate. The state owes to every church protection and full freedom
> in the pursuit of its spiritual ends. In providing for such freedom
> no ecclesiastical group or denomination should be favored by the
> state more than others. Civil government being ordained of God,

---

[42] Grudem presses this issue with vigor. He states rightly, "Any speech, in order to
be properly restricted by law, needs to *directly cause actual harm* to another person."
Politics According to the Bible, 495.

it is the duty of Christians to render loyal obedience thereto in all things not contrary to the revealed will of God. The church should not resort to the civil power to carry on its work. The gospel of Christ contemplates spiritual means alone for the pursuit of its ends. The state has no right to impose penalties for religious opinions of any kind. The state has no right to impose taxes for the support of any form of religion. A free church in a free state is the Christian ideal, and this implies the right of free and unhindered access to God on the part of all men, and the right to form and propagate opinions in the sphere of religion without interference by the civil power.

Genesis 1:27; 2:7; Matthew 6:6–7, 24; 16:26; 22:21; John 8:36; Acts 4:19–20; Romans 6:1–2; 13:1–7; Galatians 5:1, 13; Philippians 3:20; 1 Timothy 2:1–2; James 4:12; 1 Peter 2:12–17; 3:11–17; 4:12–19.

CHAPTER 5

Religious Liberty
and the Gospel

Evan Lenow

*Go, therefore, and make disciples of all nations, baptizing them in
the name of the Father and of the Son and of the Holy Spirit, teaching
them to observe everything I have commanded you.*

MATTHEW 28:19–20

Moments before Jesus ascended into heaven following his resurrection, he commissioned his disciples to preach the gospel to all
nations. The book of Acts recounts the beginning stages of the disciples
carrying out the Great Commission, and church history continues the
story of Christians taking the gospel of Jesus Christ to the uttermost parts
of the earth. Even today missionaries are scattered across the globe, faithfully evangelizing, discipling, teaching, and baptizing.

Students taking introductory courses on the New Testament or
church history will often hear about unique features of the Roman
Empire that made the spread of the gospel a little easier. The existence

of a network of roads between major trade cities, the common Greek language spoken throughout the empire, and the relative peace brought by Roman military dominance all helped missionaries such as the apostle Paul carry the message of Christ to the nations.[1] Even persecution during the early days of the church encouraged the spread of the gospel as believers dispersed to new regions. As the gospel spread, the influence of Christianity grew until it became the official religion of the empire under Constantine.

Today, the political landscape is much different than it was in the first century. No dominant empire controls the political fate of the Western world. As syncretistic as the Roman Empire may have been, it does not compare to the landscape of religious thought known around the world today. From the proliferation of Eastern religions to the rise of Islam, Christians around the world, and even in the United States, face a much different task in proclaiming the gospel. However, much as it was for the early first-century missionaries, some features of today's political climate aid in the spread of the gospel. One of those unique features is laws protecting religious liberty. While the framers of the Constitution of the United States or any other nation that has codified religious liberty into law may not have realized it, religious liberty aids the proclamation of the gospel.

The Bible, Religious Liberty, and the Gospel

Paige Patterson and Barrett Duke stated in earlier chapters that the Bible does not explicitly proclaim a doctrine of religious liberty. However, Patterson also rightly notes "that the concept is implicit on almost every page of Scripture."[2] Therefore, it is helpful to understand the context in which Scripture describes religious liberty as an aid to spreading the gospel.

---

[1] Justo L. Gonzalez, *The Story of Christianity* (San Francisco: HarperCollins, 1984), 1:13–14.

[2] Paige Patterson, "Mutually Exclusive or Biblically Harmonious? Religious Liberty and Exclusivity of Salvation in Jesus Christ," page 15 in this volume.

A Biblical Context for Religious Liberty

In the opening verses of Matthew 10, Jesus calls together his disciples and commissions them to go out and heal the sick, cast out demons, and proclaim that the kingdom of heaven is at hand. As part of that commission, we find these unusually ominous words in verses 16 to 20:

> Look, I'm sending you out like sheep among wolves. Therefore be as shrewd as serpents and as harmless as doves. Because people will hand you over to sanhedrins and flog you in their synagogues, beware of them. You will even be brought before governors and kings because of Me, to bear witness to them and to the nations. But when they hand you over, don't worry about how or what you should speak. For you will be given what to say at that hour, because you are not speaking, but the Spirit of your Father is speaking through you.

The disciples lived in a world not unlike our own. The Roman imperial government imposed no official state religion, but only appropriate expressions of worship were tolerated or sanctioned. Syncretism and emperor worship were the unifying religious expressions of the Roman Empire. Within the region of Israel, the Roman government granted the Jews a special dispensation of freedom to worship their God but often looked on this worship with suspicion.[3] They did not drive the Jews completely underground, but the state certainly did not support the Jews.

Even within Israel, the accepted form of Judaism was the one the scribes and Pharisees governed. The message of the kingdom of heaven would certainly be at odds with the ruling parties of Israel. The message of this so-called Messiah might upset the balance of power and cause the Romans to look with even more suspicion upon a people who really just wanted to be left alone.

From a larger perspective, the Roman Empire was not really all that accepting of Jesus' message of the kingdom of heaven either. Even though the government allowed a number of religions to coexist under its watchful eye, the religion du jour was a syncretistic paganism that promoted

---

[3] Gonzalez, *The Story of Christianity*, 1:14–17.

the worship of gods made in the image of humans and even the worship of humans themselves. As long as you fit within the generally accepted syncretistic paganism, you were fine. Once you moved to something more radical, no one promised to protect you.

Syncretistic paganism was the cultural context of the day for the disciples, and Jesus gave them fair warning. He first warned his disciples about the official "church" of their region. He told them, "Because people will hand you over to sanhedrins and flog you in their synagogues, beware of them" (Matt 10:17). The religious leaders of the day were sure to find the disciples' message unpalatable because it threatened the offerings given to the synagogues. People turned away from the established religion and followed after this band of radicals led by a man who claimed to be the Son of God. As a result, the disciples found themselves on trial before the Sanhedrin and scourged by the Jews. They risked being excommunicated by the religious leaders of their day.

Not only this, but Jesus also warned them regarding the government. He said, "You will even be brought before governors and kings because of Me" (v. 18). He did not mean the emperor would invite them to the palace for a state dinner. Instead, he meant they would be turned over to those who could actually kill them (as he later mentions in v. 28). The government could impose all sorts of sanctions and punishments all the way up to the death penalty for their faith. Their own countrymen and even families would turn them over to the authorities for the sake of "keeping the peace." This was the disciples' cultural context.

So what were they to do? Jesus told them in verse 16, "Look, I'm sending you out like sheep among wolves. Therefore be as shrewd as serpents and as harmless as doves." In the face of real persecution—the type that could end their lives—they still had a commission to go. The threat of persecution was not cause to abandon the mission or shudder in fear. The disciples had a message to proclaim, and these were merely the consequences of proclaiming that message.

The fact that persecution so often attends the preaching of the gospel helps us understand why religious liberty is important for a nation. Not all Christians in history have benefited from such protections, as Jesus' disciples did not. But it is easy to see how legal guarantees of religious liberty provide a context in which the gospel can move about unhindered by threat of bodily or social reprisal.

A Biblical Foundation for Religious Liberty

After having seen a biblical context for religious liberty, we now can explore a biblical foundation. One biblical text used to defend religious liberty is Jesus' parable of the Wheat and the Tares (Matt 13:24–30). In this parable an enemy sows bad seed amongst the field of wheat (vv. 24–28). Rather than pulling up the tares and risk destroying some of the wheat, the farmer tells his slaves to allow the wheat and tares to grow up together (vv. 29–30). At the time of the harvest, the farmer says, the tares will be thrown in the fire and the wheat will be stored in the barn (v. 30). This passage illustrates that there will be people who arise in the community and even the church whom the enemy sows. These are heretics and heathens who do not belong but are allowed to remain so that the true believers will not be harmed by their removal. This does not mean that believers neglect to share the gospel with these individuals, but the true judgment is left up to God. It is not the job of the government to judge and remove these people for their unbelief. God will judge them, and his judgment is final.

We also see a biblical foundation for religious liberty in the government's role of ensuring civil peace, not doctrinal purity. This particular teaching can be found in Romans 13:1–7. Notice some key concepts about government in this passage. First, government is ordained by God (v. 1). God has given government its authority, and it does not have any authority that he has not given it. Second, we are to submit to the government's authority because we submit to God (vv. 1–2, 5). To refuse to submit is to oppose the ordinance of God. Third, government functions within the scope of authority God has granted it (v. 4). The government is a minister of God for those who do what is good. It exacts punishment on those who do what is evil. This is not a theological function but a civil one. Government's role is to keep peace and restore order when that peace is violated.

The final biblical foundation for religious liberty is that we have the right to persuade others of the gospel. Consider Paul's interaction with the government of Corinth in Acts 18:12–17. We read:

> While Gallio was proconsul of Achaia, the Jews made a united attack against Paul and brought him to the judge's bench. "This man," they said, "persuades people to worship God contrary to the law!" As Paul was about to open his mouth, Gallio said to the Jews, "If it were a matter of a crime or of moral evil, it would be reasonable for me to put up with you Jews. But if these are questions about words, names, and your own law, see to it yourselves. I don't want to be a judge of such things." So he drove them from the judge's bench. Then they all seized Sosthenes, the leader of the synagogue, and beat him in front of the judge's bench. But none of these things concerned Gallio.

We see here that Paul is brought before Gallio and accused of disturbing the peace in Corinth. Notice the specific charge: he is accused of persuading people to worship God in a way contrary to the law. Before Paul can even defend himself, Gallio dismisses the case. He is not concerned with Jewish laws or customs of worship. Paul is free to do as he pleases: persuading people to follow Christ. The Jews exact their revenge on Sosthenes, but the government official is unconcerned about the religious dispute that is brought before him.

In the very next chapter, Paul spends more than two years in Ephesus speaking out boldly, reasoning, and persuading people to follow Christ. When he can no longer do so in the synagogue, he moves to a public forum. Over and over, we see the apostles reasoning and persuading men to follow Christ. No one is coerced to confess Christ on threat of their life or livelihood. They are free to reject him.

These biblical principles lay a foundation on which we build the idea of religious liberty. Implicit in the text of Scripture is the idea that government has a specific function. It cannot tell people what they are to believe about God. At the same time, the church does not have the authority to use force in converting unbelievers. Therefore, both heathens and believers coexist in this world until the day of God's judgment. It is our duty to warn, exhort, and persuade these unbelievers with the gospel, but we cannot force conversion upon them. In this way, Scripture sets the tone for our understanding of how religious liberty aids the spread of the gospel.

History, Religious Liberty, and the Gospel

Much can be said regarding the historical development of religious liberty among the theological and political mechanisms of civilization. However, this section will focus on how some influential historical figures viewed religious liberty as an aid in proclaiming the gospel. Thomas White has already discussed the Anabaptist and English Baptist roots of religious freedom, but we need to connect the dots with a historical understanding of religious liberty as aiding the gospel message.

Proclamation and Persecution of the Anabaptists

By the sixteenth century, many European governments were fully wedded to the church, often conducting trials and exacting punishments for heresy. Even among some of the Magisterial Reformers, the relationship between church and state was no different than what the Catholic Church enjoyed. However, the Anabaptists had a different vision. They wanted to see a clear distinction between the church and state, whereby the state had no influence over the religious beliefs and practices of the people. Such a vision was revolutionary in sixteenth-century Europe because many of the official churches used government power to coerce and punish those who disagreed with their doctrine and practice.[4]

The Anabaptists believed that the state's role was limited to protecting the good of society, not the doctrine of any church. Balthasar Hubmaier wrote, "The authorities judge the evildoers but not the godless, who can harm neither body nor soul but rather are useful, so that as is known God can make good out of evil."[5] Hubmaier believed that the God-given role of government excluded the state from interfering in matters of religious belief and conscience. In addition, the state could not act on behalf of the church or privilege one church over another.

Second, the Anabaptists believed that conversion came on the basis of persuasion through the Word of God rather than at the point of the

---

[4] Timothy George, *Theology of the Reformers* (Nashville: B&H, 1988), 285–86.

[5] Balthasar Hubmaier, *On Heretics and Those Who Burn Them*, in *Balthasar Hubmaier: Theologian of Anabaptism*, trans. and ed. H. Wayne Pipkin and John H. Yoder (Scottdale, PA: Herald Press, 1989), 64.

sword. Such a belief formed the basis on which Anabaptists built their understanding of religious liberty. Without a connection to the governing authorities, the church would not have the power to coerce unbelievers and heretics into doctrinal conformity. Thus, the proclamation of the gospel was central to the Anabaptist belief in religious liberty. With this liberty, those who were heretics and heathens could be convinced and persuaded of the true gospel message through the Word of God. The Dutch Anabaptist Dirk Philips wrote,

> Here is revealed that no congregation of the Lord may have domination over the consciences of people with an external sword, nor compel the unbeliever to faith with violence, nor kill the false prophets with sword and fire. But they must judge and exclude with the Lord's Word all who are within the congregation and found to be evil. Anything more than this that happens is neither Christian, evangelical, nor apostolic.[6]

Not only was the state forbidden from exercising authority over religious beliefs, but Anabaptists also proclaimed that the church could not use force to compel particular beliefs. Heretics and heathens alike were due the same freedom of conscience as those who professed faith in Christ. Such freedom should then serve as an impetus for believers to profess the truth of the gospel within the marketplace of ideas.

Because the church was no longer connected to the state and conversion was not to be found at the point of the sword, then the third Anabaptist belief was the free exercise of religion. We find this expressed in what many may consider a most unusual way. The heathens were allowed to exist in their unbelief. It was the duty of neither the state nor the church to coerce them into belief. If they could not be convinced on the basis of the Word of God, then they were to be left to continue in their false beliefs. The Swiss Anabaptist Conrad Grebel declared in a letter to Thomas Muntzer, "Whoever will not repent and believe, but resists the Word and the moving of God, and so persists in sin, after Christ and His Word and Rule have

---

[6] Dirk Philips, "The Congregation of God," in *The Writings of Dirk Philips: 1504–1568*, trans. and ed. Cornelius J. Dyck, William E. Keeney, and Alvin J. Beachy (Scottdale, PA: Herald Press, 1992), 375.

been preached to him, and he has been admonished in the company of the three witnesses and the congregation, such a man, we declare, on the basis of God's Word, shall not be killed, but regarded as a heathen and a publican, and let alone."[7] In contrast with other religious movements of the Reformation era, the Anabaptists believed that those who refused to repent when confronted with the gospel were simply to be left alone. This did not mean Christians were forbidden from proclaiming the gospel to the heathen. Instead, it simply meant that no one could be coerced into confessing a faith that was not genuine, much less executed on the basis of being a heretic. The free exercise of religion was not only for the privileged Christian church but for all people.

Of course the Anabaptists paid dearly for these beliefs. The Magisterial Reformers disagreed with their desire to remove the state from enforcing the doctrines of the church, as did the Catholics. Therefore, the Anabaptists were targets of persecution from both sides. However, such persecution did not prevent them from proclaiming the message of salvation and the benefits of religious liberty.

Religious Liberty and the Gospel in America

The development of religious liberty in America has distinctively Baptist roots that should not be overlooked. For the purpose of this chapter, we will briefly explore three Baptists in America and their understanding of the connection between religious liberty and the gospel. The common thread that we find among these Baptist leaders is that one ought to be free to share and respond to the gospel message without the forceful coercion of the government or church.

Roger Williams secured the first location for religious liberty in the early American colonies. Mark Noll reports, "Under his direction, Rhode Island became the first place in the North American colonies where freedom of religious worship was defined as a human right for all groups (or almost all—open atheists were still excluded). It was also the first American colony to attempt a separation between the institutions of religion and the

---

[7] Conrad Grebel, "Letter to Thomas Muntzer from the Swiss Brethren," in *Anabaptist Beginnings (1523–1533): A Source Book*, ed. William R. Estep Jr. (Nieuwkoop: B. De Graaf, 1976), 35.

institutions of the state."[8] This development of religious liberty as a human right was a forerunner to the First Amendment of the Bill of Rights to be adopted more than a century later.

For Williams, religious liberty had a specific connection to the gospel message. He believed that a person's conversion must not be coerced through force and that the believer should have the freedom to persuade his neighbor with the gospel. He stated that true conversion "must not be (it is not possible it should be, in truth) a conversion of people to the worship of the Lord Jesus by force of arms and swords of steel."[9] In contrast, the people of God must be free to proclaim the gospel and those who hear it have the opportunity to respond.

Williams goes on to say, "In particular, first, [true conversion] must be by the free proclaiming or preaching of repentance and forgiveness of sins (Luke 24) by such messengers as can prove their lawful sending and commission from the Lord Jesus, to make disciples out of all nations and so to baptize them or wash them . . . in the name of profession of the holy Trinity (Matt. 28:19; Rom. 10:14, 15)."[10] The reason that the messengers must freely engage others with the gospel rather than convert them by force is that Jesus did the same. Williams notes, "Jesus Christ compels by the mighty persuasions of his messengers to come in, but otherwise with earthly weapons he never did compel nor can be compelled."[11]

While Williams did not remain a Baptist for long, he offered a distinctively Baptist perspective, and his impact on religious liberty in America is essential. Williams himself was the target of persecution for his religious beliefs and practices. He knew firsthand what it meant to be compelled by force to hold a particular belief or practice, and he set the stage for a later codification of religious liberty into American constitutional law.

John Leland also played a key role in making sure religious liberty was protected by a bill of rights. Leland was a Baptist preacher who is

---

[8] Mark A. Noll, *A History of Christianity in the United States and Canada* (Grand Rapids: Eerdmans, 1992), 60.

[9] Roger Williams, *Christenings Make Not Christians*, in *On Religious Liberty: Selections from the Works of Roger Williams*, ed. James Calvin Davis (Cambridge, MA: Harvard University Press, 2008), 163–64.

[10] Ibid., 164–65.

[11] Ibid., 164.

remembered for his influence on James Madison and the politics of Virginia at the founding of the United States. While many of the young states had established churches, Leland used both his ecclesiastical and political influence to ensure that the constitution by Virginia was ratified and to elicit a promise from James Madison that a bill of rights would be added to the constitution. One of those amendments explicitly ensured religious liberty for the people.[12]

With the First Amendment's promise that "Congress shall make no law respecting an establishment of religion, or prohibiting the free exercise thereof," adherents to all faiths were guaranteed the right to the free exercise of religion. As a result, religious groups were free to take to the highways and byways to proclaim what they believed. Christians and others would have the freedom to gather for worship, change their religious beliefs, and proselytize. However, such freedom is a delicate balance. No one religious tradition can be privileged over another. The predominant religion of one generation may be the minority in the next. Therefore, it is imperative upon each generation to recognize that the religious liberty that Leland helped to secure in the infancy of the United States extends to all equally.

A third influential Baptist figure who clearly communicated his perspective on religious liberty and the gospel was E. Y. Mullins. Mullins served as president for both the Southern Baptist Theological Seminary and, from 1923 to 1928, the Baptist World Alliance.[13] In his presidential address for the latter, Mullins expounded upon the uniquely Baptist conception of religious liberty, which he said was central to all forms of liberty. He declared, "The quest for economic liberty, intellectual liberty, civil liberty, all go back to religious liberty at the root."[14] If religious liberty is at the root, several implications follow, including the free proclamation of the

---

[12] See William R. Estep, "Civil Religion and the Revolution within the Revolution," *Fides et Historia* 24 (1992): 47–49; and Mark S. Scarberry, "John Leland and James Madison: Religious Influence on the Ratification of the Constitution and on the Proposal of the Bill of Rights," *Penn State Law Review* 113 (2009): 733–800.

[13] For a summary of Mullins's address to the congress, see J. Brent Walker, "E. Y. Mullins on Religious Liberty," *Baptist History and Heritage* 43 (2008): 74–82.

[14] E. Y. Mullins, "The Baptist Conception of Religious Liberty," in *Third Baptist World Congress*, ed. W. T. Whitley (Nashville: Baptist Sunday School Board, 1923), 67.

gospel message. Mullins noted, "So also religious liberty implies the right of free utterance and propagation of truth. The evil powers of the world have ever sought to stifle men. Heroes have led the way in the witness for the truth."[15] Even when coercive governments and societal structures have attempted to silence these heroes, Mullins declared that those who stood up and proclaimed truth were the greatest people.

Mullins clearly articulated the impact of religious liberty on the gospel. True freedom of religion allows for the unfettered proclamation of truth. Mullins believed that "the right of free utterance and propagation of truth" was a human right grounded in the fact that humankind is created in the image of God.[16] We have direct access to God and can be persuaded and convinced of the truth. Mullins stated, "The second [right] is man's right to search for truth in religion. Jesus recognized this. He did not compel belief by Divine authority. He so lived and taught the truth that men discovered His Messiahship for themselves."[17] Mullins also taught that, because humans should be free to discover the truth of Jesus Christ, they should be free to deny the truth. Thus, religious liberty did not merely extend to the privileged religions of the early twentieth century, but it also extended freedom to deniers of religion. Mullins stated, "While we have no sympathy with atheism or agnosticism or materialism, we stand for the freedom of the atheist, agnostic and materialist in his religious or irreligious convictions. To God he stands or falls. He will render his account to the Eternal Judge, not to men."[18] In this way Mullins stands in solidarity with the sixteenth-century Anabaptists as they argued for the right of all to hold to their own religious beliefs without the coercion of government.

These three historical figures give us only brief snapshots of the development of religious liberty, but they provide a foundation for understanding how liberty aids the proclamation of the gospel. This review of history now leads us to consider the contemporary implications for religious liberty and the gospel.

---

[15] Ibid., 69.
[16] Ibid., 67–69.
[17] Ibid., 69.
[18] Ibid., 70.

Contemporary Implications for Religious Liberty and the Gospel

Having considered the biblical and historical foundations for religious liberty, we are left to examine the contemporary implications of religious liberty and the gospel. These implications relate to the all-encompassing nature of our faith and how we declare the message of the gospel to a lost and dying world. In so doing, we will see that religious liberty is most certainly an aid to the transmission of the gospel and a right that we should not take for granted.

An All-Encompassing Faith

The doctrines and teachings of the church are more than only ancient words written on a page. They should be taught, pondered, and lived out. Further, these teachings are more than just instructions for a worship service. They should impact every aspect of the believer's life. Our doctrine, ethics, families, jobs, and relationships should reflect the life-changing reality of union with Christ.

The current political climate in the United States and around the world does not always recognize the all-encompassing nature of Christianity. As a result, some may suggest that religious liberty ensures the right to freedom of worship and nothing more. However, the historical doctrine of this liberty implies much more. Even Pope Francis recognized the significant breadth of religious liberty during his visit to the United States in 2015. He stated, "Religious freedom certainly means the right to worship God, individually and in community, as our consciences dictate. But religious liberty, by its nature, transcends places of worship and the private sphere of individuals and families. Because religion itself, the religious dimension, is not a subculture; it is part of the culture of every people and every nation."[19] The transcending nature of faith means that Christians should live out

---

[19] Pope Francis, "Meeting for Religious Liberty with the Hispanic Community and Other Immigrants," speech at Independence Mall, Philadelphia, September 26, 2015, http://w2.vatican.va/content/francesco/en/speeches/2015/september/documents/papa-francesco_20150926_usa-liberta-religiosa.html.

their faith in both private and public. Therefore, religious liberty guarantees the right to religious expression even in the face of public disdain.

The 2015 United States Supreme Court case regarding same-sex marriage actually brought religious liberty to the forefront of public attention. In the penultimate section of the Supreme Court's majority opinion in the case *Obergefell v. Hodges*, which held that the right to marry is guaranteed to same-sex couples, Justice Anthony Kennedy offered what he believed to be comforting words to those who disagreed on religious grounds with the court's decision. He wrote:

> Finally, it must be emphasized that religions, and those who adhere to religious doctrines, may continue to advocate with utmost, sincere conviction that, by divine precepts, same-sex marriage should not be condoned. The First Amendment ensures that religious organizations and persons are given proper protection as they seek to teach the principles that are so fulfilling and so central to their lives and faiths, and to their own deep aspirations to continue the family structure they have long revered.[20]

These words offered little comfort to those who opposed the decision. In his dissent, Chief Justice John Roberts noted, "Today's decision, for example, creates serious questions about religious liberty." After offering examples of potential conflicts between the *Obergefell* decision and religious beliefs, Roberts stated, "There is little doubt that these and similar questions will soon be before this Court. Unfortunately, people of faith can take no comfort in the treatment they receive from the majority today."[21]

Those who currently work or will work within religious institutions such as churches, mission boards, or seminaries enjoy further protection while on their jobs because the nature of their work is explicitly religious. However, many people in our congregations do not have that same luxury. Their religious beliefs are not acceptable on the job. Holding a pro-life stance on abortion and birth control or a position that marriage is between one man and one woman for a lifetime could cost them a raise, a promotion, or even a job. Business owners could be forced to shut down their

---

[20] Obergefell v. Hodges 576 U.S. 32 (2015).
[21] Ibid.

businesses in the face of steep financial penalties simply for holding religious beliefs that are not acceptable in our current culture. There could come a day when denouncing abortion, sexual distortions, and all types of sin from the pulpit could be considered hate speech. This is why religious liberty is important to us.

Upholding religious liberty beyond the four walls of a house of worship allows people of faith to model the biblical life, which in turn prepares their non-Christian neighbors to hear the gospel. As culture continues to slide away from biblical norms, a tipping point will come. The consciences of people will begin to see that something is not right in the world. They will long for something different. As the apostle Paul wrote in Romans 2:14–15, "So, when Gentiles, who do not have the law, instinctively do what the law demands, they are a law to themselves even though they do not have the law. They show that the work of the law is written on their hearts. Their consciences confirm this. Their competing thoughts will either accuse or excuse them." People of faith who model God's standards will give the rest of the world the example they need to answer the questions to life's biggest problems. Thus, the burden is upon believers to live a consistent Christian life.

A Sharing Faith

There is one final application concerning religious liberty that many of us do not often consider. Religious liberty does not give Christianity a privileged position in the culture. It puts all religions (or the rejection of religion) on equal footing. Consider this for a moment. The next time Mormon missionaries knock on your door and try to convince you that the Church of Jesus Christ of Latter Day Saints restores the true church and that you need to be baptized in their church in order to enjoy the benefits of salvation, remember that they are exercising religious liberty. The next time that the Muslim community decides to build a mosque in your neighborhood (or even next door to your church), remember they are exercising religious liberty. Because religious liberty guarantees everyone the right to exercise faith freely, the government cannot coerce (what we believe to be) false religions to give up their beliefs or plans for worship. Thus, religious liberty ought to motivate us to share the gospel. In a country where religious liberty is currently protected, we should take advantage of this freedom and reason with others, persuading them to hear and receive the gospel.

What happens if we lose a robust understanding of religious liberty in the United States? Or what should you do if you find yourself in a country that does not recognize this freedom? I pray we would respond like Peter and John did in Acts 4:18–20: "So they called for them and ordered them not to preach or teach at all in the name of Jesus. But Peter and John answered them, 'Whether it's right in the sight of God for us to listen to you rather than to God, you decide; for we are unable to stop speaking about what we have seen and heard.'"

Religious liberty is the first freedom guaranteed by the US Constitution. Religious liberty is one of the first freedoms that united the early Anabaptists. And it is this first freedom that Christians today so often take for granted. Let us not do so anymore. May we exercise this freedom first and foremost by bringing the message of the gospel to a lost and dying world.

CHAPTER 6

RELIGIOUS LIBERTY AND THE PUBLIC SQUARE

Andrew T. Walker

I assume that those who cling to old beliefs will be able to whisper their thoughts in the recesses of their homes, but if they repeat those views in public, *they will risk being labeled as bigots and treated as such by governments, employers, and schools.*

JUSTICE SAMUEL ALITO,
OBERGEFELL V. HODGES
DISSENT (EMPHASIS ADDED)

The Supreme Court has a habit of marking eras in American history. From its disastrously wrong and war-sparking *Dred Scott* decision in 1857, to its unconscionable *Roe* decision in 1973, the Supreme Court has enacted horrific legal regimes that permeate American politics and culture.

On June 26, 2015, the Supreme Court's *Obergefell* decision once again ushered in a new era.[1] Hailed by marriage revisionists as the zenith of equality and a redress of past injustices, the outcome of *Obergefell* has, and will for the foreseeable future, cast a long shadow on the status of religious liberty in the public square. The dissenting voices—Justices Roberts, Alito, Scalia, and Thomas—ominously declared as much in their blistering dissents to the majority opinion authored by Justice Kennedy.[2] Rulings like *Obergefell* are the by-product of culture.

The law, like culture, is not static but dynamic and pedagogical. For good or ill, the forces of cultural opinion shape law, but, conversely, the law is an almost-unrivaled force for shaping cultural opinion. This means the future of religious liberty is caught up in a public square matrix consisting of what Justice Alito hinted at in the opening quote—cultural factors including, but not limited to, government, media, entertainment, business, education, and law. The future of religious liberty is bound up with public opinion and cultural shifts.

This chapter will explore the future of religious liberty as it relates to the public square. While this topic could be explored in a myriad of ways, here I will seek first to discern contemporary challenges facing religious liberty within our political order and, second, to develop constructive proposals explaining how Baptists and evangelicals might engage future disputes over religious liberty in light of our liberal democratic context and current cultural ethos. The principles that undergird religious freedom are timeless, yet the time-bound events I reference herein will, I believe, determine the shape and context of religious liberty within the public square for the foreseeable future.

The term *public square* is broad. For this essay, I understand it to mean a matrix and amalgamation of cultural forces that provide a horizon of meaning for public life. These forces include such arenas as media, government, entertainment, family structure, religion, education, law, and the

---

[1] Obergefell v. Hodges, 576 U.S. 32 (2015), http://www.supremecourt.gov/opinions/14pdf/14-556_3204.pdf.

[2] For excellent analyses of the majority's opinion and its consequence for undermining religious liberty, see Ryan T. Anderson, *Truth Overruled: The Future of Marriage and Religious Freedom* (Washington, DC: Regnery, 2015); see also Michael Stokes Paulsen, "The Wreckage of Obergefell," *First Things* 256 (October 2015): 33–40.

marketplace. In short, the public square is a function of our shared interaction within the institutions of culture.

Discerning Contemporary Challenges to Religious Liberty in the Public Square

It may seem strange to begin a chapter whose purpose is to develop broad principles for public square engagement with a large introductory section on the contemporary challenges facing religious liberty. But to offer constructive solutions, one must understand the presenting problems.

Religious Liberty and the Impact of Changing Public Morality and Demographics

Moral Revolution

What a society deems morally acceptable will impact or determine how it accepts countervailing moral claims made by religion. If, for example, a hypothetical religion condemned baseball as an immoral activity, it would find itself in conflict with a broad swath of America that considers baseball a historic and national pastime. Likewise, when secular morality conflicts with religious morality, conflict follows, or what Robert P. George refers to as a "clash of orthodoxies."[3] And no greater conflict surrounds our current beliefs and laws protecting religious liberty than the moral revolution in gay rights. The change in public perception and affirmation of homosexuality represents the greatest single factor in the decline of religious liberty in America. While I share the concerns of prominent Christian intellectuals Michael Gerson and Peter Wehner about the possibility that evangelicals will appear sex obsessed in our opposition to gay marriage, nonetheless, we cannot ignore the momentous impact that the gay rights

---

[3] Robert P. George, *Clash of Orthodoxies: Law, Religion, & Morality in Crisis* (Wilmington, DE: Intercollegiate Studies Institute, 2002); for a sociological-theological look at how Christianity's social crisis is tied inextricably to principles of the sexual revolution, see Rod Dreher, "Sex after Christianity," *The American Conservative*, April 11, 2013, http://www.theamericanconservative.com/articles/sex-after-christianity/.

movement has had in unsettling the foundation upon which religious liberty once stood.[4]

The gay rights movement represents one of the most successful social movements in American history. Regardless of the moment one regards as the movement's origin, the success of gay rights activists in completely reversing American culture's perception of homosexuality is nothing short of stunning. It amounts to what Baptist theologian Albert Mohler calls a "moral revolution."[5] A moral revolution occurs, according to Mohler, when "those who were once seen as upholding the high moral position are now seen as immoral, with the reverse also true—those just recently seen as engaged in sexual immorality are seen as morally superior to those who believe homosexuality to be sinful." Mohler cites Theo Hobson, a British commentator, who presciently remarked in 2007:

> The public change in attitudes towards homosexuality is not just the waning of a taboo. It is not just a case of a practice losing its aura of immorality (as with premarital sex or illegitimacy). Instead, the case for homosexual equality takes the form of a moral crusade. Those who want to uphold the old attitude are not just dated moralists (as is the case with those who want to uphold the old attitude to premarital sex or illegitimacy). They are accused of moral deficiency. The old taboo surrounding this practice does not disappear but "bounces back" at those who seek to uphold it. Such a sharp turn-around is, I think, without parallel in moral history.[6]

Hobson's claim could not have proven truer. And the impact of the gay rights revolution on religious liberty cannot be overstated. The script

---

[4] Michael Gerson and Peter Wehner, "How Christians Can Flourish in a Same-Sex-Marriage World," ChristianityToday.com, November 2, 2015, http://www.christianitytoday.com/ct/2015/november/how-christians-can-flourish-in-same-sex-marriage-world-cult.html.

[5] R. Albert Mohler Jr., "A Pink Reformation? Sexuality, Credibility, and the Church," AlbertMohler.com, February 12, 2007, http://www.albertmohler.com/2007/02/12/a-pink-reformation-sexuality-credibility-and-the-church/.

[6] Theo Hobson, "A Pink Reformation," *The Guardian*, February 5, 2007, http://www.theguardian.com/commentisfree/2007/feb/05/apinkreformation.

is still being written, largely because the fallout of *Obergefell* is not yet fully known. But efforts to enshrine sexual orientation and gender identity (SOGI) protections into civil rights legislation may result in further cultural losses for evangelicals, even as homosexuality gains continued acceptance. Such attempts to elevate sexual orientation and gender identity to protected classes—a status on par with race, sex, and other categories, guaranteeing significant constitutional protections—have precipitated a democratic crisis of values and a massive conflict between religious liberty and claims of equal protection. This rising conflict surrounds questions of public policy on every level: municipal, state, and federal. It may prove to be the pivotal hinge upon which religious liberty turns.[7]

---

[7] One needs to look no further than the Equality Act to find a site of future legislative conflicts over religious liberty. The Equality Act seeks the protections offered in the 1964 Civil Rights Act for sexual orientation and gender identity. If enacted into law, the government could discriminate against those who do not accept a sexually permissive understanding of human nature, which denies sexual complementarity and innate biological categories. It would further erode religious liberty, transform public opinion on sexuality, and harm the public perception of those who believe in traditional or biblical sexual morality. By elevating sexual orientation and gender identity to the level of race, the law would functionally equate dissenters with racists and label them perpetrators of irrational bigotry. To favor such a bill is to oppose and actively stigmatize the moral convictions that millions of Americans adhere to with abiding sincerity and deep religious precedent. The underlying philosophy that gives rise to such a bill is problematic. Passing antidiscrimination statutes on the basis of sexual orientation and gender identity lacks both the philosophical warrant and the principled necessity of protections based on, for example, immutable categories like race. Sexual orientation and gender identity are unlike race, are unapparent, and are subjective. Furthermore, the categories are constantly evolving. Both bills rely on contested, controversial categories subject to the always-evolving standards of secular ideology. The Equality Act tries to shut down debate by treating sexual orientation and gender identity as topics beyond debate. The trouble is, ambiguity persists in the social sciences over the definition, experience, and origin of sexual orientation and gender identity. Granting special rights to others while denying the religious liberty and conscience rights of others is unacceptable. There is no compelling reason to deny a gay individual access to his or her favorite restaurant. It is nonsensical to prevent a gay individual from purchasing batteries or being treated at a hospital. But that isn't what the Equality Act attempts to address, because those problems are extreme and so rare as to be virtually nonexistent. The Equality Act instead paves over the consciences of those who cannot in good faith condone conduct they believe to be immoral by providing services for a same-sex wedding ceremony. Again, such conflicts arise not over the personhood and dignity of an LGBT customer but over participation in particular conduct or ceremonies that some find morally unacceptable. Unjust discrimination is always wrong. Unfortunately, the

Religious liberty scholar Steven D. Smith argues that the paramount factor creating this conflict between religious liberty and gay rights is a consequence of "equality" as a constitutional principle run amok. In liberal taxonomy, equality necessarily denotes strict egalitarianism. According to a strict egalitarian principle, sexual orientation is interpreted as a category worthy of equal protection alongside other protected class categories— such as race—that are protected by federal nondiscrimination law. If sexual orientation receives equal protection under the law, law will necessarily treat anyone or any institution with moral concerns about the legitimacy of homosexual conduct as engaging in some form of discrimination. To warrant such protection, public morality would require unquestioned affirmation of homosexuality as morally praiseworthy conduct, which historic and orthodox Christianity finds objectionable. On this understanding of a shift in public morality, notice again the theme of moral revolution that Smith relies on:

> In this equality-oriented framework, traditional virtues and vices
> get reordered. Previously, "deadly sins" like pride, lust, and sloth

---

Equality Act does not help prevent discrimination; it only confuses persons as to what discrimination really is and punishes other citizens for historic and reasonable beliefs. It eliminates the status/conduct distinction that differentiates discrimination based on one's being and one's actions. Moreover, supposed "compromise" solutions are also problematic. The exemption thresholds for compromise solutions are arbitrary and not based in principle. Plus, later amendments could remove any exemptions altogether. At the philosophical level, the LGBT community views the Equality Act as a matter of justice and fundamental rights. And if justice requires establishing sexual orientation and gender identity as protected classes, then no amount of goodwill on this issue will prevent the LGBT community from enacting more invasive protections or rescinding proposed compromises later. Yet under no circumstance should government ever penalize or stigmatize citizens for expressing or acting upon their conviction that marriage is the union of husband and wife, that sexual relations are properly reserved for such a union, or that maleness and femaleness are objective biological realities. In the aftermath of *Obergefell*, America is searching for a way to balance competing interests. Treating millions of Americans as though they are criminals because of their beliefs about marriage, sexuality, and gender is unacceptable. For more discussion on the problematic effects of the Equality Act, see Andrew T. Walker, "The Equality Act: Bad Policy That Poses Great Harms," *Public Discourse*, July 24, 2015, http://www.thepublicdiscourse .com/2015/07/15381/. See also Russell D. Moore and Andrew T. Walker, "Is Utah's LGBT-Religious Liberty Bill Good Policy?," ERLC.com, March 6, 2015, https://erlc .com/article/is-utahs-lgbt-religious-liberty-bill-good-policy.

are displaced on the list of evils by more currently loathsome traits—bigotry and intolerance—that are thought to violate "equal respect." Consequently, a good deal of political polemics (and, for that matter, of constitutional jurisprudence) consists of efforts to show that one's opponents are acting from bigotry or prejudice, or are failing to accord "equal respect" to some disadvantaged but deserving group.[8]

Yet, as Smith perceptively notes, even a regime of strict "equality" demands a greater qualification than is typically offered by its lesbian, gay, bisexual, and transgender (LGBT) proponents. While accepting the legitimacy of equality, he observes:

> [E]quality implies that *like cases* (or, as the common phrase goes, "similarly situated" instances or classes) should be treated in the same way. But the substantive criteria for determining which cases or classes are relevantly alike or "similarly situated" cannot simply be deduced from the abstract concept of equality; they must be supplied from other sources.[9]

Smith's analysis is helpful in that it shows why equality as a blunt principle of law applied to SOGI is not self-evident. Sexual orientation and gender identity are ambiguous terms that require qualification and understanding—i.e., discriminating judgment—to determine whether such identities and practices are moral and promote flourishing. To equate sexual orientation and gender identity with race, as liberal theorists would like, requires making them equivalent. But that cannot be done prima facie. Sexual orientation and gender identity are not like race. Equality requires moral evaluation—"substantive criteria," to use Smith's term, which the term *equality* itself does not supply by its own usage. Moral evaluation is required to determine whether the cases involved are indeed *similarly situated*. And there are good, principled, and theological reasons to reject

---

[8] Steven D. Smith, *The Rise and Decline of American Religious Freedom* (Cambridge, MA: Harvard University Press, 2014), 150. For a helpful explanation of equality's leveling effects on religious liberty's decline, see pp. 147–52.

[9] Ibid., 150.

the claim that SOGI categories can be equated with race or sex based on moral agency. As Ryan T. Anderson of the Heritage Foundation argues:

> One's character is comprised of one's voluntary actions, and it is reasonable to make judgments about actions. While race implies nothing about one's actions, sexual orientation and gender identity are frequently descriptions for one's actions: "gay" denotes men who engage in voluntary sex acts with other men, "lesbian" denotes women who engage in voluntary sex acts with other women, and "transgender" denotes a biological male who voluntarily presents himself to the world as if female or a biological female who voluntarily presents herself to the world as if male. "Race" and "sex," by contrast, clearly refer to traits, and in the vast majority of cases denote no voluntary actions.[10]

Smith further argues that the work of notable liberal theorists such as Ronald Dworkin and John Rawls does not offer "any cogent justification for egalitarian commitments; usually the theorists simply assert or assume equality, or else posit that in the absence of any persuasive objection, we should adopt a 'presumption' of equal worth."[11] Recognizing the apparent deficiencies in a "presumed" equality, Smith further argues that "substantive claims about equality or moral worth will make little sense"[12] apart from "religious presuppositions" that allow for the moral evaluation of appeals to equality.

These matters demonstrate why religious liberty is so imperiled by the ascendancy of gay rights. The degree of protections afforded to sexual orientation and gender identity will largely determine the extent to which traditional Christian sexual morality is treated as suspect and perhaps contrary to federal law. This breathtaking attempt to relocate historic religious

---

[10] Ryan T. Anderson, "Sexual Orientation and Gender Identity Are Not Like Race: Why ENDA Is Bad Policy," *Public Discourse*, March 18, 2015, http://www.thepublic discourse.com/2015/03/14649/. See also Ryan T. Anderson, "Marriage, Reason, and Religious Liberty: Much Ado About Sex, Nothing to Do with Race," *The Heritage Foundation*, April 4, 2014, http://www.heritage.org/research/reports/2014/04/marriage -reason-and-religious-liberty-much-ado-about-sex-nothing-to-do-with-race.

[11] Smith, *The Rise and Decline of American Religious Freedom*, 149.

[12] Ibid., 148.

belief as outside the bounds of polite culture is flatly unacceptable. Should this course be taken, negative consequences will follow for millions of Americans whose beliefs fall within the Abrahamic tradition. Faith traditions whose systems of beliefs and ethics provided a foundational moral grammar for American social stability will be stigmatized.

We must always remember the teaching function of the law. Law communicates standards of decency, conduct, and custom. Over time, if the current ideology concerning SOGI becomes further ingrained, it will continue to subvert and undermine the idea that Christian or traditional sexual ethics are reasonable and can be sincerely held by people of goodwill.

The worldview behind LGBT activism teaches a view of human embodiment that is contrary to orthodox Christianity. Christianity embraces the body and soul as an integrated whole, and that each person is a unique creation who was created male or female. Male and female are not arbitrary, socially imposed constructs. They are rooted in our biology. In contrast, the worldview behind the sexual revolution assumes an expressive individualism where our bodies become instruments of the will, capable of being re-created according to preference and desire. Because law teaches morality, changing the law to adopt principles rooted in the sexual revolution will result in treating dissenting voices as discriminatory. This is unacceptable and will prove disastrously consequential for religious liberty.

The Impact of Obergefell v. Hodges

The impact of the *Obergefell* ruling will only accelerate the concerns mentioned above regarding religious liberty. Consider but a few examples written in the dissenting opinions to *Obergefell.*

In Chief Justice Robert's blistering dissent, he argues that the majority's opinion is disingenuous in its references to protecting religious liberty:

> Perhaps the most discouraging aspect of today's decision is the extent to which the majority feels compelled to sully those on the other side of the debate. The majority offers a cursory assurance that it does not intend to disparage people who, as a matter of conscience, cannot accept same-sex marriage. That disclaimer is hard to square with the very next sentence, in which the majority explains that "the necessary consequence" of laws codifying

the traditional definition of marriage is to "demean or stigmatize" same-sex couples. The majority reiterates such characterizations over and over. By the majority's account, Americans who did nothing more than follow the understanding of marriage that has existed for our entire history—in particular, the tens of millions of people who voted to reaffirm their States' enduring definition of marriage—have acted to "lock . . . out," "disparage," "disrespect and subordinate," and inflict "dignitary wounds" upon their gay and lesbian neighbors. These apparent assaults on the character of fairminded people will have an effect, in society and in court. Moreover, they are entirely gratuitous. It is one thing for the majority to conclude that the Constitution protects a right to same-sex marriage; it is something else to portray everyone who does not share the majority's "better informed understanding" as bigoted.[13]

According to Justice Thomas, the majority's opinion downplays the role of religious sentiment shared throughout American culture concerning marriage. He further argues that the majority's opinion represents a truncated understanding of religious liberty and a purposeful departure from our constitutional history:

In our society, marriage is not simply a governmental institution; it is a religious institution as well. Today's decision might change the former, but it cannot change the latter. It appears all but inevitable that the two will come into conflict, particularly as individuals and churches are confronted with demands to participate in and endorse civil marriages between same-sex couples. The majority appears unmoved by that inevitability. It makes only a weak gesture toward religious liberty in a single paragraph. And even that gesture indicates a misunderstanding of religious liberty in our Nation's tradition. Religious liberty is about more than just the protection for "religious organizations and persons . . . as they seek to teach the principles that are so fulfilling and so central to their lives and faiths." Religious liberty is about freedom of action in matters of religion generally, and the scope of that

---

[13] *Obergefell*, 576 U.S. at 28–29.

liberty is directly correlated to the civil restraints placed upon religious practice. Although our Constitution provides some protection against such governmental restrictions on religious practices,
the People have long elected to afford broader protections than
this Court's constitutional precedents mandate. Had the majority allowed the definition of marriage to be left to the political
process—as the Constitution requires—the People could have
considered the religious liberty implications of deviating from the
traditional definition as part of their deliberative process. Instead,
the majority's decision short-circuits that process, with potentially
ruinous consequences for religious liberty.[14]

In addition to the quote found at the beginning of this chapter, Justice
Alito accuses the justices who joined the majority opinion of sidestepping
the requirements of democratic order and thereby foisting same-sex marriage on states whose populations disagree with it:

The system of federalism established by our Constitution provides a way for people with different beliefs to live together in a
single nation. If the issue of same-sex marriage had been left to the
people of the States, it is likely that some States would recognize
same-sex marriage and others would not. It is also possible that
some States would tie recognition to protection for conscience
rights. The majority today makes that impossible. By imposing its
own views on the entire country, the majority facilitates the mar-
ginalization of the many Americans who have traditional ideas.
Recalling the harsh treatment of gays and lesbians in the past,
some may think that turn-about is fair play. But if that sentiment
prevails, the Nation will experience bitter and lasting wounds.[15]

It may seem overly dramatic to place the future of religious liberty at
the feet of the sexual revolution, and particularly *Obergefell*. But nothing
about the current predicament convinces me that my fears are exaggerated
or out of place.

---

[14] Ibid., at 15–16.
[15] Ibid., at 7.

In summary, the coming shifts in the moral landscape will determine the extent to which religious liberty will remain an accepted principle. If it is increasingly interpreted as justifying discrimination, its future will not be bright.

The Rise of the Religiously Unaffiliated

At the risk of oversimplification, religion's place in society affects the status of religious liberty. In current-day America, our increasingly irreligious demographics will prove a major obstacle to religious liberty.

American religiosity is in a state of dramatic flux. According to demographic and statistical trends, the percentage of Americans who do not identify with any religion has sharply increased. The "nones," as they are popularly referred to throughout culture, represent a growing segment of the population for whom religion is not an identifying feature of their existence. The nones represent America's first social class for whom secularism is a way of life.

Space prevents a thoroughgoing explanation of the entrenched and pervasive secularism that has given rise to this new demographic; however, the nones are but a classic example of secularism's prominent features—namely, the belief that one's existence is unaided by religious values.[16]

According to Pew Research, one of the most reliable sources for measuring religious trends in America, the number of religiously unaffiliated Americans continues to climb:

> [T]he number of religiously unaffiliated adults has increased by roughly 19 million since 2007. There are now approximately 56 million religiously unaffiliated adults in the U.S., and this group—sometimes called religious "nones"—is more numerous than either Catholics or mainline Protestants, according to the new survey. Indeed, the unaffiliated are now second in size only to evangelical Protestants among major religious groups in the U.S.[17]

---

[16] For a helpful and introductory explanation of the work of noted philosopher Charles Taylor's *A Secular Age*, see James K. A. Smith, *How (Not) to Be Secular: Reading Charles Taylor* (Grand Rapids: Eerdmans, 2014).

[17] "America's Changing Religious Landscape," Pew Research Center, May 12, 2015, http://www.pewforum.org/2015/05/12/americas-changing-religious-landscape/.

While evangelical Christians have maintained relative stability, declining as a total percentage only slightly, all signs indicate that nominal religious belief—a "religious middle"—is collapsing altogether.[18] And this is unsurprising. The predicament besetting religious conservatives in today's culture wars is social isolation. What's the value then in being halfheartedly religious if it is culturally alienating? It goes without saying that people of nominal belief would not eagerly subject themselves to such treatment.

So what are the practical consequences for religious liberty should America continue its descent into secularism? First, religion itself will decreasingly be viewed as a social good. Historically, Americans have long regarded religion as a pillar that provides social stability and moral guidance to our so-called American experiment.[19] As Americans grow less religious, however, they will overlook these benefits as well as the need to protect it. The privileged place that religion has long occupied could be over, treated instead as superstition meriting ridicule.

Second, in an increasingly secular society, religious motivation will be misunderstood. In particular, citizens acting according to deeply held convictions will be seen as odd. Even worse, religious motivation will be

---

[18] According to Pew, "The drop in the Christian share of the population has been driven mainly by declines among mainline Protestants and Catholics. Each of those large religious traditions has shrunk by approximately three percentage points since 2007. The evangelical Protestant share of the U.S. population also has dipped, but at a slower rate, falling by about one percentage point since 2007." Ibid.

[19] George Washington's farewell address at the end of his presidency is a historic example of how religion has historically been viewed in contributing to civil society: "Of all the dispositions and habits which lead to political prosperity, religion and morality are indispensable supports. In vain would that man claim the tribute of patriotism, who should labor to subvert these great pillars of human happiness, these firmest props of the duties of men and citizens. The mere politician, equally with the pious man, ought to respect and to cherish them. A volume could not trace all their connections with private and public felicity. Let it simply be asked: Where is the security for property, for reputation, for life, if the sense of religious obligation desert the oaths which are the instruments of investigation in courts of justice? And let us with caution indulge the supposition that morality can be maintained without religion. Whatever may be conceded to the influence of refined education on minds of peculiar structure, reason and experience both forbid us to expect that national morality can prevail in exclusion of religious principle." "Washington's Farewell Address," *The Papers of George Washington*, September 19, 1796, http://gwpapers.virginia.edu/documents/washingtons-farewell-address/.

interpreted as a harmful, deluded idiosyncrasy that secularism views with suspicion and condescension—something in need of correction. Consider a recent Supreme Court case involving the megachain Hobby Lobby. Its Christian owners, the Green family, objected to the portions of the federal government's health-care law that required employers to provide access to contraception and sterilization services. They believed that some forms of contraception were potentially abortion-inducing agents (abortifacients). And therefore they objected to offering these services in their employee health-care plans.

The case went all the way to the Supreme Court[20] where, thankfully, the Greens emerged victorious in a perilously narrow 5–4 win. Yet along the way the extensive media assault against the Greens demonstrated the vast scope of opposition brought forth when religious motivation is met with secular resistance and misunderstanding. To their opponents, the Greens were seen as participating in a fundamentalist conspiracy that aimed to deny access to "basic" health care to their working-class employees.

Impossible to appreciate by secular standards was the fact that the Green family goes above and beyond in compensating their employees. As Christians, they believe it is necessary to treat their employees generously and courteously. Also to the benefit of their employees, the Greens earnestly live out their Christian principles as business owners by closing on Sundays. Even the court's ruling affirmed that the Greens acted out of sincerely held beliefs. But regardless, liberal media outlets, reproductive rights activists, and secular coalitions pilloried the Greens and Hobby Lobby as perpetrating an invidious religious crusade to end contraception in America.

Misunderstood religious motivation can easily be interpreted by some as a golden ticket that can be used to cudgel opponents into submission. According to noted University of Virginia religious liberty scholar Douglas Laycock, the decline of religion in society can result in religious liberty being reduced to a form of special pleading on behalf of religious constituencies:

> A large secular minority gradually coming to public awareness
> changes the structure of the debate over religious liberty. The

---

[20] Burwell v. Hobby Lobby, 134 S. Ct. 2751 (2014).

original commitment to religious liberty was a sort of mutual non-aggression pact. Everyone had a religion, and everyone would be protected by religious liberty. Small religions were more at risk than large religions, but numbers could change, and especially in America, people could move. A right to free exercise of religion was a promise to everyone—you will not be persecuted for your religious beliefs or practices. It is still the case that everyone has a belief about religion, and that everyone should be protected by religious liberty. But many Americans do not see it that way. Much of the nonbelieving minority sees religious liberty as a protection only for believers. On that view, a universal natural right morphs into a special interest demand—and on behalf of an interest group that, to many of its opponents, seems especially undeserving. One view of the debates over gay rights and abortion is that many of the believers claiming liberty for themselves seem intent on restricting the liberty of others.[21]

Undermining Religious Liberty

I conclude this section with a brief look at the subtle ways religious liberty is being undermined within the public square. Aside from hackneyed recitations of "the separation of church and state" and the accompanying call for strict secularist regime or scare quotes around "religious liberty," a few examples demonstrate how the robust conceptions of religious liberty at our nation's founding have been slowly degraded.

First, many liberals and progressives have adopted the phrase "freedom of worship" in place of "freedom of religion," which signals a historic break with the past.[22] The consequence of this action is to restrict—intentionally or unintentionally—how religious liberty and the First Amendment's guarantee of "free exercise" are understood. In truth, the act of "worship" is a subset of the larger umbrella category of "exercise." Restricting "exercise"

---

[21] Douglas Laycock, "Sex, Atheism, and the Free Exercise of Religion," *University of Detroit Mercy Law Review* 88 (2010–11): 422.

[22] Sarah Eekhoff Zylstra, "'Freedom of Worship' Worries," *Christianity Today,* June 22, 2010, 12.

to "worship," however, restricts religious liberty to what occurs within a house of worship, as opposed to public expression, which was how the phrase was historically understood. As Yuval Levin perceptively notes, "Religious practice, in this understanding, involves the profession of faith, but it does not extend to participation in the broader life of the society. It is essentially a private intellectual exercise."[23]

Second, liberal groups have begun pushing to label religious freedom as a "license to discriminate,"[24] undermining the historical usage of "religious liberty." This accusation comes in the context of religious freedom legislation, where liberal opponents use such language to accuse advocates for religious liberty of attempting to justify discrimination by using religious liberty exemptions.

Despite the many concerns raised in the preceding section, the problems that religious liberty encounters in America pale in comparison to international concerns. In relative comparison to other regimes, religious liberty is unwaveringly strong. No American is staring down death for believing that marriage is complementary and conjugal. Christians are not routinely slaughtered outside of churches. Christians are not facing mass seaside beheadings as we've witnessed with ISIS on the nightly news. And Americans are not fleeing as religious minorities from oppressive regimes. But that doesn't mean that religious liberty occupies the place of prestige it once did. Religious liberty is in a state of flux and even devaluation.

While the future is yet to be written, religious liberty's place within the public square is at a historically low ebb in terms of understanding and sympathy. Changes in public opinion have placed religious liberty in the crosshairs. Changing demographics are breeding a new class of citizens for whom religion is foreign. The future of religious liberty is unsettled and precarious.

---

[23] Yuval Levin, "The Perils of Religious Liberty," *First Things* 260 (February 2016), 32.

[24] Mitch Smith, "Indianapolis Rallies Around Its Gay Citizens After a Law Sets Off a Flood of Support," *New York Times*, June 12, 2015, http://www.nytimes .com/2015/06/13/us/indiana-gay-community-grows-in-confidence-and-pride.html.

Constructive Proposals for Strengthening Religious Liberty in the Public Square

In view of the challenges that will determine the future and shape of religious liberty, the present task is to determine the paradigms, proposals, and strategies needed to safeguard religious liberty for another generation.[25]

When making proposals for renewing the place of religious liberty in the public square, questions of first principles are worth asking: What role does religion play in society? Is religious liberty only special pleading for Christians? What is the relationship between church and state, religion and politics? In this section, I offer a few reflections on the necessary contexts in which religion and religious liberty must advance. The struggle for religious liberty lies at the heart of the struggle to maintain a free society. As one public intellectual soberly noted: "Religious liberty is plainly essential for the endurance of our free society and for the protection of the rights and freedoms of the many millions of Americans who dissent from the caustic Gnosticism that increasingly dominates our culture. The cultural revival we yearn for is only imaginable if we fight now against the suppression of dissenting views on moral questions."[26]

Recovering Religious Liberty as a "Disciplined Public Philosophy"

If religious liberty is not intended to privilege one religion over another, then religious liberty can never be a ploy for special pleading. Tragically, conservative evangelicals have not always shown great reciprocity in their advocacy for the liberty of religious minorities. Consider one example. In 2010, efforts commenced to build a mosque at Ground Zero, the site of the

---

[25] One wishes that an entire volume, not only a section of one chapter, could be dedicated to evaluating proposals for how Baptists and evangelicals ought to engage with religious liberty in the public square. The proposals offered here are by no means to be considered exhaustive in nature. Instead, the proposals here are but an entryway into additional issues meriting further consideration. Additional considerations include the role of academic concentration on religious liberty, the future of jurisprudence, legislative strategies, electoral forecasting, and the use of coalitions in fostering momentum around religious liberty.

[26] Levin, "The Perils of Religious Liberty," 30.

attacks upon the World Trade Center in New York City on September 11, 2001. The plans were resoundingly opposed, and the whole affair ignited a fever pitch of hostility toward Islam.

While one can raise legitimate concerns about the emotional provocation of building a mosque at the site of an attack perpetrated by jihadist Islam, the unremitting effort to block such a building using legal maneuvers demonstrates the precariousness of religious liberty, and its potential subjection to the majority's preference. This is of grave concern for several reasons. First, the Constitution of the United States purposely refrains from determining whether a religion shall be granted freedom based on its popularity or number of adherents. Secondly, if a mosque cannot be built because it is disfavored or culturally unpopular, the same principle could be used to prevent a church from purchasing land or constructing new property. Evangelical Christians must more frequently stand in defense of religious minorities based on the principles of reciprocity and equality. As I've heard pithily recited: *No religious liberty for thee can eventually, over time, result in a reduction of religious liberty for me.*

While I firmly consider myself a member of a new generation of conservative Christian or "Religious Right" activist-scholars, episodes like the Ground Zero mosque make it incumbent to evaluate the previous application of religious liberty to determine whether it was appropriated fairly.

According to Carl Henry, conservative Christianity's track record of protecting religious liberty is not without its problems:

> The Religious Right eagerly appealed to religious liberty and increasingly declared it to be basic to all other human freedoms. Yet it specially invoked religious liberty to protest encroachments on evangelical freedom, and to advance legitimate evangelical concerns. But a disciplined public philosophy would stress religious freedom for all persons of whatever faith, as at the same time the best guarantee of religious liberty for Christians.[27]

Henry's concern that religious liberty function as a "disciplined public philosophy" accurately captures what must occur if religious liberty is to retain importance and viability. Far too often, conservative Christianity

---

[27] Carl Henry, "The New Coalitions," *Christianity Today*, November 17, 1989, 27.

has treated religious liberty as its own special province used to prop up a Christian social order. That can no longer be the case. The struggle for religious liberty is no longer a struggle over securing cultural prestige but over providing cultural space for religion to freely flourish on the basis that duty is owed to one's Creator. In James Madison's famous *Memorial and Remonstrance Against Religious Assessments,* he offered these historic words about religion's preeminence to the claims of government and culture:

> It is the duty of every man to render to the Creator such homage and such only as he believes to be acceptable to him. This duty is precedent, both in order of time and in degree of obligation, to the claims of Civil Society. Before any man can be considered as a member of Civil Society, he must be considered as a subject of the Governour of the Universe: And if a member of Civil Society, who enters into any subordinate Association, must always do it with a reservation of his duty to the General Authority; much more must every man who becomes a member of any particular Civil Society, do it with a saving of his allegiance to the Universal Sovereign.[28]

To sustain religious liberty for future generations, more effort must be exerted to defend religious liberty for all religions as a condition of our constitutional order. That Christianity and its sexual ethics continue to be the ridicule of elite culture may teach Christians the importance of standing for religious freedom on principle, and not simply to preserve their own cultural status.

Seen in this vein, religious liberty as *hospitality* and religious liberty as *accommodation* must become the operating protocol moving forward. Treating religious minorities with hospitality makes religious liberty a picture of America's welcoming embrace. Valuing religious diversity separates the American constitutional regime from regimes that cause religious minorities to seek refuge. The idea of accommodation denotes a preference and care for multiple religious expressions, thus allowing each the freedom to flourish. Accommodation requires the public square to be marked by

---

[28] James Madison, *Memorial and Remonstrance Against Religious Assessments,* June 20, 1785, papers 8:298–304, http://press-pubs.uchicago.edu/founders/documents /amendI_religions43.html.

understanding, pluralism, and respect. If we don't value religious liberty for others, it must be because we've not experienced for ourselves how deep religious conviction runs.

Recovering the Connection between Religious Liberty and Natural Rights

Treating religious liberty as a "disciplined public philosophy" requires retrieving the historical meaning of religious liberty, beginning with our nation's founding. This will necessitate invigorating the ethos and intellectual milieu that birthed American principles, namely, natural rights.

What did famed Reagan speechwriter Peggy Noonan call the "most important speech so far in the 21st century?"[29] It was a speech given by the conservative agnostic and public intellectual George Will at Washington University in St. Louis. While Will refers to himself as religiously unaffiliated in the speech, he argues nonetheless that it is "indubitably the case that natural rights are especially firmly grounded when they are grounded in religious doctrine."[30]

The influence of religion would be impossible were it not free and ennobled. An important function of religion in our society is to help secure the rights that make democracy possible. To do this, religion must be given freedom to flourish in order to communicate the truths that are essential to our democratic order. Commenting on how the founders understood the importance of religion to democratic order, Will observes:

> They understood that Christianity, particularly in its post-Reformation ferments, fostered attitudes and aptitudes associated with, and useful to, popular government. Protestantism's emphasis on the individual's direct, unmediated relationship with God and the primacy of individual conscience and choice subverted

---

[29] Peggy Noonan, "The Most Important Speech So Far in the 21st Century?" blog, *Wall Street Journal*, December 29, 2012, http://blogs.wsj.com/peggynoonan/2012/12/29/the-most-important-speech-so-far-in-the-21st-century/.

[30] George F. Will, "Religion and the American Republic," *National Affairs* 16 (Summer 2013), 111.

conventions of hierarchical societies in which deference was expected from the many toward the few.

Beyond that, however, the American founding owed much more to John Locke than to Jesus. The founders created a distinctly modern regime, one respectful of pre-existing rights—rights that exist before government and so are natural in that they are not creations of the regime that exists to secure them.[31]

Now, at this point, one must caution against the pure instrumentalization of religion. Religion is itself its own good, worthy of pursuit for its own end.[32] It must not be co-opted or subverted for political ends. But that is not the point at issue here. For it is also paramount to recognize the distinct and historic role of religion in American society. When religion is allowed to function voluntarily and sincerely, not as an appendage of the state, it nourishes the principles that undergird our political order. The connection between natural rights and religion acts to rebuff the claims of absolute state sovereignty.

Will goes on to argue that biblical religion is inextricably bound to America's rights regime. It is important to consider that George Will is no token "God and Country" conservative looking to baptize the founding fathers as Americanized super-apostles. No, Will is an analytic skeptic. He argues that the rights that the Constitution worked to secure were best intelligible within a milieu of Christianity. Speaking of the "Creator" found in the Declaration of Independence, he writes that:

> This is the Creator who endows us with natural rights that are inevitable, inalienable, and universal—and hence the foundation of democratic equality. And these rights are the foundation of limited government—government defined by the limited goal of securing those rights so that individuals may flourish in their free and responsible exercise of those rights.
>
> A government thus limited is not in the business of imposing its opinions about what happiness or excellence the citizens

---

[31] Ibid., 113.

[32] See Robert P. George, "What Is Religious Freedom?," *Public Discourse*, July 24, 2013, http://www.thepublicdiscourse.com/2013/07/10622/.

should choose to pursue. Having such opinions is the business of other institutions—private and voluntary ones, especially religious ones, that supply the conditions for liberty.[33]

Will argues that "the founders did not consider natural rights reasonable because religion affirmed them; rather, the founders considered religion reasonable because it secured those rights."[34] Will's last statement may sound problematic to some because he could be construed as arguing that religion's primary value is to guarantee our rights. But the purpose of Will's essay isn't to argue for the legitimacy of Christian orthodoxy. Instead, the value of Will's argument is found in his demonstration of the variegated nature of civil society, in which he sees religion as a powerful, historic, and meaningful contributor to the story of America's dedication to natural rights. The importance of Will's insights are multiplied precisely because he is not religious himself. As an "objective" observer, Will nonetheless shares an affinity and deep appreciation for the role that religion plays in fostering and securing the rights that our founders deemed essential for a people in a free society.

The argument for a limited government circumscribed by preexisting natural rights makes plain the necessity of free and flourishing religion. Only a limited government can refrain from overriding the rights that religion ensures. Thus, it is incumbent upon Baptists and other evangelical Christians to employ expansive "rights" language as an important component of our public discourse surrounding religious liberty. Natural rights secure the foundation of ordered liberty. Thus, in contrast to an overzealous secularism that would attempt to undermine "rights" as a prepolitical reality, Christians must insist, alongside Will, that "government's primary purpose is to secure pre-existing rights. Government does not create rights; it does not dispense them."[35] And neither should government dispense *of* them.[36]

---

[33] Will, "Religion and the American Republic," 118.

[34] Ibid.

[35] Ibid., 119.

[36] Will concludes this section with a wonderful summary of Christianity's importance to the American project of ordered liberty: "A nation such as ours, steeped in and shaped by Biblical religion, cannot comfortably accommodate a politics that takes

Opposing Secular Orthodoxies

The unavoidable result of successful opposition to religious liberty is the undermining of other precious First Amendment freedoms. And this means other state-enforced orthodoxies will be adopted.

Policies come to us with principles attached to them. When debating public policy, we should consider the principles included not only in the legislation that has passed but also those principles that have been rejected. Few are discussing where the principles inherent in secular liberalism's opposition to religious liberty will lead. Responsible statecraft involves examining a principle's logical conclusion. In the case of secular liberalism, the conclusions to which its principles lead help us see just how deeply opposed those principles are to the constitutional order we've inherited.

When secular liberalism works to undermine religious liberty, it invites compelled speech. When photographers are forced, under threat of fines, to shoot weddings or religious services that they believe are immoral, the assumption is that compelled speech is obligatory. The state becomes the arbiter of what acceptable speech is. The instances where photographers, bakers, and florists are forced to provide services for same-sex marriage ceremonies, for example, may seem insignificant or harmless. But the requirement that they render such services despite protest means that "they are more like religious believers under compulsion in a society with an established church than like believers simply denied the freedom to exercise their religion. Only now the compulsive state religion, or at least our new civil religion, is supposed to be progressive liberalism."[37]

---

its bearings from the proposition that human nature is a malleable product of social forces, and that improving human nature, perhaps unto perfection, is a proper purpose of politics. Biblical religion is concerned with asserting and defending the dignity of the individual. Biblical religion teaches that individual dignity is linked to individual responsibility and moral agency. Therefore, Biblical religion should be wary of the consequences of government untethered from the limited (and limiting) purpose of securing natural rights." "Religion and the American Republic," 121.

[37] Levin, "The Perils of Religious Liberty," 33. Levin continues: "Of course, liberalism is not literally becoming a religion—but it is approaching the question of society's moral order from the point of view of a dominant established power that expects to command formal assent to its views in the public square. People are allowed to believe

When secular liberalism works to undermine religious liberty, it welcomes the erosion of free association. When the state can deem codes of conduct or membership statements to be rooted in irrational prejudice, it diminishes the ability of citizens to associate or to organize for a cause.

When secular liberalism works to undermine religious liberty, it invites the derogation of religious motives underpinning free expression. It allows the state to determine which beliefs warrant legal action.

This leads to the final point: When secular liberalism works to undermine religious liberty, it invites the imposition of state-enforced morality. Secular liberalism requires obedience and punishes dissent. It insists that all citizens must, against their will, act only in a manner that liberalism judges to be accommodating and politic.

Baptists and evangelicals must begin opposing orthodoxies of every sort that stymie freedom and intimidate citizens.

Recovering the Role of Religion in Society: Humane Democracy

In March 2015, President Obama and other national leaders traveled to Selma, Alabama, to commemorate the fiftieth anniversary of the historic march from Selma to Montgomery, Alabama. The events of that day in particular, and of the civil rights movement in general, remind us of an important truth: religion and politics do go together—a democratic version of the latter cannot be sustained without the former.

Martin Luther King Jr. recognized that American law was accountable to divine law—much in the same way that Richard John Neuhaus spoke of "under God" in the Pledge of Allegiance as meaning that America is a nation committed to God's judgment over it. The civil rights movement awakened the nation and revealed America's brutality and barbarism. The civil rights movement invoked God as the judge over the affairs of humans. And the religious roots of the civil rights movement made America a more humane place.

---

what they want, but when they act together in public, they must abide by the beliefs of the established order." Ibid.

King understood that one aspect of the church's mission was to help America be a better version of itself and that, in return, the church would live out its calling. King wrote timeless words for the church's relationship to the state: "The church must be reminded that it is not the master or the servant of the state, but rather the conscience of the state. It must be the guide and the critic of the state, and never its tool. If the church does not recapture its prophetic zeal, it will become an irrelevant social club without moral or spiritual authority."[38]

"Freedom's chances coincide with those of the evangelical message," wrote Jacques Maritain in *Christianity and Democracy*.[39] The project of democracy is nourished by institutions that stand between the individual and the state, institutions that guide both the individual and the state into what Francis Schaeffer referred to as "true truth"[40]—institutions that work to combat the dictatorship of relativism. Apart from the religious truths that hold the state accountable through its citizenry, there is no lasting democracy but simply majoritarianism. A state unaccountable to its actions is no longer a state but a god.

Richard John Neuhaus spent the majority of his career laboring for this truth that democracy requires the rich interaction of religious values in order to succeed. For Neuhaus, "politics is an inescapably moral enterprise."[41] As he poignantly observed, democracy doesn't just welcome religion; it requires certain manners of its exercise: "First, democratic government is premised upon the acknowledgment of transcendent truth to which the political order is held accountable. Second, democracy assumes the lively interaction among people who are acting from values that are, in most instances, grounded in specific religious belief."[42]

The lessons of King, Maritain, and Neuhaus remind us there is no intelligible hope or sustainable vision for achieving a humane democracy—at

---

[38] Martin Luther King Jr., *Strength to Love* (New York: Harper & Row, 1963), 62.

[39] Jacques Maritain, *Christianity and Democracy, and The Rights of Man and Natural Law* (San Francisco: Ignatius Press, 2012), 24.

[40] Francis Schaeffer, *He Is There and He Is Not Silent*, 30th ed. (Wheaton: Tyndale House, 1972), 42.

[41] Richard John Neuhaus, *The Naked Public Square: Religion and Democracy in America*, 2nd ed. (Grand Rapids: Eerdmans, 1988), 125.

[42] Ibid., 120.

least one that does not descend into barbarism—apart from mediating institutions grounded in and motivated by transcendent authority. This means religion and politics must inexorably relate to one another. The exercise of religion requires nothing more and nothing less than a legal order that does not co-opt religion for state purposes nor impede the church's mission.

Few claims are more controversial in American life today than the call to replenish our public life with *more* religion, not less. But there's no claim more necessary for reviving our democratic order than the claim that the democratic order is not an end in itself.

The symbolism of Selma should inspire us to commit to what Maritain calls the "common task of heroic renewal."[43] It is a commitment to vigilantly denounce the latent barbarisms that would tear our democratic order asunder. Religion affords the best opportunity to ensure that no man-made orthodoxies are allowed to trump the canons of transcendent justice. The place of religion in society is to ensure that state power remains checked and buffered by transcendent authority—an authority that ennobles justice and fertilizes the conditions for humane democracy to occur.

I never voted for Barack Obama. I was, however, deeply moved when I saw President Obama speaking against a backdrop that included the Edmund Pettus Bridge, an icon that symbolizes one of America's past and ongoing tensions. It was the best of America's religious character that helped to install President Obama as the chief executive of this land—a character worth guarding and perfecting still.[44]

Conclusion

Before embarking on his missionary journey to India, William Carey famously told Andrew Fuller, "I will go down into the pit, if you will hold

---

[43] Maritain, *Christianity and Democracy, and The Rights of Man and Natural Law*, 10.

[44] Adapted from Andrew T. Walker, "Selma and Humane Democracy," *First Things*, March 10, 2015, http://www.firstthings.com/web-exclusives/2015/03/selma -and-humane-democracy.

the ropes."[45] Many Baptists remember Carey as one of the fathers of the modern missionary movement. But fewer still remember Fuller as the man who organized, raised funds, and built a lasting enterprise to ensure the success of gospel endeavors.

Today, missions movements are still enabled by rope holders—committed believers who pray, send money, and staff organizations that equip and send missionaries to foreign lands. But there's another aspect of gospel advance that also goes unnoticed: the fight for religious liberty, that first freedom, which is now under threat.

What does an issue tied to the First Amendment have to do with a bloody cross? After all, asserting "rights" seems contrary to the witness of Christ, who set aside his rights for the sake of others, an action we are called to imitate. Even worse, some opponents claim (falsely) that religious liberty is a license or weapon to discriminate against homosexuals. The people of God, however, cannot walk away from such controversies.

Today, some Christians even seem to long for persecution, viewing it as a mark of true Christian identity. It is such a mark, that's true. We serve a Savior who, by his own life and death, calls us to come and die—and the church is built on the blood of martyrs. But for some in this longing-for-persecution camp, the persecuted and underground churches of Asia are trotted out as moral exemplars, as they teach Christians that "rights" are extraneous to embracing the sufferings of the cross.

While I have some degree of sympathy to these concerns, I fear that they root in a well-intentioned but naive romanticism that some American Christians have adopted toward persecution. Virtue is in solidarity, of course. But imagine you are a thirty-six-year-old pastor of an underground church in China with twelve members. You cannot publicly identify as a Christian. There are no seminaries, so you can't receive further education in the Scriptures. You cannot safely have a Bible tucked beneath your arm. The governing authorities view you with suspicion, even contempt. Your best friend, another pastor, "disappeared" when his church failed to evade authorities.

---

[45] Peter J. Morden and Ian M. Randall, *Offering Christ to the World: Andrew Fuller (1754–1815) and the Revival of Eighteenth-century Particular Baptist Life* (Cumbria, UK: Paternoster, 2003), 136.

Ask yourself: Would you rather persist in this state of hardship? Or, instead, would you rather have the freedom to exercise your religion openly? Would you rather subject your church to the margins? Or would you rather conduct your affairs without a hint of government meddling?

I could be wrong, but I bet that most would choose the latter. Religious liberty is like a lineman who clears the way for a running back or like asphalt that paves the road to a destination or like a machete that clears the brush through the jungle.

Christ is building his church, so the gospel will advance, regardless. Yet I see no virtue in embracing obstacles that impede the message and bring hardship to its messengers.

Paul modeled this well, both as a faithful apostle and as a Roman citizen. While he reminds us of our ultimate and true citizenship in heaven, he was not shy about asserting his rights as a Roman citizen to escape punishment and stand before Caesar (Acts 22). Paul and most of the apostles did not escape the sword of the state, but it is not as if they joyfully requested martyrdom. Persecution may purify the church, but freedom gives space for gospel advance.

A small state and a large church—this is why Paul instructed Timothy to pray for a government that would allow space for the church to pursue its gospel mission (1 Tim 2:2). Governments that allow religious freedom, whether they acknowledge it or not, are doing the work of God. They are self-policing by restricting themselves from spheres where they have no reign or jurisdiction. As H. Richard Niebuhr so rightly articulated: "Religion, so understood, lies beyond the provenance of the state not because it is a private, inconsequential, or other-worldly matter, but because it concerns men's allegiance to a sovereignty and a community more immediate, more inclusive, and more fateful than those of the political commonwealth."[46]

God instituted government, yes, but there is precedent for resisting a government that invades the human conscience. Jesus taught us that Caesar has limited authority. He is not God and we are not made in Caesar's likeness (Matt 22:20–22).

---

[46] H. Richard Niebuhr, *Radical Monotheism and Western Culture* (New York: Harper & Row, 1960), 70–71.

So Christians who advocate for religious liberty in the public square are holding the ropes for those who labor to plant churches, evangelize, and equip the body of Christ. Such advocacy also helps to ensure a more humane democracy. As Southern Baptists, we point, with pride, to the work of two unrelenting Baptists, John Leland and Isaac Backus, who fought tirelessly for religious liberty during the colonial period. Their influence, along with that of others, like Roger Williams, helped enshrine religious liberty in the Bill of Rights.

Those of us living under the umbrella of freedom, working to spread the gospel in our communities, would do well not to forget the work of these pioneers. They tilled the cultural ground so we might see a harvest of spiritual fruit. In view of our historical connection to the efforts to secure religious liberty as a public-square virtue, minimizing the fight for liberty would needlessly and foolishly insult those who once held *our* ropes.

Those who advocate for religious liberty and those who preach the gospel every week in local churches are partners together. Their work is not at odds. So to our gospel-loving colleagues, who labor faithfully in communities across the country, we say, "As you go down, we *will* hold the ropes."

Religious liberty is an embattled right in America today. While America retains a rich ecology that welcomes religious values in the abstract, today religious motivation is vastly misunderstood. Worse, it is cast as an invidious exponent of discrimination seeking special rights. Ensuring that America retains its commitment to religious liberty will require Christians to navigate increasingly secular waters with greater dexterity and to be committed to responsible pluralism. Future success for religious liberty will mean retrieving the principles of our past.[47]

Finally, let us agree that it is critical to protect religious liberty within the public square. Indeed, all Christians should see it as their missional obligation to work for the flourishing of religious liberty in order that the gospel might advance unaided by government privilege and without injury by government edict. For the freedom to believe is the freedom to flourish. Let us fight to maintain these rights for all.

---

[47] Neuhaus, *The Naked Public Square*, 21.

PART 3

Contemporary Challenges to Religious Liberty

CHAPTER 7

CONSERVATIVE CHRISTIANS IN AN ERA OF CHRISTIAN CONSERVATIVES

Reclaiming the Struggle for Religious Liberty
from Cultural Captivity

Russell D. Moore

First of all, then, I urge that supplications, prayers, intercessions, and thanksgivings be made for all people, for kings and all who are in high positions, that we may lead a peaceful and quiet life, godly and dignified in every way. This is good, and it is pleasing in the sight of God our Savior, who desires all people to be saved and to come to the knowledge of the truth. For there is one God, and there is one mediator between God and men, the man Christ Jesus, who gave himself as a ransom for all, which is the testimony given at the proper time. For this I was appointed a preacher and an apostle (I am telling the truth, I am not lying), a teacher of the Gentiles in faith and truth.

> *I desire then that in every place the men should pray, lifting*
> *holy hands without anger or quarreling; likewise, also that women*
> *should adorn themselves in respectable apparel, with modesty*
> *and self-control, not with braided hair and gold or pearls or costly*
> *attire, but with what is proper for women who profess godliness—*
> *with good works.*
>
> 1 TIMOTHY 2:1–10 ESV

For too long cultural commentators have talked about conservative Protestant Christians as only another electoral interest group or identifiable American subculture. That, in itself, is not that problematic. What is problematic is the fact that many conservative Protestant Christians see themselves in precisely the same way. After a half century of political isolationism, many of our churches seem to identify what it means to be a Christian more with specific policy proposals than with theological identity. This is dangerous, not only for the mission of the church but for the preservation of religious liberty in the Western world.

The struggle for religious liberty has never been principally about politics or culture. The Baptist struggle for religious freedom has been from the beginning first and foremost about the Great Commission calling of the church. If we see religion—or even religious liberty—as principally a cultural or political concern, we will lose not only the resources to protect the "first freedom," but we will also lose the distinctiveness of our Christian witness.

While we must engage politically to protect our own inalienable religious rights as well as those of our neighbors, we must do so first as conservative *Christians* and not first as Christian *conservatives*. We must call the state to justice, but our ultimate concern should be for a place at the table at the Marriage Supper of the Lamb, not a place at the table of a political party platform committee meeting. As we find in Paul's discourse in 1 Timothy 2:1–10, our concern for the temporal political order is built on our much more significant concern for the gospel and the covenant community. If we will further our Baptist commitment to religious liberty, we must turn our attention to our theology—specifically our concepts of salvation and the church.

Regeneration, Not Just Reformation

One of the most helpful contributions to contemporary political thought in the post–September 11 era has come from conservative voices reminding us that ideas are behind religious movements and regimes, not only economic or cultural factors. Behind Islamic jihadism there is a particular ideology—grounded in theology—that must be understood before it is confronted.[1] Thus, the reason "they hate us" is not simply economic envy. We cannot rid the world of terrorism simply by supplanting third-world economies with more money. As a matter of fact, when American capitalism meets Islamic fascism, the result is more terrorism—since the Islamic terror lords conceive of American capitalism in terms of the cultural rot of trash reality television. Just as we had to understand the pseudo-theological ideology behind Marxist communism, we must understand the pseudo-ideological theology behind Islamic jihad.

In our own context, however, many look at conservative evangelicalism—particularly the Southern Baptist Convention—through the grid of culture rather than theology. For much of the nineteenth and twentieth centuries, Southern Baptists could assume a common culture rooted in the relative safety of the Bible-Belt South. There was a day in which Southern Baptist identity meant that one knew the difference between a GA and an Acteen,[2] a day in which every Southern Baptist meeting would serve sweet tea. That day is gone, and mostly for the good, because it means that Southern

---

[1] See, for example, Natan Sharansky, *The Case for Democracy: The Power of Freedom to Overcome Tyranny and Terror* (New York: Public Affairs, 2004).

[2] "GA" refers to "Girls in Action," a missions education program designed for females of elementary school age. "Acteens" is a similar program designed for older girls. "RAs" are "Royal Ambassadors," a missions education program designed for boys. These organizations were promoted by the Woman's Missionary Union and the Brotherhood Commission of the SBC. In Southern Baptist churches, RAs and GAs typically met on Wednesday night for activities, fellowship, and lessons on missionaries and cooperative support for the Great Commission. They also served as a Baptist version of Cub Scouts or Campfire Girls, complete with badges, awards, and summer retreats. The organizations are now in decline. This is seen not only in local church statistics but also in the fact that the editors asked me to define GAs and Acteens in this footnote. A Broadman Press book of my father's generation probably no more felt the need to spell these things out than to explain the meaning of the letters *USA*.

Baptists are engaging globally in the Great Commission task, and that we are impacting all of North America, not just Dixie. But it also means that we must take more careful heed in definition—heed to the theological commitments that define us. We must approach religious liberty in a different way than the Anti-Defamation League or the Seventh-day Adventists—even when we share the same policy goals. We must teach our people that religious liberty is not only about self-interest or American constitutionalism. It flows instead from our deepest and most theological commitments.

The apostle Paul's Spirit-inspired communiqué to his young disciple Timothy is instructive here. Paul calls on the church under Timothy's care to pray not simply for people in general but specifically for "kings and for all those who are in authority." It is important that twenty-first-century Southern Baptists understand the reasons behind this interest in political structures. It is not for power or for domination. It is instead because of the Great Commission. Paul notes that kings have much to do with whether "we may lead a peaceful and quiet life." The question for us is, who is the "we"? There is no doubt that, for Paul, the "we" is the church of the Lord Jesus.

Moreover, Paul immediately turns from prayers for kings to his central concern: the mediation of Christ, who gave himself for all people, and the desire of the Father that all persons come to know the gospel. He longs for political tranquility because he wants the church to be the church—and to spread the gospel of the kingdom across the creation. Caesar's decisions make a difference about whether we have access to the nations to baptize, and whether we can meet in freedom to worship our King Jesus. We must pray for these things. Now Paul's admonition has a special application to citizens of a democratic republic. We are not only the church in this context; we are also those who are kings and in authority. Christians have a responsibility to be politically engaged and civically active. But we must not forget that religious liberty is about the Great Commission and not the other way around. If we blur this reality, we will become just another political interest group. And we will lose religious liberty along the way.

This is something our Baptist forebears from Isaac Backus to John Leland to George W. Truett understood well. For years the Baptist left has sought to copyright religious liberty and separation of church and state—importing into these terms the content of the latest platform of the Democratic National Committee or the latest fund-raising letter of the American Civil Liberties Union. And yet, any historical investigation will reveal that the trail of blood was left by persecuted Baptists and Anabaptists crying out for a free church in a free state who were *not* posing against the "religious right." They *were* the "religious right." They insisted on religious liberty precisely because they believed in personal regeneration, a regenerate church, the convicting authority of the Holy Spirit, and the supernatural origins of Christianity.

If we abstract religious liberty and political engagement from the Great Commission and the gospel of personal regeneration, we will have begun walking down a dark and treacherous path. Right now scads of "evangelical" political parachurch organizations exist with detailed policy proposals but virtually no theological consensus. They stand united against same-sex marriage and for a pro-life ethic, but they haven't a clue why. Some "pro-family" organizations say far more about the president than Jesus of Nazareth.[3] Indeed, some of our churches have more of a consensus on foreign policy than on the inerrancy of Scripture.

Evangelical groups find themselves uniting for conferences on saving America with the likes of evangelist Joyce Meyer. Yes, Meyer is right on abortion and on the definition of family and so forth, but she is theologically aberrant to the core.[4] Some evangelical Christians align themselves in pro-Israel causes with the likes of John Hagee—without qualms that Hagee is a prosperity gospel teacher with a track record of numerous false prophecies, who has remained notoriously unclear about whether Jewish people can be saved apart from faith in Christ. This is not to say that we cannot unite with those who disagree with us theologically for specific policy purposes, especially for religious liberty. We can work with Mormons, for instance, to work against zoning laws that unfairly penalize churches. But we must make sure that our churches understand that religious liberty

---

[3] For a further discussion of how Christian theism must be theologically grounded in order to avoid being politically identified, see Russell D. Moore, *The Kingdom of Christ: The New Evangelical Perspective* (Wheaton: Crossway, 2004).

[4] Joyce Meyer is among the most successful contemporary manifestations of the "prosperity gospel" movement popularized in the twentieth century by preachers such as Oral Roberts, Kenneth Copeland, and Fred Price. For an analysis of the "word of faith" movements, see D. R. McConnell, *A Different Gospel: Biblical and Historical Insights into the Word of Faith Movement* (Peabody, MA: Hendrickson, 1995).

flows from the gospel—and then spend years of discipleship and teaching to make sure they grasp the content and glory of that gospel.

Religious liberty and political engagement are not incidental to our calling as the church. Our Chinese and Sudanese brothers and sisters in Christ cannot send missionaries to the nations because they are hunted like animals by predatory governments.[5] In the "free world," religious liberty means more than simply making sure no one goes to jail for preaching the gospel. It also means understanding that political decisions often transform culture, and that culture then transforms the context in which we preach the gospel.

The abortion issue, for instance, is about more than saving the lives of babies (although that would be reason enough to obligate us to stand against it). How are we to preach the gospel of everlasting life in a culture that celebrates death? We must change minds about abortion because the abortion culture is more than a political problem. It is a satanic conspiracy that drives people away from wisdom and toward death itself (Prov 8:36). This means that if we are going to make a difference on the abortion issue, we need to cultivate more than pro-life voters. Too often people assume that we oppose abortion because we want to vote Republican. Rather, for most of us, we so often vote Republican because of the abortion issue—and the issues that cluster around it. To fight for religious liberty and Christian freedom, we must cultivate churches that are in love with the gospel itself.

Churches that try to isolate themselves from speaking into the broader culture, under the guise that they're "only here to preach the Word," are not being completely faithful to the gospel. The call to repentance is a necessary word that shows up both in our private actions and in our corporate decisions and in the systems we put in place to perpetuate our sin so that we will not have to think consciously about such things. There will always be those who see a social ethic as a challenge to the gospel of justification. But where there is sin, no matter the form, the gospel speaks a word. This requires a "both/and" approach from the church, recognizing both the

---

[5] For a discussion of persecution of Christians across the world, see Allen D. Hertzke, *Freeing God's Children: The Unlikely Alliance for Global Human Rights* (Lanham, MD: Rowman and Littlefield, 2004).

vertical and horizontal aspects of our sin, both the personal and social. A church member who embraces white supremacy or a "pro-choice" position on abortion is not principally a political statistic but a failure of Christian discipleship. Likewise, a Christian who longs for a coercive state church or who does not care about religious persecution in the Islamic world does not have just a skewed political ideology but also an apathetic heart for the nations, a heart that does not understand the freeness of the gospel or the task of the Great Commission.

Only with a firm grasp of the gospel—what Paul explains in mysterious glory to Timothy—can we motivate regenerate hearts to press for religious liberty. We come to Caesar not as supplicants seeking our rights. We come to Caesar, when he obstructs the freedom to worship or evangelize or live peaceably, with a warning, "No sir, you will not come this far." The reason we do so is because, more than anyone else, we understand that Caesar's authority is derivative and strictly limited (Rom 13:1–7). We also understand that religious liberty—or even constitutional rights as citizens—are not ends in themselves; they are means to an end. They enable us to preach more freely and persuade and pray and worship and live in ecclesial community. "Just as I Am" is a religious liberty anthem.

Counterculture Peace, Not Only Culture Wars

Secondly, in order to preserve our heritage of advocacy for religious liberty, we must protect the centrality of the church. Many contemporary Christians argue that social and political engagement is for individual Christians, not for churches. The problem with this argument is that there is no understanding in the New Testament of a Christian who is not ecclesiastically located. A churchless Christian is, for the apostles, simply lost (Heb 10:23–31; 1 John 2:19). All of the Christian life is situated within the life of the community, a covenant community that models for the world the realities of the coming kingdom of Christ. The fight for religious liberty means more than just advocacy by Christians for protection from the government. It means maintaining the freedom for churches to be the church before the watching culture.

This is why Paul, after commanding the church to pray for ruling authorities in the context of the free offer of the gospel, turns to what it looks like for a free church to live "godly and dignified in every way" (1 Tim 2:2). The men of the congregation must not be quarrelers. They must be holy. They must pray diligently. The women of the congregation, meanwhile, must likewise not be conformed to the culture around them. They must not be entranced by outward beautification. They must not usurp the headship of men. In short, Paul calls on the church not only to attend to the culture, chiefly through prayer, but also to attend to forming, through the Spirit and the Word, a counterculture.

If we are to preserve our commitment to religious liberty, we must confront within our own people what they get perpetually from the culture and the state—the notion that they are autonomous individuals living individual stories and claiming individual rights. Too often even Christians see themselves as isolated individuals who come together at the voting booth to decide who runs the Congress, or who come together at a congregational business meeting to decide whether to buy a lawn mower. Is it any wonder that we often find community more in our political commonalities than in the church?

The spirit of Jim Crow laws fell in Southern Baptist churches not because civil rights activists appealed to the Fourteenth Amendment. White supremacy fell because churches appealed to Ephesians 2 and Ephesians 3 and Galatians 3—passages on the unity of the people of God in the church. This carries the weight not of a political agenda but the weight of the authority of God himself, as revealed in his inerrant Word. We need not only the religious liberty to live out the calling of the church; we also need to live out that calling. We need not only to claim the rights to have crisis pregnancy centers; we should have them. We need not only to claim the rights of elderly people and orphans to live; we should take them in and care for them. We need not only to maintain that the welfare of the impoverished is principally the role of the church and not the state; we need to take care of the poor as churches. We need not only to express outrage when a renegade court forbids students from freely gathering to pray; we need to engage our churches to teach teenagers to be praying men and women.

Creating countercultural Christian churches also implies that our political alignments will be provisional and loosely held. We should never feel too comfortably at home with any political movement—or even with American culture itself. If Christian conservatism is going to "conserve" a Christian counterculture, we must understand the ways in which our interests are subverted not only by an overreaching government but by an overreaching socioeconomic culture as well.[6] After all, it is not tax policy alone causing hordes of evangelical and Roman Catholic mothers to pursue full-time careers while their children sit in day-care centers watching *Veggie Tales*. And do not be deceived; it will take much more than a weekly hour of Sunday school and moralistic lessons from singing vegetables to transform the character formation built into a child by two parents chasing the corporatist vision of the American dream into the fruits of the Spirit.

Most conservative Christians would concede that there is more to life than what is advertised on the high-definition television screens at Walmart. But do our churches and our pastors lead them to ask whether there might be something *different* to life than this? Yes, we believe that children are a gift from the Lord. But do our own congregants roll their eyes in dismay at the godly Christian husband and wife who actually seek to raise a multitude of Christian children, or at least a "multitude" as defined by our antiseptic contraceptive culture? How can we decry Planned Parenthood if the way our churches view family size and parenting is being formed by the culture of death Planned Parenthood promotes, and our pastors say nary a word (1 Tim 2:15)?

If we are to be a church that maintains religious liberty, we need to love the religion as much as the liberty—indeed more so. And that means we will be increasingly odd in American culture. We may have less and less in common with libertarian Republicans and libertine Democrats. If the outside culture pronounces this anathema, so be it—it always has. And if Caesar decides to add his sword to the disapproval of the culture, so be it—he has done it before. The church still stands. We will claim our mantle of dissent not simply by standing in the public square demanding our rights—though we must sometimes do that. We claim it first of all by being an alternative community, the people of Christ.

---

[6] For an excellent survey of the social and economic factors involved in family breakdown, see Brian C. Robertson, *Forced Labor: What's Wrong with Balancing Work and Family* (Dallas: Spence, 2002); and Allan Carlson, *The Family in America: Searching for Social Harmony in the Industrial Age* (New Brunswick, NJ: Transaction, 2003).

Conclusion

Maintaining religious liberty has more to do with vacation Bible school than with the Supreme Court. If we are to ensure that the next generations of churches have liberty, we must remember why we claim that liberty: for the gospel and for the church. We must therefore rear a generation of children and grandchildren who so love the gospel, who so love the church, that they are willing, when soldiers with AK-47s line them up against the walls for the faith, to go to their deaths for the Christ who is alone King. They will not learn to do that through a weekly diet of "how to" sermons and moralistic Sunday school drivel. They will not do that for a political party, or even a cultural way of life. They will learn to do it through identifying with the same gospel and same churches that our ancestors carried in their hearts as they were drowned for insisting that they would baptize the way Jesus ordered, not the way the state church commanded. They will find religious liberty—and every kind of liberty—not in the word of the Constitution or in the "natural rights" of humanity—but by being hidden in Christ, and living together in his Body. They will be free only if they realize that they must be conservative Christians, not just Christian conservatives.

CHAPTER 8

THE GATHERING STORM

Religious Liberty in the Wake of the
Sexual Revolution

R. Albert Mohler Jr.

In the first volume of his history of World War II, Winston Churchill looked back at the storm clouds that gathered in the 1930s portending war and the loss of human freedom. Churchill wisely and presciently warned Britain of the tragedy that would ensue if Hitler were not stopped. Churchill's actions were courageous, and the world was shaped by his convictional leadership. We are not facing the same gathering storm, but we are now facing a battle that will determine the destiny of priceless freedoms and the very foundation of human rights and human dignity.

Speaking thirty years ago, Attorney General Edwin Meese warned that "there are ideas that have gained influence in some parts of our society, particularly in some important and sophisticated circles, that are opposed to religious freedom and freedom in general. In some areas there are some people that have espoused a hostility to religion that must be recognized for what it is, and expressly countered."[1]

Those were prophetic words, prescient in their clarity and foresight. The ideas of which Mr. Meese warned have only gained ground in the past thirty years, and with astounding velocity. A revolution in morality now seeks not only to subvert marriage but to redefine it, and thus to undermine an essential foundation of human dignity, flourishing, and freedom.

Religious liberty is also under direct threat. During oral arguments in the *Obergefell* case, the solicitor general of the United States served notice before the Supreme Court that the liberties of religious institutions will be an open and unavoidable question. Already, religious liberty is threatened by a new moral regime that exalts erotic liberty and personal autonomy and openly argues that religious liberties must give way to the new morality, its redefinition of marriage, and its demand for coercive moral, cultural, and legal sovereignty.

These are days that will require courage, conviction, and clarity of vision. We are in a fight for the most basic liberties God has given humanity, every single one of us, made in his image. Religious liberty is being redefined as mere freedom of worship, but it will not long survive if it is reduced to a private sphere with no public voice. The very freedom to preach the gospel of Jesus Christ is at stake, and thus so is the liberty of every American. Human rights and human dignity are temporary abstractions if they are severed from their reality as gifts of the Creator. The eclipse of Christian truth will lead inevitably to a tragic loss of human dignity. If we lose religious liberty, all other liberties will be lost, one by one.

Religious Liberty and the Challenge of Same-Sex Marriage

Even though same-sex marriage is new to the American scene, the religious liberty challenges became fully apparent even before it became a national reality. Soon after the legalization of same-sex marriage in the state of Massachusetts, several seminars and symposia were held in order

---

[1] Edwin Meese, *Major Policy Statements of the Attorney General, Edwin Meese III, 1985–1988* (Ann Arbor: University of Michigan Library, 1989), 168.

to consider the religious liberty dimensions of this legal revolution. The Becket Fund for Religious Liberty sponsored one of the most important of these events, which produced a major volume with essays by prominent legal experts on both sides of this revolution. The consensus of every single participant in the conference was that the normalization of homosexuality and the legalization of same-sex marriage would produce a head-on collision in the courts. As Marc D. Stern of the American Jewish Congress stated, "Same-sex marriage would work a sea change in American law."[2] He continued, "That change will reverberate across the legal and religious landscape in ways that are unpredictable today."[3]

Nevertheless, he predicted some of the battlefronts he saw coming and addressed some of the arguments that could already be recognized. Even then, Stern saw almost all the issues we have recounted, and others yet to come. He saw the campuses of religious colleges and the work of religious institutions as inevitable arenas of legal conflict. He pointed to employment as one of the crucial issues of legal conflict and spoke with pessimism about the ability of religious institutions to maintain liberty in this context, and for which he advocates. As Stern argued, "The legalization of same-sex marriage would represent the triumph of an egalitarian-based ethic over a faith-based one, and not just legally. The remaining question is whether champions of tolerance are prepared to tolerate proponents of the different ethical vision. I think the answer will be no."[4]

Stern did not wait long to have his assessment verified by legal scholars on the other side of the debate. One of the most important of these, Chai R. Feldblum, presented rare candor and revealed that an advocate for same-sex marriage and the normalization of homosexuality could also see these issues coming. Feldblum pointed to what she described as, "the conflict that I believe exists between laws intended to protect the liberty of lesbian, gay, bisexual, and transgender (LGBT) people so that they may live lives of dignity and integrity and the religious beliefs of some individuals

---

[2] Marc. D. Stern, "Same-Sex Marriage and the Churches," in *Same-Sex Marriage and Religious Liberty: Emerging Conflicts*, ed. Douglas Laycock, Anthony R. Picarello, and Robin Fretwell Wilson (Lanham, MD: Rowman and Littlefield, 2008), 1.

[3] Ibid., 1.

[4] Ibid., 57.

whose conduct is regulated by such laws."[5] She went on to state her belief that "those who advocate for LGBT equality have downplayed the impact of such laws on some people's religious beliefs and, equally, I believe those who sought religious exemptions in such civil rights laws have downplayed the impact that such exemptions would have on LGBT people."[6]

As Feldblum argued, she called for society to "acknowledge that civil rights laws can burden an individual's belief liberty interest when the conduct demanded by these laws burdens an individual's core beliefs, whether such beliefs are religiously or secularly based."[7] Thus, in Feldblum's argument, we confront face-to-face the candid assertion that an individual's "belief liberty interest" must give way to what are now defined as the civil rights of sexual minorities. Feldblum believed she saw the future clearly and that the future would mean "a majority of jurisdictions in this country will have modified their laws so that LGBT people will have full equality in our society, including access to civil marriage or to civil unions that carry the same legal effect as civil marriage."[8] In that future, religious liberty would simply give way to the civil liberties of homosexuals and same-sex couples.

Feldblum, then a professor at Georgetown University Law Center, also understood that this moral revolution would mean that the government is "taking sides" in a moral conflict, siding with the LGBT community. This necessarily puts government on the side of that moral judgment, which is precisely the point Feldblum is insisting we must recognize. Once government is on that side of the moral judgment, its laws and its coercion will require those who hold to a contrary moral system, whether based in religious or secular convictions, to give way to the new moral judgment affirmed by the government.

In her revealing argument, Feldblum struggles to find a way to grant recognition and a level of liberty to those who disagree with the normalization of homosexuality, especially on religious grounds. Nevertheless, as

---

[5] Chai R. Feldblum, "Moral Conflict and Conflicting Liberties," in Laycock, Picarello, and Wilson, *Same-Sex Marriage and Religious Liberty*, 124–25.

[6] Ibid., 125.

[7] Ibid.

[8] Ibid., 126.

she shares quite openly, she is unable to sustain that effort, given her prior commitment to the absolute imposition of the new morality by means of the law and the power of the state. Appointed and later confirmed as commissioner of the US Equal Employment Opportunity Commission, nominated by President Obama, Feldblum stated in a different context that the end result of antidiscrimination legislation would mean the victory of sexual rights over religious liberty. She commented that she could not come up with a single case in which, at least hypothetically, religious liberty would triumph over coercion to the new morality.

It is crucially important that we understand the moral judgment being made and enforced by legal mechanisms in the wake of this revolution. Feldblum, a lesbian activist who has advocated for same-sex marriage and the legalization of polygamy, fully understands the law teaches and reinforces a morality. She insists that the law must allow no deviation in public life from the dictates of the new morality. In this case, this means allowing virtually no exemptions to regulations prohibiting discrimination on the basis of sexual orientation or gender identity.

In her presentation at the Becket Fund event, Feldblum cited the writings of Judge Michael McConnell, who offered both support for same-sex marriage and the assurance that the religious liberty of Christians and other religious citizens must be protected. McConnell's argument is straightforward:

> The starting point would be to extend respect to both sides in the conflict of opinion, to treat both the view that homosexuality is a healthy and normal manifestation of human sexuality and the view that homosexuality is unnatural and immoral as conscientious positions, worthy of respect, much as we treat both atheism and faith as worthy of respect. In using the term 'respect,' I do not mean agreement. Rather, I mean the civil toleration we extend to fellow citizens and fellow human beings even when we disagree with their views. We should recognize that the 'Civil Magistrate' is no more 'competent a Judge' of the 'Truth' about human sexuality than about religion.[9]

---

[9] Ibid., 133.

Feldblum dismissed his argument by accusing McConnell of failing to recognize "that the government *necessarily* takes a stance on the moral question he has articulated every time it *fails* to affirmatively ensure that gay people can live openly, safely, and honestly in society."[10]

In other words, there must be no exceptions. Religious liberty simply evaporates as a fundamental right grounded in the US Constitution and recedes into the background in the wake of what is now a higher social commitment: sexual freedom.

Conflict of Liberties: Religious Liberty versus Erotic Liberty

We now face an inevitable conflict of liberties. In this post-*Obergefell* context of acute and radical moral change, the conflict of liberties is excruciating, immense, and eminent. In this case, the conflict of liberties means that the new moral regime, with the backing of the courts and the regulatory state, will prioritize erotic liberty over religious liberty. Over the course of the past several decades, we have seen this revolution coming. Erotic liberty has been elevated as a right more fundamental than religious liberty. Erotic liberty, foreign to the founders of this nation, now marginalizes, subverts, and neutralizes religious liberty—a liberty highly prized by the builders of this nation and its constitutional order. We must remember that the framers of the Constitution did not believe they were creating rights within the Constitution but rather acknowledging rights given to all humanity by "nature and nature's God."

Erotic liberty emerges directly from arguments made in opinions handed down by the United States Supreme Court. The *Griswold* case and William O. Douglas's "finding" of the right to privacy, and thus a right to birth-control pills, within the Fourteenth Amendment of the United States Constitution laid much of the groundwork for the advancement of erotic liberty. As Douglas acknowledged, this right is by no means explicit or even present in the text of the Constitution. It is drawn from penumbras emanating from the Constitution. Similarly, in the *Planned Parenthood of Southeastern Pennsylvania v. Casey* decision on abortion in 1992, Justices

---

[10] Ibid.

Sandra Day O'Connor, Anthony Kennedy, and David Souter declared, "At the heart of liberty is the right to define one's own concept of existence, of meaning, of the universe, and of the mystery of human life."[11]

A direct line can be drawn from the 1992 case to the 2003 *Lawrence v. Texas* decision striking down all laws against sodomy. In this case, Justice Kennedy authored the majority opinion. Quoting from the *Casey* decision, Kennedy asserted:

> These matters [personal decisions relating to marriage, procreation, contraception, family relationships, child rearing, and education], involving those most intimate and personal choices a person may make in a lifetime, choices central to personal dignity and autonomy, are central to the liberty protected by the Fourteenth Amendment. At the heart of liberty is the right to define one's own concept of existence, of meaning, of the universe, and of the mystery of human life. Beliefs about these matters could not define the attributes of personhood were they formed under compulsion of the State.

He then added, "Persons in a homosexual relationship may seek autonomy for these purposes, just as heterosexual persons do."[12] In the end, not only can a direct line be drawn from *Griswold* to the *Lawrence v. Texas* decision, but further a direct line can be drawn from these two cases to the *Obergefell* case. Consistent throughout all of these legal arguments is the assumption that erotic liberty is central to the project of defining "one's own concept of existence, of meaning, of the universe, and of the mystery of human life."[13]

The use of that language demonstrates how erotic liberty typifies the freedom most cherished by the culture and most respected by the courts in the context of the secular age. A liberty that did not even exist when the Constitution was written now supersedes protections that are explicit in the Constitution. This explains the trajectory of court decisions and

---

[11] Planned Parenthood of Southeastern Pennsylvania v. Casey, 505 U.S. 833 (1992).
[12] Lawrence v. Texas, 539 U.S. 558 (2003).
[13] Ibid.

developments in the law and, at the same time, reveals the trajectory we can expect in the future.

We should also hear the clear voices attempting to moderate or ameliorate the impact of the sexual revolution on religious liberty. Jonathan Turley, known for his defense of the legalization of both same-sex marriage and polygamy, states:

> I believe (and hope) that the nation will evolve toward a greater protection of homosexuals and greater recognition of civil unions. This evolution will not, however, occur if the government is viewed as unfairly trying to pre-determine the debate or harass one side. Finally, the progress made toward same-sex marriage and homosexual rights is due in large part to the protection of free speech and associational rights. The rights of gay citizens will be secured not simply with legal but also with cultural changes. The latter will depend on greater, not lesser protection of speech and association on both sides of the same-sex marriage debate.[14]

The moderating words of Professor Turley are almost entirely swept away now that same-sex marriage is a legal reality and not only a hypothetical possibility. In the wake of the legalization of same-sex marriage, it is clear that the sexual revolutionaries are going to assume a "take no prisoners" approach concerning dissent, only offering exceptions to non-discrimination policies somehow won and defended, even in hostile courts.

Before leaving Professor Feldblum, we need to recognize that she can help us see the scope and scale of what confronts Christians and other religious citizens concerning the religious liberty challenge. Feldblum insists that lesbians and gay men, along with other sexual minorities, will only achieve equality if the negative moral judgment against their sexual behavior is eliminated from public consideration. She concedes that a majority of Americans, as recently as a decade ago, indicated both a negative moral judgment against homosexual behaviors and a growing acceptance of gay rights. She described this as a form of "moral bracketing" that Americans

---

[14] Jonathan Turley, "An Unholy Union: Same-sex Marriage and the Use of Governmental Programs to Penalize Religious Groups with Unpopular Practices," in Laycock, Picarello, and Wilson, *Same-Sex Marriage and Religious Liberty*, 75–76.

considered part of a generally tolerant attitude. Nevertheless, she asserts that moral bracketing, though useful to the gay rights movement, cannot satisfy the demand of the LGBT community for full dignity. That dignity can only come if all moral censure of their sexual behaviors, as well as their relationships, is removed from the public square. She insists that the movement cannot be satisfied until Americans believe that "sexual orientation is a morally neutral trait" and that "acting consistently with one's sexual orientation is a morally good act."[15]

Accordingly, Feldblum has argued that gays and lesbians "must force the conversation—in personal, political, and public media settings—that an individual's sexual orientation is a morally neutral characteristic and that an individual who acts consistently with his/her orientation is acting in a morally good manner."[16] As she continues her argument, she boldly asserts that government "has the obligation, through its public policies, to create societal frameworks that advance a set of moral goods."[17] Thus, having asserted that homosexual acts should be recognized as a moral good, she then asserts that the government has a positive duty to create societal frameworks (laws) that advance those moral goods. In other words, she wants frameworks that would infringe on religious liberty for the sake of erotic liberty.

Responding to the Challenges

Christians must always remember that marriage is a prepolitical institution, recognized and solemnized throughout history by virtually every human culture and civilization. But we are living in an age in which everything is political, and nothing is honored as prepolitical.

This has all been made possible by a breakdown in the immune system of human society—and this breakdown was no accident. Immunologists will explain that one of the wonders of human life is the fact that each of us

---

[15] Chai R. Feldblum, "The Moral Values Project: A Call to Moral Action in Politics," in *Moral Argument, Religion and Same-Sex Marriage*, ed. Gordon Babst, Emily Gill, and Jason Pierceson (Lanham, MD: Rowman and Littlefield, 2009), 216.

[16] Ibid., 215.

[17] Ibid., 217.

receives from our mother an amazing array of defenses within our immune system. Throughout time, we develop further immunities to disease, or we grow sick and vulnerable. A severely compromised immune system leads to chronic disease, constant vulnerability, and potentially death. If this is true for an individual, it is also true of a society or civilization.

We have forfeited our immunity against the breakdown of marriage, the family, and the integrity of human sexuality. We can point to others who have been the prophets and agents of this self-injury to society, but we must recognize that we have all contributed to it—in so far as we have embraced essentially modern understandings of love, romance, liberty, personal autonomy, obligation, and authority. Furthermore, the separation of the conjugal union and openness to the gift of children has further undermined both our conscience and our credibility in the defense of marriage. We separated sex from marriage and marriage from reproduction. We sowed the seeds of the current confusion. At the very least, we did not address this confusion with sufficient moral clarity and credibility.

Marriage is the most basic unit of civilization. In fact, it is the basic molecular structure of human society. The redefinition of marriage will bring great human unhappiness. As Pascal Bruckner reminds us, this is true of heterosexual divorce.[18] It promised happiness but has produced misery and brokenness. It declared itself to be liberation, but it imprisons all moderns in its penitentiary of idealized and unattainable romance and sexual fulfillment.

The family, as properly prepolitical as marriage, is now the great laboratory for human social experimentation. Children are routinely sacrificed to the romantic whims and sexual demands of their parents, who may or may not be married, may or may not stay married, and may or may not include both a father and a mother at any point.

The epidemic of fatherlessness is well documented and no longer even denied, but there is no social consensus to address a phenomenon that has wrought incalculable human costs, both individually and socially.

A basic principle of Christian theology was once written into the moral immune system of Western civilization—what God commands and

---

[18] Pascal Bruckner, *Has Marriage for Love Failed?*, trans. Steven Rendall and Lisa Neal (Cambridge: Polity Press, 2013).

institutes is what leads to genuine human flourishing. Our civilization now lives in open revolt against that affirmation.

The moral revolution we are now witnessing on the issue of homosexuality is without precedent in human history in terms of its scale and velocity. We are not looking at a span of centuries, or even the length of one century. This revolution is taking place within a single human generation. I argue that no moral revolution on this scale has ever been experienced by a society that remained intact, even as no moral revolution of this velocity has yet been experienced. We can now see more clearly where this revolution began. It is virtually impossible to see where it ends.

But, for the first time in the experience of most Americans, the moral revolution revolving around marriage, the family, and human sexuality is now clearly becoming a religious liberty issue. The rights of parents to raise their children according to their most basic and fundamental theological and moral convictions are now at stake. Courts have ruled in some jurisdictions that parents cannot even "opt out" their children from sex education driven by moral revisionism. Legislatures in California and New Jersey have made it illegal for mental health professionals to tell minors that there is anything wrong with homosexual sexuality, orientation, or relationships. Parents are put on notice. How long will it be before the moral authority of the secular state is employed to allow children to "divorce" their parents? How long before the logic of sexual revolution and sexual self-expression leads to parents being told what they must allow and facilitate with their own children when it comes to sex, gender, and sexual orientation? The logic of moral change by legal coercion is already on full display in many modern legal debates. How long will a respect for parental rights and religious liberty hold back the flooding river of this moral revolution?

Religious liberty is already severely compromised by modern political regimes that claim to be democratic and respectful of human rights. Given the shape of current arguments for sexual expression and liberty, religious institutions—especially schools, colleges, universities, welfare agencies, and benevolent ministries—are under fire and under warning. Some have already been forced to make a decision: forfeit your convictions or forfeit your work. Some have chosen one, some the other. One way leads to an honorable extinction, the other to a dishonorable surrender. Both are violations of religious liberty.

The conflict of liberties we are now experiencing is unprecedented and ominous. Forced to choose between erotic liberty and religious liberty, many Americans would clearly sacrifice freedom of religion. How long will it be until *many* becomes *most*?

There is a gathering storm, and its threat is urgent and real, but there are arguments to be made, principles to be defended, rights to be respected, truths to be cherished, and permanent things to be preserved. We face the danger of a new Dark Age marked by the loss of liberty and the denial of human dignity. Thus, there is a battle to be joined and much work to be done. Together, may we be found faithful to these tasks. As Churchill reminded us, in every gathering storm there is a summons to action.

CHAPTER 9

RELIGIOUS LIBERTY AND THE CHRISTIAN UNIVERSITY

Thomas White

"Do not be afraid," Scripture tells us. Abram, Moses, the shepherds, Peter, Paul, and others were reminded to fear not.[1] Far too often, cultural pressures or human wisdom leave little hope, but in the lowest moments, God calls followers to exercise faith. Consider Joshua. Several times God tells him, "Haven't I commanded you: be strong and courageous? Do not be afraid or discouraged, for the LORD your God is with you wherever you go" (Josh 1:9).

Imagine the possible criticism and discouragement. Crossing an overflowing river at harvest season raised questions about the timing. Joshua had no ten-year strategic plan for conquering the wall of Jericho and other fortified cities. When the human perspective gave reason for concern and

---

[1] See Gen 15:1; Num 21:34; Luke 2:10; 5:10; Acts 18:9.

hopelessness, those words—"be strong, be courageous, do not be afraid, and do not be discouraged"—must have echoed through Joshua's mind.

Today, Christian universities look across the tumultuous cultural rivers of the sexual revolution, understanding that contemporary times have placed sexual freedom above religious freedom. They read articles from popular journalists calling for the end of their tax-exempt status, to cease federal funding, or to prohibit them from being accredited academic institutions. The rising pluralistic worldview does not appreciate the exclusive nature of biblical truth. Like the three Hebrew captives in Babylon standing before the supreme court of Nebuchadnezzar and being told to bow to an idol, Christian universities feel the pressure to bow to the false god of sexual freedom. Yet God fearers cannot do this without violating the authority of Scripture. They must stand firm and repeat the declaration of Shadrach, Meshach, and Abednego: that our God "can rescue us . . . but even if he does not," we will not bow down to anyone but the one true God (Dan 3:17–18).

So while we look in this chapter at an unfavorable cultural landscape with challenges on many fronts, we do not worry, because God is still on his throne and not surprised. In the current state of affairs, we must prepare ourselves. We must demonstrate compassionate conviction as we clearly articulate a biblical worldview in the face of adversity. Culture has provided an opportunity to testify to the reason for the faith within us. Our Christian universities exist for such a time as this: a time when rejecting the easy path of compromise and change for the hard path of faithful submission to the authority of God's Word provides a clearer and louder testimony of faith in the gospel than years of prosperity could ever do. Let us not waste this opportunity. Let us prepare well to understand the coming challenges and then let us glorify God with the truth of our testimony.

Toward that end, this chapter will offer some considerations by looking at the major consequences of eroding religious liberty facing Christian universities. We will look at challenges to tax-exempt status; the challenge of Title VII; Title IX, federal funding, and transgender orientation; exemptions from Title IX; and the challenge of accreditation, as well as other narrower challenges, before making some recommended responses.

Ultimately, we must recognize that our duty and calling in this life is not to preserve earthly institutions but to be faithful to our heavenly Father. It is the prayer of this author that the words of this chapter will encourage and equip those involved in or supportive of Christian education to operate with compassionate conviction, maintain an eternal perspective, and clearly present the truth of a biblical worldview.

Potential Consequences of Eroding Religious Liberty

The new battle lines have been drawn. No longer is the discussion over the legalization of same-sex marriage. Now, proponents of the LGBT movement seek not only acceptance but also endorsement by everyone. In order to achieve this goal, religious freedom must take a backseat to sexual freedom. The argument centers on what defines a human being. LGBT proponents contend that sexual freedom defines at least part of who a person is. A biblical worldview contends that being created in the image of God defines a person, and that each person contains a sinful nature inherited from Adam and Eve, which causes us to run away from God and seek our own sinful inclinations.[2] While the LGBT movement sees embracing same-sex attraction or transgender orientation as being true to one's self, a biblical worldview sees those same actions as sinful rebellion against our Creator, with true peace and fulfillment being found only in salvation by grace through faith in Jesus Christ alone.

These two worldviews will never agree on which freedom should have priority. A biblical worldview contends that religious freedom, which entails every person's God-given right to live out religious beliefs, is the first freedom. Yet some lawmakers are considering classifying the

---

[2] A biblical worldview contends that God created humankind and established marriage between one man and one woman (see Genesis 2), mysteriously representing the gospel (Eph 5:31–32). It also contends that God established all of our days before any one existed, and that he created us male and female in the womb (Ps 139:13–16). Because of the sinful rebellion of Adam and Eve in the garden, all humankind inherits a sinful nature and affirms Adam's sin with personal rebellion against God (Genesis 3; Rom 5:12). A biblical worldview contends that the inward desire toward same-sex relationships or transgender orientation comes from the sinful nature and is rebellion against our Creator (Romans 1–2). All humankind has sinful inclinations, such as pride, lying, stealing, coveting, sexual immorality of all forms, and anger, to mention only a few. Any sin separates a person from God, and all have sinned (Rom 3:23). Sinners must repent and believe in Jesus Christ alone to be saved by grace through faith (Rom 6:23; Eph 2:8–9). Jesus will return to create a new heaven and a new earth, and Christians will enjoy eternity with him forever for his glory.

expression of the biblical view of human sexuality as hate crimes.[3] Telling someone the truth about their creation, purpose, potential for a relationship with God, and eternal destiny should not be considered hate speech but an expression of true concern for that person's soul. The United States must allow freedom for all nonviolent worldviews and encourage spirited engagement of differing ideas without considering those disagreements as creating hostile environments.

Those who oppose a biblical worldview will threaten Christian educational institutions with the loss of tax-exempt status, federal funding, or accreditation in order to encourage them to compromise, be silent, or cease operation. Christian universities must recognize that our struggle is not against individual people but against principalities and powers, and we must continue to treat all people with dignity and respect even when they seek to end our institutions. At the same time, we must prepare to communicate our ideas clearly and prepare for the success of our institutions. The mission to train the next generation with a biblical worldview to live for God's glory must not cease.

Tax-Exempt Status[4]

During the oral arguments in *Obergefell et al. v. Hodges, Director, Ohio Department of Health et al.*, Justice Samuel A. Alito Jr. referenced the 1983 *Bob Jones* Supreme Court decision when asking Solicitor General Donald B. Verrilli Jr. a question: "In the *Bob Jones* case, the court held that a college was not entitled to tax-exempt status if it opposed interracial marriage or interracial dating. So would the same apply to a university or a college if it opposed same-sex marriage?" The response from the representative of the Obama administration was, "I don't think I can answer that

---

[3] R. Albert Mohler, "Same-Sex Marriage and Christian Higher Education," *The Weekly*, June 24, 2015, https://erlc.com/article/same-sex-marriage-and-christian -higher-education.

[4] Some of the research for this chapter comes from John Hart and Robert Vaughn, who serve as counsel and assistant counsel for Cedarville University. They have helped gather relevant court cases and explain important precedents to me. I greatly appreciate their research. Any errors in the wording, documentation, or explanations in this chapter are my own.

question without knowing more specifics, but it's certainly going to be an issue. I don't deny that. I don't deny that, Justice Alito. It is going to be an issue."[5] Christian universities took note of the testimony. Seventy leaders of Christian colleges and schools wrote congressional leaders citing the solicitor general's statement and asked Congress to enact a law protecting the religious liberty of these institutions, highlighting their current policies on same-sex relationships.[6]

Two days before the *Obergefell* decision, the *New York Times* ran an article entitled, "Schools Fear Gay Marriage Ruling Could End Tax Exemptions."[7] The nature of the case, the recognition that Christian universities are not churches even if they are religious institutions, and the *Bob Jones* precedent sparked fears and discussion in the world of higher education.[8] The decision two days later in favor of same-sex marriage only heightened those fears.

Justice Anthony Kennedy, writing the majority opinion, sought to calm fears by stating that the First Amendment provides proper protection for religious organizations. He wrote:

> Finally, it must be emphasized that religions, and those who adhere to religious doctrines, may continue to advocate with utmost, sincere conviction that, by divine precepts, same-sex marriage should not be condoned. The First Amendment ensures that religious organizations and persons are given proper protection as

---

[5] Scott Jaschik, "The Supreme Court Ruling and Christian Colleges," *Inside Higher Ed.*, June 29, 2015, https://www.insidehighered.com/news/2015/06/29/will-supreme-court-decision-same-sex-marriage-challenge-or-change-christian-colleges.

[6] Laurie Goodstein and Adam Liptak, "Schools Fear Gay Marriage Ruling Could End Tax Exemptions," *New York Times*, June 24, 2015, http://www.nytimes.com/2015/06/25/us/schools-fear-impact-of-gay-marriage-ruling-on-tax-status.html?_r=1.

[7] Goodstein and Liptak, "Schools Fear Gay Marriage Ruling Could End Tax Exemptions."

[8] Bob Jones University v. United States, 461 U.S. 574 (1983), https://www.oyez.org/cases/1982/81-3. The *Bob Jones* case provides precedent and in some ways encouragement that the loss of tax-exempt status would not be the demise of Christian universities. In this case, the IRS revoked tax-exempt status over discrimination, and in 1982 the Burger-led Supreme Court upheld the decision by an 8–1 vote. While there is no doubt that losing tax exemption would create financial pressure on an institution, Bob Jones University still exists more than thirty years after this decision.

they seek to teach the principles that are so fulfilling and so central to their lives and faiths, and to their own deep aspirations to continue the family structure they have long revered.[9]

Yet his efforts did not keep Justice Clarence Thomas from noting the threat to religious liberty in his dissent.[10] Additionally, Chief Justice John Roberts in his dissent cited the solicitor general's testimony and what Roberts perceived as the looming future court battles over tax exemptions and religious institutions:

> Hard questions arise when people of faith exercise religion in ways that may be seen to conflict with the new right to same-sex marriage—when, for example, *a religious college* provides married student housing only to opposite-sex married couples, or a religious adoption agency declines to place children with same-sex married couples. Indeed, the Solicitor General candidly acknowledged that the *tax exemptions of some religious institutions would be in question if they opposed same-sex marriage.* See Tr. of Oral Arg. on Question 1, at 36–38. There is little doubt that these and similar questions will soon be before this Court. Unfortunately, people of faith can take no comfort in the treatment they receive from the majority today.[11]

Just two days after the Supreme Court ruling, Mark Oppenheimer, writer for the "Beliefs" column in the *New York Times*, published an article titled

---

[9] Obergefell v. Hodges, 556 U.S. 32 (2015).

[10] Justice Thomas writes, "Aside from undermining the political processes that protect our liberty, the majority's decision threatens the religious liberty our Nation has long sought to protect." He later states, "It [Opinion of the Court] makes only a weak gesture toward religious liberty in a single paragraph, ante, at 27." In footnote 7, Thomas writes, "Concerns about threats to religious liberty in this context are not unfounded. During the hey-day of antimiscegenation laws in this country, for instance, Virginia imposed criminal penalties on ministers who performed marriage in violation of those laws, though their religions would have permitted them to perform such ceremonies. Va. Code Ann. §20–60 (1960)."

[11] Obergefell, 556 at 28–29, emphasis added.

"Now's the Time to End Tax Exemptions for Religious Institutions."[12] In his article, Oppenheimer proposes his solution, as he writes, "Rather than try to rescue tax-exempt status for organizations that dissent from settled public policy on matters of race or sexuality, we need to take a more radical step. It's time to abolish, or greatly diminish, their tax-exempt statuses."[13] Other sources of higher education news also noted the concern that schools refusing to compromise on same-sex relationships might face challenges to their tax-exempt status at some point in the future but not immediately.[14] Political agendas have rarely had implications this important for Christian education.

The loss of tax exemptions would at a minimum mean the following increased financial hardships for Christian universities:

- They would no longer be able to issue tax-deductible receipts for gifts or trusts. This would potentially affect endowment, building campaigns, scholarships, mission trips, sports contributions, and other areas where donations are given.
- When trusts mature, the funds paid would be subject to corporate income tax.
- Investment income would become subject to corporate income tax.
- Property and sales tax and income tax on tuition would be levied.
- Lower rates on tax-exempt loans would no longer be an option.
- 403b and 401a pension plans would need to be closed and 401k plans created.

The minimal list above would force institutions to become creative. One option might be developing separate 501(c)(3) organizations to minimize the loss of tax exemptions. These organizations could be created to assist students with paying tuition. Unfortunately, such creativity would likely not help with donations to new buildings or new programs. Universities rely on generous donors to help offset start-up costs when launching new

---

[12] Mark Oppenheimer, "Now's the Time to End Tax Exemptions for Religious Institutions," http://time.com/3939143/nows-the-time-to-end-tax-exemptions-for-religious-institutions/.

[13] Ibid.

[14] Scott Jaschik, "The Supreme Court Ruling and Christian Colleges."

programs, building new facilities, or expanding land holdings. The loss of tax-exempt status would basically stifle growth in this important minority voice in higher education. Those schools not able to find additional revenue streams may struggle to stay competitive in the market of higher education.

Good reasons exist for continuing tax exemptions for Christian universities. At a time when higher education accreditation desires more diversity and lawmakers decry the high cost of education, it would be counterintuitive to eliminate the minority voice of Christian education or to drive up costs, increasing student debt. Removing tax exemptions would likely impact churches around the country, igniting fear and frustration among millions of Americans. Religious organizations do a lot of unseen good in this country, and losing tax exemptions would be detrimental to several causes of compassion.

Title VII

The Equal Employment Opportunity Commission (EEOC) enforces Title VII of the Civil Rights Act of 1964, which contains a provision making discrimination on the basis of gender illegal. Title VII noncompliance carries monetary consequences. Strong EEOC support for the LGBT movement has been clear for some time.

As Chai Feldblum stated in 2006, "There can be a conflict between religious liberty and sexual liberty, but in almost all cases the sexual liberty should win."[15] In 2010, Feldblum, who was on a mission to advance the LGBT agenda, was confirmed as commissioner of the EEOC.[16] On April 20, 2012, the EEOC issued an opinion that transgender orientation or "gender-identity" discrimination is covered by Title VII. The five-member

---

[15] Maggie Gallagher, "Banned in Boston: The coming conflict between same-sex marriage and religious liberty," *The Weekly Standard*, May 15, 2006, http://www.weekly standard.com/banned-in-boston/article/13329. The article states, "Chai Feldblum, for example, is a Georgetown law professor who refers to herself as 'part of an inner group of public-intellectual movement leaders committed to advancing LGBT equality in this country.'"

[16] Feldblum was nominated by President Barack Obama and confirmed by the Senate. She is currently in her second term, which is set to expire in 2018.

commission issued this decision without objection, and it applies to all fifty-three field offices throughout the country and binds all federal agencies and departments.[17] Shannon Minter, National Center for Lesbian Rights legal director, described the ruling by saying, "This is huge. This is a real sea change."[18] Minter correctly notes the shift in trajectory to be increasingly hostile to the religious freedom of Christian institutions to operate by their religious convictions.

More recent EEOC actions have continued pushing for LGBT protections under the Civil Rights Acts of 1964, including litigation in late 2014 and a February 3, 2015, memorandum titled, "Update on Intake and Charge Processing of Title VII Claims of Sex Discrimination Related to LGBT Status." The memo instructed that "complaints of discrimination on the basis of transgender status or gender-identity-related discrimination should be accepted under Title VII and investigated as claims of sex discrimination."[19] Applying this understanding, a July 15, 2015, EEOC decision stated, "sexual orientation is inherently a 'sex-based consideration.'"[20] According to one journalist, "While only the Supreme Court could issue a definitive ruling on the interpretation, EEOC decisions are given significant deference by federal courts."[21]

Christian universities may find some hope in the *Hosanna-Tabor Evangelical Lutheran Church and School v. EEOC* Supreme Court decision. The court decided in favor of the school, upholding the "ministerial exception."[22] Essentially, the court held that teachers who are "ministers" at religious schools do not have the protections of Title VII. Thus, schools

---

[17] Chris Geidner, "Transgender Breakthrough," *Metro Weekly*, April 23, 2012, http://www.metroweekly.com/2012/04/transgender-breakthrough/.

[18] Ibid.

[19] Chris Geidner, "The Growing Effort to Protect LGBT People from Discrimination Under the Civil Rights Act of 1964," *Buzzfeed*, February 18, 2015, http://www.buzzfeed.com/chrisgeidner/the-growing-effort-to-protect-lgbt-people -from-discriminatio.

[20] Chris Geidner, "Sexual Orientation Discrimination is Barred by Existing Law, Federal Commission Rules," *Buzzfeed*, July 16, 2016, http://www.buzzfeed.com /chrisgeidner/sexual-orientation-discrimination-is-barred-by-existing-law.

[21] Ibid.

[22] Hosanna-Tabor Evangelical Lutheran Church and School v. EEOC, 565 U.S. __ (2012), https://www.oyez.org/cases/2011/10-553.

that characterize teaching from a biblical worldview as "religious service" and demonstrate ministerial responsibilities as opposed to lay responsibilities may find relief in those positions from the EEOC or its independent federal counterpart, the National Labor Relations Board (NLRB).[23] It would, however, be difficult to justify a "ministerial exception" for every job at a Christian university.

Decades ago, the Supreme Court held that schools operated by churches to teach both religious and secular subjects are not within the NLRB's jurisdiction.[24] Having the NLRB determine which employees are clergy and which are not would "give rise to entangling church-state relationships of the kind the Religious Clauses sought to avoid."[25] This has been applied on a case-by-case basis to educational institutions of all levels.[26] Thus, the NLRB developed a test to determine if institutions possessed "substantial religious character." In trying to apply this to the University of Great Falls, the NLRB determined the Catholic institution did not possess religious character and fell under its jurisdiction.[27] The courts reversed the NLRB's findings and determined that the NLRB does not have jurisdiction if an institution holds itself out as providing a religious educational environment, organizes as a nonprofit, and has affiliation with a religious organization or reference to religion.[28] In recent cases, the NLRB has not adopted this ruling and continues to exert jurisdiction specifically at Manhattan College and Saint Xavier University and to apply the "substantial religious character" test. While the final outcome remains undetermined, Christian universities appear to be best served when they clearly differentiate themselves from secular institutions. Boldness as a Christian university rather than playing both sides of the fence will help pass the "substantial religious character" test.

---

[23] The Supreme Court, in the case of NLRB v. Catholic Bishop of Chicago, 440 U.S. 490 (1979), held that schools operated by churches to teach both religious and secular subjects are not within the NLRB's jurisdiction. *Id.*, at 503, citing Lemon v. Kurtzman, 403 U.S. 602 (1971). This has been applied on a case-by-case basis to educational institutions of all levels. *St. Joseph's College*, 282 NLRB 65 (1986).

[24] NLRB v. Catholic Bishop of Chicago, 440 U.S. 490 (1979).

[25] *Id.*, at 503, citing Lemon v. Kurtzman, 403 U.S. 602 (1971).

[26] *St. Joseph's College*, 282 NLRB 65 (1986).

[27] *Great Falls*, 331 NLRB 188 (2000).

[28] University of Great Falls v. NLRB, 278 U.S. __ (2002).

Anyone interested in Christian education should take note of the agendas the EEOC and the NLRB are pushing. If this trajectory continues, they will try to make it impossible for Christian universities to operate in accordance with their faith.

Title IX, Federal Funding, and Sexual/Transgender Orientation

Most Christian universities accept millions of dollars in federal funding in the form of Pell Grants and deferrable loans distributed to students through approved schools. Some, like Barry W. Lynn, the executive director of Americans United for Separation of Church and State, believe federal funding will likely not continue for schools with religious convictions against same-sex marriage. He says, "For starters, can federally supported educational institutions bar married same-sex couples from living together in student housing? I doubt it."[29]

Some schools could not exist without federal funding. Depending on tuition, financial aid, and students' financial situations, approximately one-fourth or more of an institution's budget may come from federal funding. Some could survive by replacing federal loans with private, low-interest, deferrable loans. Schools such as Grove City College and Hillsdale College have determined not to receive federal funding and have made other arrangements. Schools whose students have high default rates would pose greater risk. Moreover, not all schools could find willing private investors.

The most likely place of religious freedom infringement and the threatened loss of federal funding will come through the Office of Civil Rights (OCR), which operates under the US Department of Education and enforces Title IX.[30] Title IX is a portion of the United States Education

---

[29] David R. Wheeler, "Gay Marriage and the Future of Evangelical Colleges," *Atlantic*, July 14, 2015, http://www.theatlantic.com/education/archive/2015/07/evangelical-colleges-struggle-gay-marriage-ruling/398306.

[30] "The U.S. Department of Education's Office for Civil Rights enforces, among other statutes, Title IX of the Education Amendments of 1972. Title IX protects people from discrimination based on sex in education programs or activities that receive Federal financial assistance." More information online at http://www2.ed.gov/about/offices/list/ocr/docs/tix_dis.html (accessed December 22, 2015).

Amendments of 1972, which states, "No person in the United States shall, on the basis of sex, be excluded from participation in, be denied the benefits of, or be subjected to discrimination under any education program or activity receiving Federal financial assistance."[31] The major question, then, is whether Title IX covers transgender orientation. The Department of Education has already issued guidance letters stating that transgender orientation is covered under Title IX, but legal rulings on the matter conflict, once again requiring a Supreme Court resolution or adjudication.

The Office of Civil Rights, in a significant guidance document, answers the question, "How do the Title IX requirements on single-sex classes apply to transgender students?" by stating:

> All students, including transgender students and students who do not conform to sex stereotypes, are protected from sex-based discrimination under Title IX. Under Title IX, a recipient generally must treat transgender students consistent with their gender identity in all aspects of the planning, implementation, enrollment, operation, and evaluation of single-sex classes.[32]

Statements like this seem to have encouraged more schools to apply for exemptions in order to stay true to their religious beliefs, but not all courts have followed the guidance document. For instance, Judge Kim Gibson wrote in an opinion in *Johnston v. University of Pittsburgh* that Title IX "does not prohibit discrimination on the basis of ***transgender*** itself because ***transgender*** is not a protected characteristic under the statute."[33] Gibson notes that Title IX allows for sex-segregated bathrooms, locker rooms, and living spaces based on a students' natal or birth sex so long as they are comparable.[34]

Judge Gibson denied that transgender orientation was protected as a suspect classification under the Equal Protection Clause and embraced the

---

[31] For the entire text of Title IX, see http://www.justice.gov/crt/title-ix-education-amendments-1972 (accessed December 22, 2015).

[32] U.S. Department of Education Office for Civil Rights, "Questions and Answers on Title IX and Single-Sex Elementary and Secondary Classes and Extracurricular Activities," question 31, p. 35.

[33] Johnson v. Univ. of Pittsburgh, 359 U.S. 12–19 (2015). Bold and italics added.

[34] Ibid., 13. See also: 34 C.F.R. § 106.33; 34C.F.R. § 106.61; and 20 U.S.C. § 1686.

definition established by the Seventh Circuit Court of Appeals in *Ulane v. E. Airlines*, which denied that Title VII covered cases where a person was discontent with the sex into which they were born.[35] Gibson summarized the case well:

> This case presents one central question: whether a university, receiving federal funds, engages in unlawful discrimination, in violation of the United States Constitution and federal and state statutes, when it prohibits a *transgender* male student from using sex-segregated restrooms and locker rooms designated for men on a university campus. The simple answer is no.[36]

In a more recent case, Judge Robert G. Doumar rendered a similar decision. *Gavin Grimm v. Gloucester County School Board* in Virginia was decided on September 17, 2015, but now awaits appeal toward the end of January 2016, with the Obama administration backing Grimm to overturn the decision.[37] The opinion by Judge Doumar notes the previously mentioned "Guidance Document" from OCR as well as an additional letter of guidance and concluded, "The Department of Education's interpretation does not stand up to scrutiny."[38] Doumar indicates that the Department of Education must follow procedure to amend its regulations by providing

---

[35] Ulane v. E. Airlines, Inc., 742 U.S. 1081, 1085 (1984). As noted in Judge Kim R. Gibson, *Johnson*, 359 at 8, states, "The words of Title VII do not outlaw discrimination against a person who has a sexual identity disorder, i.e., a person born with a male body who believes himself to be female, or a person born with a female body who believes herself to be male; a prohibition against discrimination based on an individual's sex is not synonymous with a prohibition against discrimination based on an individual's sexual identity disorder or discontent with the sex into which they were born." In a footnote, the court recognizes that other courts have declined to follow the definition articulated in *Ulane* such as Smith v. City of Salem, Ohio, 378 U.S. 566, 573 (2004).

[36] Johnson, 359 at 1. Bold and italics added.

[37] Chris Geidner, "Federal Judge Rules That Sexual Orientation Discrimination Is Sex Discrimination," *Buzzfeed*, December 20, 2015. http://www.buzzfeed.com /chrisgeidner/federal-judge-rules-that-sexual-orientation-discriminatio. See also Chris Geidner, "Obama Administration Supports Transgender Student in Federal Appeals Court," *Buzzfeed*, October 28, 2015, http://www.buzzfeed.com/chrisgeidner /obama-administration-supports-transgender-student-in-federal.

[38] Gavin Grimm v. Gloucester County Sch. Bd., U.S. 7 (2015).

noticeandacommentperiodinaccordancewiththeAdministrativeProcedure Act.[39] The appeals court disagreed and ruled in favor of Grimm.[40]

Worthy of note, Doumar advises that sex-segregated bathrooms may in fact protect a constitutional right previously extended to prisoners, which logically should extend to students. He writes, "In protecting the privacy of the other students, the School Board is protecting a constitutional right. The Fourth Circuit has recognized that prisoners have a constitutional right to bodily privacy. *Lee v. Downs, 641 F.2d 1117, 1119 (4th Cir. 1981)*."[41]

In a case involving a high school, Kelsey Harkness writes about six girls who spoke out after "seeing their high school back down to threats that the U.S. Department of Education would strip away federal funding, and watching school officials overrule their parents."[42] These girls discussed with the school board how hard it was at fifteen and sixteen years old to change in front of women, much less a person still anatomically male, and said in a joint statement, "It is unfair to infringe upon the rights of others to accommodate one person."[43] In this particular case, OCR ruled that the school discriminated against the transgender student by forcing the student to use a separate locker room.[44]

In a far-reaching decision, Judge Dean Pregerson may have become the first federal judge to determine that sexual orientation discrimination is sex discrimination.[45] In a ruling pertaining to a lawsuit against Pepperdine University, Pregerson wrote the following:

---

[39] Ibid. Doumar notes *5 U.S.C. § 553*.

[40] Richard Fausset, "Appeals Court Favors Transgender Student in Virginia Restroom Case" *New York Times*, April 19, 2016.

[41] Grimm, U.S. 7 at 10.

[42] Kelsey Harkness, "Why These High School Girls Don't Want a Transgender Student in Their Locker Room," *Daily Signal*, December 21, 2105, http://dailysignal .com/2015/12/21/why-these-high-school-girls-dont-want-transgender-student-a-in -their-locker-room/.

[43] Ibid.

[44] OCR Case No. 05-14-1055, published by the *Chicago Tribune*, November 2, 2015, http://www.chicagotribune.com/ct-doe-report-on-district-211-20151102-htmlstory.html.

[45] Geidner, "Federal Judge Rules That Sexual Orientation Discrimination Is Sex Discrimination."

After further briefing and argument, the Court concludes that
the distinction is illusory and artificial, and that sexual orientation discrimination is not a category distinct from sex or gender
discrimination. Thus, claims of discrimination based on sexual
orientation are covered by Title VII and IX, but not as a category
of independent claims separate from sex and gender stereotype.
Rather, claims of sexual orientation discrimination are gender
stereotype or sex discrimination claims.[46]

This ruling, should it stand, would provide legal precedent for extending
Title IX and Title VII to cover transgender claims. Pregerson continued, "It
is impossible to categorically separate 'sexual-orientation discrimination'
from discrimination on the basis of sex or from gender stereotypes; to do
so would result in a false choice."[47]

With differing legal opinions and different weight given to Department
of Education guidance documents, the Supreme Court, after allowing
time for the arguments to mature, will likely make the final determination. Barring some sort of preemptive legislation, the court would have to
determine whether transgender discrimination equals sex discrimination,
how the rights of one interact with the rights of many, and whether sex
is determined by birth or internal orientation. It seems only logical that
anatomy determines gender rather than inclinations that may change during a person's lifetime. If society rejects the objective standard of anatomy
for internal inclinations of feeling, then chaos will follow. A person could
claim to be any race, any sex, a combination of sexes, or even other animals
if they felt like it.

---

[46] Haley Videckis and Layana White v. Pepperdine University. Case No. CV
15-00298 DDP (JCx), p. 12, lns. 16–28, https://assets.documentcloud.org
/documents/2648492/Pepperdine-Title-IX-Ruling.pdf. Michael Schramm believes this
ruling "could be the first step toward a radical change in the Title IX law," as in "Judge's
Ruling Against Pepperdine Win for LGBT Community," *USA Today*, December 22,
2015, http://college.usatoday.com/2015/12/22/judges-ruling-against-pepperdine/.

[47] Ibid., 15 lns. 14–15. See also Nick DeSantis, "Title IX Covers Bias Based on
Sexual Orientation, Judge Rules," *Chronicle of Higher Education*, December 22, 2015,
http://chronicle.com/blogs/ticker/title-ix-covers-bias-based-on-sexual-orientation
-judge-rules/107566.

Finally, federal funding should never be in jeopardy for Christian universities because the government issues these funds to individual citizens who choose how to use them. To tell these citizens that rightfully obtained awards cannot be used at institutions only because they teach a biblical worldview would not only violate religious freedom but also come quite close to the establishment of the religion of secular humanism. In order for students to be able to receive these funds, the school must meet certain criteria (which includes accreditation, proper protocol concerning fund distribution, and other regulations). Imposing a religious test as an additional criterion would violate the constitutional rights of the individual. Again, it is important to note that the taxpayer funds are granted to the individual through the institution and not directly to the institution. Some want to make the claim that their taxpayer dollars should not go to religious institutions, but because the funds go to individuals such concern has no legitimate foundation.

Exemptions from Title IX

Consequently, with guidance documents claiming that Title IX covers transgender orientation, many schools have applied for and received exemptions from Title IX, which has a provision that allows institutions controlled by religious organizations to waive parts of the law that conflict with religious tenets. The exception clause states, "This section shall not apply to an educational institution which is controlled by a religious organization if the application of this subsection would not be consistent with the religious tenets of such organization."[48] The Department of Education has released a list of 226 colleges that have received waivers since 1976, including twenty-one pending requests from the past year.[49] Approximately fifty-six colleges in twenty-six states collectively enrolling nearly 120,000

---

[48] This falls under number (3) Educational institutions of religious organizations with contrary religious tenets, http://www.justice.gov/crt/title-ix-education-amendments-1972 (accessed December 22, 2015).

[49] "Religious Exemptions Current and Pending (Current as of 12/14/15)," available at http://static.politico.com/1f/b8/2bb4bf5f4c1587d9c07cf2df09c3/title-ix-religious-exemptions.pdf.

students have requested exemptions since 2013.[50] It appears clear that schools controlled by a religious organization will receive an exemption, but what is not clear is whether independent Christian universities with self-perpetuating boards of trustees will be granted exemptions. These universities should also receive exemptions if they operate consistently by a trustee-adopted statement of faith, and the applications of Title IX would not be consistent with that statement.

The Human Rights Campaign (HRC), the nation's largest LGBT civil rights organization, has taken notice of the increase in exemptions and requested that the Department of Education take at least three actions.[51] These actions include

- Regularly report which educational institutions have been granted Title IX religious exemptions and the scope of the exemptions;
- Add Title IX religious exemptions as a searchable feature on College Navigator; and
- Provide the following information on individual school landing pages as a part of College Navigator:
  - When an exemption has been received;
  - The characteristics or behaviors to which the exemption applies;
  - The scope of the exemption; and
  - A statement explaining that students are still protected under all other provisions of Title IX.[52]

Responding to the HRC's request, Andrew Walker, director of policy studies for the Ethics and Religious Liberty Commission, argues, "In

---

[50] Eric Kelderman, "*How Does a College Get an Exemption from Title IX?*," *Chronicle of Higher Education,* December 21, 2015, http://chronicle.com/article/How-Does-a -College-Get-an/234674.

[51] They have released a report, http://hrc-assets.s3-website-us-east-1.amazonaws .com//files/assets/resources/Title_IX_Exemptions_Report.pdf (accessed December 21, 2015). See also http://www.hrc.org/press/hrc-calls-on-department-of-education-to -take-action-following-anti-lgb2.

[52] Sarah Warbelow and Remington Gregg, "Hidden Discrimination: Title IX Religious Exemptions Putting LGBT Students at Risk," (Washington, DC: Human Rights Campaign, 2015) 17, http://hrc-assets.s3-website-us-east-1.amazonaws.com// files/assets/resources/Title_IX_Exemptions_Report.pdf.

effect, HRC wants the Department of Education to publicly list these unsanctioned dissenters, require these institutions to confess their sins publicly, and to be held accountable for any sins committed."[53] David French comments that "these universities aren't 'seeking a license to discriminate,' they're exercising their *right* to exercise their religious faith, a right so clear that the language of Title IX doesn't even apply to these schools."[54] The HRC claims they want clarity for prospective students, but institutions like Cedarville University, where I have the privilege of serving, have clear statements in the student handbook, doctrinal statement, and bylaws, not to mention a motto that declares, "For the Word of God and the Testimony of Jesus Christ" on our landing page.[55] The HRC desires much more than clarity.

Walker continues, "In effect, HRC knows that it cannot deny religious colleges the rights to such waivers, but, in their thinking, who needs a law when you have unelected administrative bureaucracies that can unlawfully intrude and intimidate those with religious views that are found unacceptable?"[56] The HRC ultimately wants to reshape faith to accept a pro-LGBT position. They fail to understand that for true evangelical Christians supporting the LGBT movement is not possible. Submission to the authority of God's Word will always trump cultural opinion. Scripture itself states that, while the flowers fade and the grass withers, the Word of God will stand forever (see Isa 40:8).

---

[53] Andrew T. Walker, "Human Rights Campaign Calls on Christian Colleges to Repent of Their Christianity," *National Review*, December 18, 2015, http://www .nationalreview.com/article/428771/christian-colleges-religious-freedom.

[54] David French, "LGBT Lobby: How Dare Christian Colleges Exercise Their Right to Religious Liberty!" *National Review*, December 11, 2015, http://www .nationalreview.com/corner/428404/lgbt-lobby-how-dare-christian-colleges-exercise -their-right-religious-liberty-david.

[55] See www.cedarville.edu.

[56] Walker, "Humans Rights Campaign Calls on Christian Colleges to Repent of Their Christianity." See also Kelsey Harkness, "LGBT Group Calls on Government to Address 'Disturbing Trend' on Religious College Campuses." *Daily Signal*, December 21, 2015, http://dailysignal.com/2015/12/21/lgbt-group-calls-on-government-to -address-disturbing-trend-on-religious-college-campuses/.

Accreditation

The biggest fear and the fatal blow for all Christian universities would be a loss of accreditation. Potential students would not spend money on schools without accreditation because credits will not transfer, certifications for areas like nursing or education would not be possible, and most graduate schools will not accept an unaccredited degree. Loss of accreditation means a loss of students and the end of a university. However, it would be difficult for accreditors who value diversity to stamp out the minority voice of a biblical worldview in higher education. Yet this would be more likely if the government combined regional accreditors into a unified national accreditation agency operated by the Department of Education. Combining regional accreditors would be marketed under the guise of efficiency, quality control, and consistency, but would place accreditation too close to the political process and open the door for sweeping and frequent partisan changes. Christian education supporters should oppose any attempts to unify accreditation at the national level.

A more likely concern comes from discipline-specific accreditation, which can be more liberal, depending on the field of study. For example, if those who accredit schools of education, psychology, or social work determined to enforce embracing same-sex relationships and transgender orientation, then Christian universities would have to decide whether to keep those majors. Having an unaccredited major would produce unemployable graduates. Such moves by discipline-specific accreditors would do more harm than good as students at Christian universities see their vocation as a calling more than an occupation. Additionally, if these fields become increasingly hostile to a biblical worldview, people of faith may pursue other vocations, leaving a shortage of skilled workers in important societal services.

The most immediate challenge to accreditation will come from a more liberal regional accreditor applying pressure to a school within that particular region. This has already occurred at Gordon College in Massachusetts. President Michael Lindsay signed a letter asking President Obama to include religious exemptions in his executive order banning sexual orientation discrimination in federal contracting. The reaction to this modest request was swift. The Lynn public schools refused to receive

Gordon's education students, and the New England Association of Schools of Colleges (NEASC) met to determine whether Gordon's actions violated its standards for accreditation.[57] The NEASC gave Gordon one year to review its policy on homosexuality and respond.[58] The two issued a joint statement on April 25, 2015, which referenced a report outlining fourteen initiatives the institution "plans to take to further enhance its support for the LGBTQ student."[59]

David French, attorney and staff writer for the *National Review*, sees this result as a win for Gordon College, but biblical scholar Robert Gagnon sees reason for concern: "Let us not be naïve here. The usual effect (if not purpose) of such measures is to inhibit vigorous critique of homosexual practice. They generally replace calls to repentance (now deemed insensitive at best, bullying at worst) with 'dialogue' until such time as the new view can enforce intolerance."[60] Christians must join Gordon College in fighting for religious liberty if for no other reason than to deter the increasing infringement upon the right of religious expression.

Peter Conn, an English professor at the University of Pennsylvania who has served as a member of an accreditation visit team, calls for a stop to accrediting religious colleges altogether. He writes, "I want to raise a different and, in my view, far more important objection to accreditation as codified and practiced now. By awarding accreditation to religious colleges, the process confers legitimacy on institutions that systematically

---

[57] David French, "Gordon College Keeps Its Faith and Its Accreditation," *National Review*, March 1, 2015, http://www.nationalreview.com/article/417788 /gordon-college-keeps-its-faith-and-its-accreditation-david-french.

[58] Mary Moore, "Accreditation Board Gives Gordon College a Year to Review Policy on Homosexuality," *Boston Business Journal*, September 25, 2014, http:// www.bizjournals.com/boston/news/2014/09/25/accreditation-board-gives-gordon -college-a-year-to.html.

[59] For the statement, see https://cihe.neasc.org/sites/cihe.neasc.org/files /downloads/Public_Statement/Joint_Statement_by_Gordon_College_and_CIHE.pdf.

[60] Robert A. J. Gagnon, "Gordon College Wins—and Loses?," *First Things*, May 5, 2015, http://www.firstthings.com/web-exclusives/2015/05/gordon-college-winsand -loses. Gordon College also provides further explanation on their website with two documents answering questions. Those pages can be found here: http://www.gordon .edu/faqcommunityrelations and http://www.gordon.edu/faqworkinggroup (accessed December 28, 2015).

undermine the most fundamental purposes of higher education."[61] He continues: "Skeptical and unfettered inquiry is the hallmark of American teaching and research. However, such inquiry cannot flourish—in many cases, cannot even survive—inside institutions that erect religious tests for truth. The contradiction is obvious."[62] The problem, according to Conn, comes when Christian universities have confessions of faith that force faculty members to consent "to such scientifically preposterous propositions as, for example, that God created Adam and Eve, who were real historical figures and who are the actual ancestors of all humanity."[63] Others have asked whether "Christian college" is an oxymoron.[64]

Conn has been taken to task over his comments. Baylor University professor Alan Jacobs states, "It would take me another ten thousand words to exhaustively detail Conn's errors of commission and omission."[65] It seems Peter Conn and those of his brand of higher education desire toleration for all but the Christian worldview. Further, instead of judging students by learning and outcomes, there is a worldview test where Conn's scientific or humanistic view must survive to the exclusion of a biblical worldview—so much for freedom of inquiry. Writing at *First Things*, Joseph Knippenberg says, "It would also be helpful for Professor Conn to become acquainted with the history of American higher education, so that he could learn how much of our higher learning depends upon institutions with religious roots."[66] Stanton Jones from Wheaton College leveled many critiques at the article, including his observation "that all knowing starts somewhere in faith."[67] It

---

[61] Peter Conn, "The Great Accreditation Farce," *Chronicle of Higher Education*, June 30, 2014, http://chronicle.com/article/The-Great-Accreditation-Farce/147425/.

[62] Ibid.

[63] Ibid.

[64] Steven Conn, "Is 'Christian College' an Oxymoron?," *Huffington Post*, July 2, 2014, http://www.huffingtonpost.com/steven-conn/is-christian-college-an-o_b_5551355.html.

[65] Alan Jacobs, "An Academic Farce," *Text Patterns*, July 3, 2014, http://text-patterns.thenewatlantis.com/2014/07/an-academic-farce.html.

[66] Joseph Knippenberg, "Accreditation and Religious Colleges," *First Things*, July 1, 2014, http://www.firstthings.com/blogs/firstthoughts/2014/06/accreditation-and-religious-colleges.

[67] Stanton L. Jones, "All Knowledge Starts Somewhere in Faith," *Chronicle of Higher Education*, July 3, 2014, http://chronicle.com/blogs/conversation/2014/07/03/all-knowledge-starts-somewhere-in-faith.

seems that secular humanists find their presuppositions so irrefutable that
they fail to recognize them as presuppositions and then label people of faith
who operate from a different set of presuppositions as ignorant and closed-
minded. If this trend continues, then expect to see accreditation agencies
issue more and more challenges against Christian universities.

Affordable Care Act, Student Housing, NCAA, and Other Challenges

Other challenges to religious liberty have arisen, such as the contraception mandate in the Affordable Care Act. The Green family, who owns
and operates more than five hundred Hobby Lobby stores with about
13,000 employees, sued the US government over the Patient Protection
and Affordable Care Act's mandate that required them to cover certain
types of contraceptive methods that may end life after conception, violating the free exercise of the Green's religious beliefs. The Supreme Court
decided 5–4 that Congress intended the Religious Freedom Restoration
Act to apply to corporations, and thus provided protection against the
contraception mandate and upheld religious liberty.[68]

The Affordable Care Act provides an accommodation to religious nonprofit organizations, but many believe the accommodation is insufficient
and have filed lawsuits.[69] The Supreme Court agreed on November 6, 2015,
to hear the case of the *Little Sisters of the Poor v. Burwell*. A total of seven
plaintiffs exist for this case, including Geneva College, Southern Nazarene
University, and East Texas Baptist University.[70] I suspect the challenges will

---

[68] Burwell v. Hobby Lobby Stores, 573 U.S. __ (2014), https://www.oyez.org/cases/2013/13-354.

[69] Many court cases have arisen. This press release from Houston Baptist
University discusses three institutions prepared to fight: "Three Religious
Institutions Appeal to Supreme Court, Say They Will Fight to Protect Their
Faith," July 8, 2015, https://www.hbu.edu/News-and-Events/2015/11/17/Three
-Religious-Institutions-Appeal-to-Supreme-Court-Say-They-Will-Fight-to-Protect
-Their-Faith.

[70] Emma Green, "The Little Sisters of the Poor Are Headed to the Supreme Court,"
Atlantic, November 6, 2015, http://www.theatlantic.com/politics/archive/2015/11
/the-little-sisters-of-the-poor-are-headed-to-the-supreme-court/414729/. The number
of and nuances of the legal struggles between Christian universities and the Affordable

only broaden beyond abortifacient drugs to include insurance coverage for same-sex spouses, euthanasia, and, with further scientific advances, genetic modification. An increasingly nationalized system of health-care forces the government to entangle itself in medical decisions with ethical and religious implications.

Additionally, Christian universities have and will continue to face LGBT housing challenges. In 2014, George Fox University dealt with this issue when a transgender student, born anatomically female but later recognized by the state of Oregon as a male, wanted to live with male friends. The university offered her single-person housing that she found unacceptable. Under threat of a Title IX filing, George Fox applied for and received a Title IX exemption on May 23, 2014. But the Justice Department then began looking into whether George Fox's transgender policy violated non-discrimination clauses in the federal housing law.[71]

For married housing, schools must have clear guidelines. Even then they may face challenges for barring legally married same-sex couples from living in married housing. Responding to this issue, Barry Lynn of the Americans for Separation of Church and State stated, "I think even now that would be on the edge of the indefensible."[72] I disagree with Lynn. Private schools have the right to establish community covenants and expectations for campus housing voluntarily agreed to by those enrolling. Those policies must be well written, clear, consistently enforced, and prominent in the recruiting and admissions process to minimize legal challenges and liability.

Care Act cannot be covered here, but the Becket Fund for Religious Liberty has many helpful resources on its website, http://www.becketfund.org/hhsinformationcentral / for information on several cases related to the HHS mandate.

[71] Joshua Hunt and Richard Perez-Pena, "Housing Dispute Puts Quaker University at Front of Fight Over Transgender Issues," *New York Times*, July 24, 2014, http://www.nytimes.com/2014/07/25/us/transgender-student-fights-for-housing-rights-at -george-fox-university.html.

[72] Lauretta Brown, "Barry Lynn: Christian College Denying Married Housing to Same-Sex Couples 'Would be on the Edge of Indefensible,'" *CNSNews*, July 7, 2015, http://www.cnsnews.com/news/article/lauretta-brown/barry-lynn-christian-college -denying-married-housing-same-sex-couples. Barry Lynn serves as the executive director of Americans United for Separation of Church and State.

For Christian universities, the National Collegiate Athletic Association may present yet another challenge to religious liberty. The NCAA or individual conferences could choose to bar schools that do not embrace the LGBT agenda from participating.[73] With lucrative scholarships available, I suspect it is only a matter of time until a mediocre male athlete declares himself a female in order to earn a scholarship to attend a university. Whether the transgender inclination is sincere or not, questions will be raised. Will Christian universities be forced to play teams with transgender athletes? How will Christian universities handle the preoperative transgender fan that desires to use a restroom opposite birth sex, and will "public accommodation" apply in such instances?

University administrators must also consider "public accommodation" laws when making decisions on selling tickets, concessions, and other auxiliary enterprises that could increasingly place the institution in the same category as restaurants and hotels rather than private nonprofits. Two courts in California have considered the issue of whether public accommodation laws apply to Christian schools.[74] In one of these, a preoperative anatomical male who indicated female sex on an application sued California Baptist University for dismissing him based on false information on his application. While California Baptist won the case, the court ruled that certain portions of its operation were "business establishments" and fell under the California civil rights act.[75] As a result, California Baptist

---

[73] NCAA President Mark Emmert criticized Indiana's Religious Freedom Restoration Act saying, "[Inclusion and diversity] are values that are fundamental to what college athletics are all about and what higher education is all about." He continued, "For us personally in the NCAA, this is a big deal. We're very proud of the inclusive environment in our office. We're very proud of the environment that we've created here and we don't want to lose that. We don't want to have it put at risk." Cindy Boren, "NCAA's Mark Emmert on Indiana anti-gay law and Final Four: 'This is a very big deal,'" *Washington Post*, March 30, 2015, https://www.washingtonpost .com/news/early-lead/wp/2015/03/30/ncaas-mark-emmert-on-indiana-anti-gay -law-and-final-four-this-is-a-very-big-deal/. If this is how the NCAA feels about a city with religious freedom protections, then it is only a matter of time until confrontation occurs with a university banning LGBT activity.

[74] Doe v. California Lutheran High School Ass'n, 170 Cal. App.4th 828, 88 Cal. Rptr.3d 475 (2009) and Cabading v. California Baptist University, Case No. RIC 1302245 (Cal. Sup. Ct., Co. of Riverside, July 11, 2014).

[75] *Cabading* at 1–2.

could not restrict access to public areas like its restaurant, theater, and library, while it could establish restrictions in the admissions process.

Finally, challenges like walking with students through sexual temptations have become more difficult in the current sexual climate. Christian universities desire to walk alongside students struggling with temptation. Historically, avoiding sexual temptation involved males and females living in separate dorms. The sexual revolution and a sexually charged society have led to more frequent cases of students struggling with same-sex attraction. These students live immersed among temptation. If you isolate someone struggling against temptation by moving him or her out of a same-sex dormitory, then you run the risk of stigmatizing the individual with unequal punishment, yet alleviating the temptation may be the best action for spiritual health. Further, chapel speakers calling same-sex activity sinful can be perceived as creating a hostile environment even if the sin is treated equally with other sins like pornography, lust, adultery, or fornication. The complexity of LGBT issues creates challenges for even the best Christian institutions desiring to serve their students well.

Protecting Religious Liberty

Christian universities must work at the state and federal levels to protect religious liberty. The Religious Freedom Restoration Act (RFRA) enacted in 1993 by bipartisan votes in Congress provides good protection for religious liberty at the federal level.[76] We must, therefore, work to keep RFRA strong at the federal and state levels, both among the twenty-one states with RFRA laws and among those that need similar legislation. Additionally, universities should develop relationships with state politicians and local communities to encourage religious liberty protections.

The Christian Legal Society and the Ethics and Religious Liberty Commission have websites with resources to help Christian schools and churches review policies and procedures to minimize legal liabilities.[77]

---

[76] 42 U.S.C. §2000bb-1.

[77] For more information, see http://clsnet.org/school-guidance and https://erlc .com/article/protecting-your-church-against-sexual-orientation-and-gender-identity -lawsu (accessed December 28, 2015).

The Bill of Rights Institute provides brief reviews of Supreme Court cases affecting religious liberty.[78] Because state and local regulations differ, each institution must prepare differently and should consult legal counsel on institutionally specific circumstances. However, general lists can be helpful in thinking through preparation. Toward that end, I offer the following steps that we have and continue to take at Cedarville University. This list is neither exhaustive nor inerrant, but I hope you will find it helpful.

Guiding Documents

Bylaws

- Reviewed and clarified statements on LGBT issues. We have the following:
  - "We uphold God's design for human sexuality as clearly revealed in His Word and enforce policies that support this biblical teaching. God created humans, male and female, in His image. Human life, sexual identity and roles are aspects of God's creative design. From creation marriage is a covenant between a man and a woman. The advocacy for or act of homosexuality, transgender expression, or alteration of one's birth gender identity through medical transition are prohibited. (Genesis 1:26–28; 2:18–25; Romans 1:18–32; 1 Corinthians 6:9–20)."
- Ensured in bylaws that doctrinal and moral beliefs are based on Scripture.
- Added a statement on religious liberty:
  - "The University reserves the right to make decisions and policies that permit it to carry out its mission consistent with Biblical principles and religious freedom, as is its right and provided for under the United States Constitution."
- Incorporated a statement in the bylaws clearly articulating that the Board of Trustees is the final authority for interpretation of doctrinal matters.

---

[78] See https://billofrightsinstitute.org/cases/ for information (accessed December 28, 2015).

Statement of Faith

- Included positive statements on our beliefs of gender and marriage:
  - "God created humans, male and female, in His image. Human life, sexual identity and roles are aspects of God's creative design. From creation, marriage is a covenant between a man and a woman that should be marked by sexual purity, by sacrificial male leadership, and by recognizing the divine blessing of children, including preborn children."[79]
- All Cedarville University employees and members of the Board of Trustees are required to affirm the doctrinal statement each year.

Mission Statement

- Made sure our mission statement adequately communicates our religious commitment:
  - "Cedarville University is a Christ-centered learning community equipping students for lifelong leadership and service through an education marked by excellence and grounded in biblical truth."[80]

Policies, Procedures, and Handbooks

- Added the following paragraph to all policies and procedures to point back to our guiding documents and prevent us from having multiple changes anytime a guiding document was amended:
  - "This policy/document should be viewed in light of Cedarville University's educational mission and theological distinctives. All applications of this policy are governed by the University's Bylaws, Doctrinal Statement and Statements of Standards and Conduct as adopted and amended by the University's Board of Trustees as the final interpretive authority on these matters. Any discrepancies should be resolved in favor of these controlling documents of the University, which reserves the

---

[79] Article 4 of the doctrinal statement, online at https://www.cedarville.edu /About/Doctrinal-Statement.aspx (accessed January 7, 2016).

[80] Our mission and additional portrait statements may be found at: http://www .cedarville.edu/About/Mission.aspx (accessed January 7, 2016).

right to make decisions that permit it to carry out its mission consistent with biblical principles."

Employment Policies

- Reviewed our religious employment criteria, including the annual affirmation of the doctrinal statement, community covenants, and church membership, making sure it clearly stipulates that failure to comply constitutes grounds for termination.
- Reviewed job descriptions to make sure they accurately and clearly delineate the spiritual and ministerial components of the job.
- Included a statement on Christian resolutions of disputes, including Matthew 18, 1 Corinthians 6, and Christian arbitration.
- Reviewed policies for explaining the importance of repentance and the lack of repentance in violations, which may explain different punishment for similar offenses.

Education, Spiritual Growth, and Teaching from a Biblical Worldview

- Reviewed class descriptions to accurately communicate education from a biblical worldview.
- Made sure our faculty handbook clearly indicates the requirement of biblical integration in the classroom:
  - "In addition to professional competencies, teaching skills, scholarly activities, and service to the University and the community, the faculty member will be evaluated in his or her progress toward an understanding of and commitment to the integration of Scripture and knowledge which is intended to lead to building up students in the Christian faith and developing Christian character. Cedarville University faculty members must be involved in an ongoing process of deepening their knowledge and the understanding of Scripture with its implications for their fields of study."
- Communicate clearly about our Center for Biblical Integration and its role in promoting biblical integration throughout curriculum, teaching, and research.
- Require an integration paper as part of tenure- and nontenure-track evaluation, which includes the following:

- "The faculty member's Christian worldview (e.g., beliefs concerning God, creation, man, and epistemology) and the correlation between Scripture or scriptural principles and his or her discipline."
- "The faculty member's role in and commitment to Christian higher education, the relationship between faith and practice as demonstrated in teaching philosophy and lifestyle, and the goals and objectives for communicating these beliefs in the classroom."

- Ensured the mandatory Bible minor for every undergraduate major is included as a Cedarville distinctive in marketing materials.
- Ensured that chapel five days a week focused on spiritual development for every undergraduate full-time student is included as a Cedarville distinctive in marketing materials.
- Ensured our student life core values of Love God, Love Others, Integrity in Conduct, and Excellence in Effort are included as a Cedarville distinctive in marketing materials.

Facilities

- Reviewed facility use policy to clarify that only uses consistent with our mission and guiding documents are allowed:
  - "Cedarville University is a Christ-centered learning community equipping students for lifelong leadership and service through an education marked by excellence and grounded in biblical truth. Consistent with this mission, all facility uses— including non-University activities held on campus—must align with and uphold the University's Community Covenant as well as the community lifestyle guidelines outlined in The Cedarville Experience Student Handbook, and are not permitted for persons or groups who publicly hold, advocate or engage in beliefs or practices that contradict the University's governing documents, including the Doctrinal Statement and statements of Standards of Conduct, as determined by the University. The University reserves the right to make appropriate application of its policies that permit it to carry out its mission consistent with Biblical principles."

- Eliminated renting facilities to outside constituents for weddings while allowing for executive leadership to approve rare exceptions for internal constituents.
- Reviewed single housing policies for clarity on transgender issues and married student housing for clarity on same-sex issues.
- Clarified that room guests in residence hall are for same birth gender or anatomical gender only.

Student Handbook: *The Cedarville Experience*

- Reviewed for consistency and clarity.
- The following statement on same-sex behavior is in "The Cedarville Experience":
  - "Consistent with our desire to teach and model a biblical approach to sex, the University prohibits same-sex dating behaviors and public advocacy for the position that sex outside of a biblically defined marriage is morally acceptable. We seek to help students who face all types of sexual temptation, encouraging single students to live chaste, celibate lives, and encouraging married students to be faithful to their marriage and to their spouse."[81]
- The following statement on transgender orientation or advocacy is in "The Cedarville Experience":
  - "Consistent with our commitment to God's design for gender identity, the public advocacy for or act of altering one's original gender identity through medical transition or transgender expression is prohibited. This commitment to gender identity also applies to—but is not limited to—the use of bathrooms, locker rooms, student housing, and participating in gender-specific University groups, clubs, and organizations."[82]
- In "The Cedarville Experience" we explain "Biblical Principles that Influence Our Approach to Discipline," how we handle

---

[81] The student handbook can be viewed online at http://publications.cedarville .edu/brochures/studentlife/studenthandbook/ (accessed January 7, 2016).

[82] Ibid.

students voluntarily seeking help, and the levels of discipline. This allows those operating outside a biblical worldview to understand why we might give grace resulting in two different penalties for similar offenses based on whether the student is repentant or not.

Marketing, Recruiting, and Admissions

- Reviewed marketing and admissions materials to make sure we emphasize the religious character of our education.
    - Returned to our historic tagline of "for the Word of God and the Testimony of Jesus Christ," which more clearly expressed our mission and distinguishes us from secular institutions.
    - Adopted a clearer Christian marketing emphasis ("Be Bold: Pursue Your Passion. Proclaim Christ").
- Clarified statements on our application for admission to request gender at birth.
- Require a written testimony for each applicant and an explanation of how one becomes a believer in Jesus Christ.
- Require applicants affirm that they agree to honor the Cedarville Covenant and Community Lifestyle Guidelines.
- Require applicants to review the university doctrinal statement and agree to respect the teachings of the university.

NCAA Athletics

- Reviewed our NCAA and athletic policies and procedures for clarity and consistency.
- Review conference policies and bring the issue up within the conference to allow for faith-based institutions to operate within beliefs.

On-Campus Communications

- Sent an email after the Supreme Court decision with a commitment to stand by our biblical beliefs.
- Addressed the biblical view of marriage in our all faculty/staff meetings, clearly articulating the university's position.

- Addressed the biblical view of marriage in a student chapel, clearly articulating the university's position and having it recorded and placed online for clear communication to potential students.

In addition to reviewing policies, every Christian university should build a consensus determined to stand for a biblical worldview. I encourage trustees, administrators, donors, alumni, and friends of various institutions to have conversations about the following suggestions to distinguish yourself from secular institutions and clearly identify your Christian mission.

Faculty and Staff Affirm the Guiding Documents

Requiring faculty and staff members to affirm the doctrinal statement, community covenants, and church membership on an annual basis will help both to set the institution apart from secular institutions and to ensure a biblical worldview across all disciplines. If faculty and staff do not affirm the doctrinal statements, then one can assume that these statements will simply become historic or guiding documents not supported in classroom content. For consistent Christian education, institutions need teachers who embrace the doctrinal and moral commitments of the school and passionately communicate those truths to students. This can be done through yearly faculty reviews in the academic division and electronically by the human resource department for staff members.

Two objections usually arise. First, some do not like signing a statement. Second, some will argue you cannot find qualified applicants. Neither of those objections is valid. In response to the first, employment is voluntary, and it would be counterintuitive for an institution to hire employees who do not support their core beliefs. Second, it may require more work to find qualified applicants, but they exist, and it is worth it. A college or university's leadership might begin this journey by allowing its faculty and staff to discuss how they think the institution could distinguish and maintain its Christian identity. They could start with a modified doctrinal statement that includes only essential elements in order to minimize problems. Or they could begin with the executive leadership and Bible department. If the executive leadership and Bible department cannot affirm the doctrinal statement, then the university really does not have one.

Biblical Worldview and a Bible Minor

If the National Labor Relations Board came to your university to apply the "substantial religious character" test, what would they determine? What distinguishes Christian university education from secular education? The answer must be that we teach from a biblical worldview and that we teach the Bible as God's authoritative Word. While we offer similar classes as secular institutions and reach similar outcomes as required by our regional accreditors, we achieve those outcomes in a distinctive way. A Christian university's faculty handbook, its hiring documents, its faculty reviews, and even its tenure and nontenure evaluation process all should ensure that every faculty member seeks to incorporate a biblical worldview in discipline-specific material. Such things will help to establish a substantive difference between a Christian university and everything else.

Most Christian universities require at least Old Testament and New Testament, but even secular schools offer those as elective literature classes, though taught from a critical viewpoint. Christian universities must articulate the difference—they affirm the authority of Scripture as more than mere literature, and they teach the text expecting life change. By requiring more, like a fifteen-hour Bible minor for every undergraduate degree, Christian universities can further distinguish themselves from secular institutions. These three classes could replace electives in degree programs or be added to degree programs. Some areas may push back and question whether this will hurt enrollment, but the students enrolling know they are coming to a distinctively Christian institution. Making that distinctive more apparent may actually improve recruiting efforts. A Bible minor should be a selling point and not a detriment. Additionally, it provides three more classes for nine hours additional revenue per student at institutions not on block pricing. Most importantly it equips students to live for Christ and allows Christian universities to accomplish their mission of equipping the next generation to glorify God wherever he places them.

Make Chapel Vibrant, Discipleship Focused, and Life Changing

We require chapel five days a week for our students, and it consistently ranks as the one thing to never change from current students and alumni. No matter how frequent a school's chapel services are, Christian universities must make sure that chapels focus on spiritual growth and move away from offering credit for cultural events. Cultural appreciation can come from class requirements. Chapel should consist of passionate preaching of the Scripture or gospel-centered testimonies that call students to live radically for Christ. I believe that chapel is the heartbeat of a Christian university, and that it reflects the values of an institution. Furthermore, vibrant chapels archived online provide a school with a recruiting tool and another way to demonstrate that it is a Christian university in deed and not only in name.

Requiring a Profession of Faith from Students

Not all Christian universities require a profession of faith. Some Christian universities intentionally focus on evangelism and admit non-Christians for that reason. I respect those intentional decisions, but I encourage Christian universities to focus on discipleship, too. The environment, the classroom experience, the depth of the discussion, even the class material presented changes depending on whether the students profess to be believers or not. By requiring a statement of faith, the school creates an intense community of discipleship to train the next generation.

If an institution currently does not require a profession of faith because of enrollment pressure, I encourage it to intentionally discuss whether it wants to focus on evangelism or discipleship in the long term. If discipleship, then a school should begin with Bible-related majors and work to build consensus on moving broader. In these times of enrollment struggles, I do not promote sudden changes unless absolutely necessary. Legally speaking, requiring a profession of faith clearly communicates the religious nature of an institution, limits the type of student it attracts, and differentiates the institution from a secular university.

Conclusion

Over the coming years the United States will see a major shift in the land-scape of religious education. Schools will either determine to stand firm or to compromise with culture. Either way, the impact will be far reaching. "According to the U.S. Department of Education's National Center for Education Statistics, there are approximately 29,000 religiously-affiliated pre-schools, elementary schools and high schools in the United States. In addition, there are more than 1,700 religiously-affiliated colleges and universities in our country, the majority of which hold to religious traditions that celebrate sexual intimacy within the bonds of marriage between one man and one woman."[83] These schools must decide, as in the days of Joshua (Josh 24:15), whom they will serve. If culture is king, then they will compromise. But if Jesus is Lord, then they will demonstrate compassionate conviction no matter the consequences.

Gone are the days when an educational institution could identify as Christian in order to gain a marketing advantage, fulfill a niche in the educational sector, or increase community relations. In this age, operating under biblical authority, standing for the biblical view of marriage, and implementing consistent biblical policies across the campus will likely result in legal entanglements. While some may fear the extinction of the Christian university, we have reason for hope. Our hope rests in the gospel of Jesus Christ, and the hope for Christian education is that we will in unison refuse to render unto Caesar that which belongs to God. If we stand against the logic of the day and in the face of popular opinion with a firm conviction upon the Word of God, then we will be universities of light, shining brightly on a hill. We have a unique opportunity to clearly articulate a biblical worldview. Let's be found faithful. As for me and my university, we will serve the Lord.

---

[83] Samuel W. Oliver, "The Future of the Christian University: It's Going to Be an Issue," *First Things*, July 2, 2015, http://www.firstthings.com/web-exclusives/2015/07 /the-future-of-the-christian-university.

CHAPTER 10

INTERNATIONAL LAW, RELIGIOUS FREEDOM, AND APOSTASY LAWS IN MAJORITY-MUSLIM COUNTRIES

Travis Wussow

B y nearly any measure, 2015 was the worst year in generations to be a Christian around the globe. Religious liberty is in a precarious place in the United States, of course, but that situation, serious though it is, pales in comparison to the plight of our brothers and sisters around the world. As the world is coming to recognize, the Islamic State has been carrying out a genocide against Christians, Yazidis, and other religious minorities in Iraq and Syria. Christians are routinely subjected to mob violence with impunity and state-sanctioned prosecutions for blasphemy. Converts to Christianity from Islam face criminal prosecution or honor violence around the world, even in the West.

When we look at the Middle East today, whether the problem is genocide or ethnic cleansing of a particular religious group or sectarian violence between Sunni and Shia Muslims, one of the fundamental problems is a lack of religious liberty, a deficit of pluralism. There are many other drivers of the violence and sectarianism, from politics to natural resource distribution to tribalism. But we should not make the mistake of believing that these other issues are the only issues—there is, in fact, a religious dimension to this problem.

This essay explores these questions: What does international law have to say about the lack of religious liberty in many parts of the world? What can Christians in the United States or other parts of the West do to help our brothers and sisters in Christ around the world? What hope is there for the growth of religious liberty in the Middle East and North Africa?

To answer these questions, this essay will provide a brief survey of how international law and international treaty practice works, walk through the history of international protections for religious liberty, and flesh out the current international legal obligations some states have entered into with respect to religious liberty. Armed with this information, the essay will examine a case study: apostasy and blasphemy laws in majority-Muslim societies. The essay will conclude with recommendations for moving forward.

But before diving in to a background on international law, a brief comment on the theory of international relations is in order. To borrow E. H. Carr's framework, one way of understanding the debate is to compare realists and utopians.

Jack Goldsmith and Eric Posner epitomize the realist pole of the debate over the role of international law in the world. Their principle argument is that states are not—as a matter of empirical fact—constrained in any way by international law. Realists argue, working from economic game theory, that states always behave according to self-interest and will violate international law when it fits their interests. International law, then, does not serve as a constraint on state power but rather represents the instances where two or more states' interests happen to coincide.[1] In other words, it is power, not law, that serves as the primary constraint on state action. States only obey international law when they are forced to do so by power. Because law per se does not organize state behavior, material inducement—sanctions, monetary assistance, use of force—are the only ways to control state action.

Those on the other side of the debate, the utopians, believe in the power of persuasion on the international level. In 1939, Carr defined utopian thinking in this way: "Reason could determine what were the universally valid moral laws; and the assumption was made that, once these laws were determined, human beings would conform to them just as matter conformed to the physical laws of nature. Enlightenment was the royal road to the millennium."[2]

According to modern utopians, persuasion is the necessary ingredient for states to conform to international norms on human rights. President Barack Obama's speech to the United Nations in September 2015 illustrates this point of view well. President Obama argued that the way to defeat Daesh[3] is with "better ideas": "This means defeating their ideology. Ideologies are not defeated with guns. They are defeated by better ideas—a more attractive and compelling vision."[4] That utopian foreign policy was on the rise at the same time that Daesh rose from the ashes of the Arab Spring to perpetuate a genocide against Yazidis, Christians, and

---

[1] Jack L. Goldsmith and Eric A. Posner, *The Limits of International Law* (Oxford: Oxford University Press, 2005).

[2] E. H. Carr, *The Twenty Years' Crisis* (London: Palgrave Macmillan, 2001), 25.

[3] *Daesh* is the Arabic term for the terrorist organization known as the Islamic State, ISIS, or ISIL. At the time of this writing, the usage of *Daesh* is on the rise, so I use it here.

[4] Gardiner Harris and Eric Schmitt, "Obama's Call at U.N. to Fight ISIS with Ideas Is Largely Seen as Futile," *New York Times*, September 29, 2015, http://www.nytimes.com/2015/09/30/world/middleeast/at-the-un-obama-states-his-case-for-fighting-isis-with-ideas.html; President Barack Obama, remarks by President Obama at the Leaders' Summit on Countering ISIL and Violent Extremism, September 29, 2015, https://www.whitehouse.gov/the-press-office/2015/09/29/remarks-president-obama-leaders-summit-countering-isil-and-violent.

other religious minorities will surely be remembered as one of history's great tragic ironies.[5]

Two other perspectives, which sit somewhere between the two poles, are worth mentioning. The first is Christian realism, developed by Reinhold Niebuhr.[6] The foundation of Christian realism is a recognition of the depravity of humankind. But like Posner's realism, the perspective emphasizes the limitation that international law can play in constraining the "law of man." Its focus is therefore also on material inducement and emphasizes the role of the state over the role of the church in making peace.

The last perspective, put forward by Ryan Goodman and Derek Jinks, is called acculturation. Acculturation examines the relationship of a state actor to a group of states or to the "wider cultural environment."[7] An acculturation model does not preclude the use of material inducement and emphasizes the role that the international community as a whole has on state behavior. Indeed, acculturation holds that what we might think of as social factors—networks, relationships, even friendships—play a role in developing state behavior over time.

Before moving on to the question of how international law works, let us remember, however, that Christians are, or at least ought to be, utopians in a sense. It is true that sin has ravaged our fallen world, that humankind's depravity gives rise to evil that must be stopped and will not be persuaded. But let us not allow this realist vision of the world to cloud our hope for the world that is yet to come. Isaiah gives us this vision of the "latter days":

> He will settle disputes among the nations
>   and provide arbitration for many peoples.

---

[5] The American response focused in part on freedom of information, like Twitter accounts and Cold War-style pirate radio stations, ultimately creating a power vacuum that allowed Russia to fill the power void in the Syrian Civil War in late 2015. As of this writing in early 2016, Syria and Iraq are still a long way away from peace, but what seems certain is that the US will not be the leader or facilitator of any peace that ultimately comes.

[6] See Reinhold Niebuhr, *The Children of Light and the Children of Darkness: A Vindication of Democracy and a Critique of Its Traditional Defense*, 8th ed. (Chicago: University of Chicago Press, 2011).

[7] Ryan Goodman and Derek Jinks, *Socializing States: Promoting Human Rights Through International Law* (Oxford: Oxford University Press, 2013), 26.

> They will turn their swords into plows
>> and their spears into pruning knives.
> Nations will not take up the sword against other nations,
>> and they will never again train for war. (Isa 2:4)

These verses have found their way onto a monument outside the United Nations building in New York City. Surely our hope cannot be found in the UN, but our hope can be found in the promise that the kingdom is coming. We surely know that the kingdom is not fully here yet. But make no mistake: it is coming.

And so as we turn to discuss international law and its role in defining and protecting religious liberty, let us remember that while it is the work of God to bring peace on earth, the kingdom is already here, although not yet fully.

How Does International Law Work?

Before discussing the way in which international law addresses religious liberty, a broad overview of international law—and specifically international human rights law—is in order.

Although there are other sources of international law, this discussion will focus on *express written agreements* between two or more states.[8] These written agreements can be referred to as treaties, conventions, or other terms, but the underlying point is that two or more states came together to agree on something, reduced the agreement to writing, and signed the writing.

Some written agreements can give rise to international nonstate bodies that then have a role in enforcing, reporting, and developing further the international norms that were the subject of the underlying treaty.

---

[8] The other two categories are *customary international law* and *soft law.* Customary international law is the set of state practice that develops over time and eventually ossifies into legal obligation. The best example of this is international maritime law, much of which has never been the subject of a treaty. Soft law emerges through formal and informal standards for international commerce and practice. Over time, soft law may or may not become customary international law, depending on the rate and extent of international adoption of the norm.

The most obvious example of this is the United Nations, but several regional international bodies also exist, such as the European Union, the Organization of American States, and the African Union. It is important to note, however, that these international nonstate bodies are created only through state action and agreement; they could be dissolved at any time by agreement of the states that gave rise to the organization in the first place.[9]

International human rights law (IHRL), in the history of the law of nations, is a new idea—indeed, a new experiment. This is because IHRL is focused on the rights of individuals relative to the state, not the rights of states relative to each other. Until the mid- to late-twentieth century, international law defined and ordered the relationships between states and had little to say about the way that states related to their own subjects. IHRL seeks to establish universal norms for the way states treat the people within their borders. Put differently, proponents of IHRL seek to reach into the sovereignty of individual states to place a check on the way that states may treat their own subjects. This move—the proposed reach into the affairs of sovereign states through international mechanisms—is not without controversy.[10]

IHRL is principally expressed in three categories of international law: the UN Charter system, UN-based treaties, and regional intergovernmental organization systems.[11] The UN Charter itself, which was signed and

---

[9] A notable example of this is the Organization of African Unity, which was dissolved in 2002 and replaced with the African Union.

[10] See, e.g., Goldsmith and Posner, *The Limits of International Law*. For a defense of international law and in particular a critique of US withdrawal from international institutions during the Bush Administration, see Jens David Ohlin, *The Assault on International Law* (Oxford: Oxford University Press, 2015), 89. Much of Ohlin's argument is focused on enhanced interrogation techniques and extraordinary rendition policies in the early years of the War on Terror.

[11] This essay does not discuss these regional intergovernmental organizations, although they are important for the development of IHRL in part because limited geographical reach leads to greater cultural homogeneity and deeper sharing of cultural and religious values. The European Commission of Human Rights has issued a large number of decisions on religious liberty. For a deeper discussion, see Malcolm D. Evans, *Religious Liberty and International Law in Europe* (Cambridge: Cambridge University Press, 1997), 263–362. This chapter also omits discussion of the International Criminal Court, which is an intergovernmental adjudicative body of growing importance worldwide. The United States has not signed or ratified the Rome Statute, which created the ICC. Further, the ICC's jurisdiction is narrowly defined

ratified in San Francisco in 1945, contains a small number of human rights provisions, although during previous negotiations, the majority of explicit provisions related to human rights were removed and dealt with in separate treaties.[12] The most notable human rights provisions relate to the empowerment of the Economic and Social Council to "make recommendations for the purposes of promoting respect for, and observance of, human rights and fundamental freedoms for all."[13] However, there was general consensus at the ratification of the UN Charter that the UN lacked the authority to monitor human rights abuses by countries, as those matters fell "essentially within the domestic jurisdiction" of member states.[14] Accordingly, a year after the UN Economic and Social Council created the Commission on Human Rights (CHR), the Economic and Social Council announced that the CHR was not competent to even investigate, to say nothing of acting upon, petitions submitted to it related to human rights abuses. Although early on the CHR did not play a critical role in investigating human rights abuses, the CHR did lead the international effort in drafting and ratifying what is now known as the International Bill of Rights.

---

to the most serious crimes of concern: genocide, crimes against humanity, and war crimes—this excludes violations of religious liberty unless that violation is related to genocide, crimes against humanity, or war crimes. See Nicolas Michel and Katherine del Mar, "Transnational Justice," in *The Oxford Handbook of International Law in Armed Conflict*, ed. Andrew Clapham and Paola Gaeta (Oxford: Oxford University Press, 2014), 863; Erika de Wet, "*Jus Cogens* and Obligations *Erga Omnes*," in *The Oxford Handbook on International Human Rights Law*, ed. Dinah Shelton (Oxford: Oxford University Press, 2013), 554.

[12] While there was initial discussion about the protection of human rights, from the Dumbarton Oaks Conference on the UN Charter onward, there was nearly no discussion of human rights from the Big 3 powers. In the history of the drafting of the UN Charter, the Dumbarton Oaks Conference constituted the final significant negotiation before the United Nations Conference in San Francisco. See Samuel Moyn, *The Last Utopia* (Cambridge, MA: Harvard University Press, 2012), 58–59. Moyn quotes Reinhold Niebuhr's article in the *Nation* on the Dumbarton Oaks negotiations to support the idea that human rights provisions were simply not included in the late drafts of the UN Charter: "Nor would the Dumbarton Oaks agreements be substantially improved by the insertion of some international bill of rights which has no relevance, and would have no efficacy, in a world alliance of states." Ibid.

[13] UN Charter art. 62, para. 4.

[14] UN Charter art. 2, para. 7; see also Nigel S. Rodley, "The Role and Impact of Treaty Bodies," in Shelton, *The Oxford Handbook of International Human Rights Law*, 621.

From the 1970s, the CHR took on an expanding role in monitoring and reporting on human rights abuses around the world. However, the CHR experienced sharp resistance in these efforts, facing increasing complaints of bias and politicization in its decision-making processes. In 2006, the UN General Assembly dissolved the Commission on Human Rights and created the new Human Rights Council, which is today the primary clearinghouse for human rights within the UN.[15] To some extent, however, the fact that the CHR over time began to reach into matters "essentially within the domestic jurisdiction" of member states can be explained by the fact that these member states had entered into a number of sweeping human rights treaties, thereby subjecting themselves to international scrutiny. It is to these treaties that we turn next.

For this discussion on religious liberty, our focus is on the International Bill of Rights, which is made up of three treaties: the Universal Declaration on Human Rights (UDHR), the International Covenant on Civil and Political Rights (ICCPR), and the International Covenant on Economic, Social, and Cultural Rights (ICESCR).[16] These treaties create mechanisms to monitor and report on state practice. This monitoring is carried out by new organs created by the treaty that fit within the larger UN framework. As with any treaty, only those states that have signed and ratified the treaty are subject to such scrutiny. Because the negotiation and history of the UDHR and ICCPR are illustrative of the major ideological conflicts related to religious freedom internationally, additional details about these treaties are below.

One's understanding of how IHRL came into existence in the first place is critical for understanding what IHRL is and is not. The received narrative of the history of IHRL goes something like this: In response to

---

[15] Miloon Kothari, "From Commission to Council: Evolution of UN Charter Bodies," in Shelton, *The Oxford Handbook of International Human Rights Law*, 589–93.

[16] Seven other treaties touch on human rights: International Convention on the Elimination of All Forms of Racial Discrimination; Convention on the Elimination of All Forms of Discrimination against Women; Convention against Torture and Other Cruel, Inhuman or Degrading Treatment or Punishment; Convention on the Rights of the Child; International Convention on the Protection of the Rights of All Migrant Workers and Members of Their Families; International Convention for the Protection of All Persons from Enforced Disappearance; and the Convention on the Rights of Persons with Disabilities.

the horrors of war experienced during World War II, and in particular the atrocity of the Holocaust, the international community banded together to vow that such atrocities would never occur again. The United Nations was formed, treaties were drafted and ratified, and all nations together agreed to subjugate their sovereignty under the UN Security Council to ensure that another world war never occurred. This led to the drafting of the UDHR, the UN Charter, and the ICCPR, which brings us up to the present day.

As Samuel Moyn has forcefully argued, there was in fact a brief moment at the end of World War II when it appeared that the world powers were committed to a broad agenda of human rights, but this moment sputtered out with the drafting of the UDHR.[17] From 1945 to the 1970s, those who would ultimately become human rights advocates were focused on decolonization and only turned to human rights as an instrument for social change when the process of decolonization ran its course, leading to the formation of a number of brutally authoritarian states.[18]

This alternative narrative helps to explain one of the major conceptual problems with international human rights law as *law*: the problem of enforcement. If the society of nations truly did come together after World War II, intending to corporately restrict their sovereignty to ensure that no individual human rights would be infringed upon, why does IHRL contain so few enforcement mechanisms? If a person's human rights are taken away, what recourse does she have? The truth is, an individual has almost no right to appeal to the international order to receive justice if her human rights are abused.

This answers the question of what IHRL is not. So then, what is IHRL? If international human rights are not individual entitlements, then what are they?

One way of answering this question is to say we don't know yet. Some argue that the apparatus and rhetoric of IHRL will eventually overwhelm the system itself, leading to its collapse. On the other hand, the institutions that develop international human rights norms are robust, and most states arguably have an interest in preserving them. Further, it is difficult to argue

---

[17] Moyn, *The Last Utopia*, 80–83.
[18] Ibid., 85.

that these institutions have not produced some valuable results. Although there are good arguments that states never intended to allow the United Nations to speak to domestic matters, today every country in the world has submitted to a peer-reviewed process administered by the Human Rights Council to put their records on human rights on the public record.[19]

What seems obvious, particularly when assessing the situation from a realist perspective, is that international human rights law is created and sustained by sovereign states who only submit to the international human rights regime because they gain some benefit from it: legitimacy, access to humanitarian aid, and international prestige, to name a few. Bad actor states will only continue to engage with international human rights institutions to the extent that these institutions serve their interests.[20] What this means is that IHRL cannot deliver on utopian promises to create a perfect world; if advocates of IHRL push too far, the entire regime could come crashing down.

So what can IHRL deliver on today? Certainly not the guarantee of individual human rights. Such a guarantee lies only within the province of sovereign states; no international order can achieve this without stripping individual states of their sovereignty. However, the international human rights regime today does provide research and reporting, develops and shares best practices, networks and coordinates states that might not otherwise interact with each other or share interests, shines daylight on and provides condemnation for bad actors, and applies pressure (even if unevenly) on states that violate broadly shared norms and values.

This is far short of a guarantee of rights, and this can never deliver utopia; Christians know that no international regime can do that anyway.

---

[19] Referred to as the Universal Periodic Review, this is a process whereby each state conducts an internal review of its human rights record and submits the report to the UNHRC. Each UN member state goes through this process every few years.

[20] It should be acknowledged that the interests of states themselves were the primary factor in the development of IHRL. The late Antonio Cassese has argued that "the states convening in The Hague [to draft the Hague Conventions of 1899 and 1907] were animated not only by a humanitarian spirit . . . [but also] to safeguard politico-military interests," agreeing on the rules of the game that preserved the interests and power of the larger states at the negotiating table. Antonio Cassese, "Current Challenges to International Humanitarian Law," in Clapham and Gaeta, *The Oxford Handbook of International Law in Armed Conflict*, 5.

Indeed, the global enforcement of human rights would require a new transnational authority that no one should want.

Religious Liberty under International Law

Many discussions regarding the protections for religious liberty under international law essentially begin and end with article 18 of the Universal Declaration of Human Rights. But in order to understand the full meaning of article 18, it is critical to get first an understanding of the role that religious liberty has played throughout the history of the law of nations.

A Brief History of Religious Freedom under International Law

Religious freedom is one of the oldest subjects of international law. Some of the earliest international treaties and legal instruments were directly concerned with protecting religious freedom between members of different faiths, and particularly the way that subjects of two different powers would be treated when those subjects were traveling in the territory of the other powers.

One of the earliest examples of religious freedom being granted to the subjects of an empire is the Edict of Milan. Emperor Constantine issued the edict in AD 313, granting religious freedom to Christians in the Roman Empire.[21] Throughout the second and third centuries AD, the Roman Empire oscillated between persecuting the early Christian church and tolerating it. But it was not until Constantine that Christians were granted true religious liberty:

> All who choose [the Christian] religion are to be allowed and to continue therein, without let or hindrance and are not in any way to be molested. . . . At the same time all others are to be accorded the free and unrestricted practices of their religions; for it accords with the good order of the realm and the peacefulness of our times that each should have the freedom to worship God after his own

---

[21] Urfan Khaliq, "Freedom of Religion and Belief in International Law: A Comparative Analysis," in *Islamic Law and International Human Rights Law: Searching for Common Ground?* ed. Anver M. Emon, Mark S. Ellis, and Benjamin Glahn (Oxford: Oxford University Press, 2012), 184–85.

choice; and we do not intend to detract from the honour due to any religion or its followers.[22]

In AD 532, the Byzantine Empire, led by Emperor Justinian I, entered into a peace treaty with the Persian Empire that ended hostilities between the two empires, one of the earliest examples of two empires negotiating with each other on religious liberty. The treaty stipulated that Christians living in the Persian Empire would have the right to worship in their churches and be free from forced participation in Zoroastrianism, the official religion of the Persian Empire.[23]

The Religious Peace of Augsburg in 1555 was the first in a series of treaties created in the bloody aftermath of the Reformation that began to lay a foundation for pluralism between Catholic and Protestant Christians. The Peace of Augsburg allowed the princes of the Holy Roman Empire to choose between Catholicism and Lutheranism when determining the religion of their territory. A provision known as the *Declaratio Ferdinandea* allowed those living in Catholic territories who had previously converted to Lutheranism to continue practicing their faith.[24]

An uprising in the Low Countries in 1576 against Spain led to the Pacification of Ghent, which accommodated the Catholic faith of most Spanish provinces and permitted Calvinist dominance in Holland and Zeeland.[25] The Pacification specifically provided that "individuals were to enjoy freedom of religion and no one was to be persecuted or questioned concerning their religion."[26] The peace was not long lived, as Catholic and Protestant divisions within the Holy Roman Empire continued to ossify, eventually resulting in the Thirty Years' War.

The Peace of Westphalia, which effectively brought an end to the Thirty Years' War, included a number of treaty provisions that addressed religious liberty. Within the Holy Roman Empire, minority Catholics and Lutherans were to be "patiently suffered and tolerated, without any

---

[22] Evans, *Religious Liberty and International Law in Europe*, 19.

[23] Ibid., 59, citing Arthur Nussbaum, *A Concise History of the Law of Nations* (New York: Macmillian 1954), 48.

[24] Evans, *Religious Liberty and International Law in Europe*, 45–48.

[25] Ibid., 48–49.

[26] Ibid., 48.

hindrance or impediment in both public and private worship" but only for a period of five years.[27] After that period, the prince of the city or territory had the right to require the minority Catholic or Lutheran to move elsewhere.[28]

The treaty language of the Peace of Westphalia certainly left much to be desired by today's standards. Indeed, the Treaty of Osnabrük specifically provided that, while tolerance would issue for "those who call themselves Reformed" and Catholics, "besides these religions no other shall be received or tolerated in the Sacred Roman Empire."[29] However, Westphalia did end up being a turning point for religious tolerance within Europe; after Westphalia, changes in territorial control were generally accompanied by respect for the existing religious practices of their new subjects.[30] This trend is observed in state practice, not prescribed by treaty obligations. For instance, the treaties signed at the Congress of Vienna in 1815 had comparatively little to say about religious liberty.[31]

Treaty practice between Europe and the predominantly Muslim Ottoman Empire also provide an interesting reference point. For instance, the Treaty of Karlowitz in 1699 between the Ottoman Empire and the Austrian Habsburgs guaranteed Roman Catholics the right to establish their own religious communities; exercise self-government in matters of marriage, inheritance, and personal status; and enjoy free and public worship.[32] The Treaty of Kutschuk-Kainardji in 1774 extended these same rights to orthodox Christians.[33]

This pattern continued as the Ottoman Empire began to disintegrate in the nineteenth century. The European powers facilitated the slow breakup of the empire, and the emergent states were required to guarantee freedom of religion, protect principles of nondiscrimination, and preserve the preexisting rights of any religious communities living in the territory.[34]

---

[27] Ibid., 52 (internal quotation marks omitted).
[28] Ibid.
[29] Ibid.
[30] See discussion ibid., 54–59.
[31] Ibid., 58–59.
[32] Ibid., 60–62.
[33] Ibid.
[34] Ibid., 66.

For instance, the Treaty of Constantinople in 1881, which ceded territory to Greece from the Ottoman Empire, required that "the lives, property, religion, and customs of those of the inhabitants of the localities ceded to Greece who shall remain under the Hellenic administration will be scrupulously respected."[35]

Over nearly two millennia, a trend emerges of increasing specificity and increasing international appetite for pluralism. Even at much-celebrated Westphalia, no Muslims or Jews were to be "received or tolerated" in the sacred Roman Empire. But by the end of the nineteenth century, the emerging international treaty practice guaranteed freedom of worship and equal protection within the new ethnically and religiously diverse states carved out of the Ottoman Empire. To be sure, the "sick man of Europe" had little choice but to accept these treaty obligations forced upon him by the European powers. But nonetheless, these treaties became the precedents drawn upon after World War II when drafting the UN Charter and the UDHR. It is to the latter document that we turn next.

The Universal Declaration of Human Rights

The Universal Declaration of Human Rights, ratified by the United Nations General Assembly in 1948, sought to provide the definitive articulation of human rights for the world, the standard to which all states should aspire. For this reason, article 18 of the UDHR, which provides for freedom of religion, has emerged as the dominant reference point for what religious liberty is internationally.

After all, religious liberty can be an elusive concept. As the debate about religious liberty in the context of the debate on same-sex marriage in the United States has made clear, no widespread consensus exists about where this right begins and ends and in what ways other rights can limit it.

Sometimes the discussion about what religious liberty is plays out as a battle of prepositions: is religious liberty the freedom *of* religion or *for* religion or *from* religion? Ultimately, these formulations cannot provide the specificity needed to actually define the right that I am addressing.

The right to religious liberty, like most rights, is best explained as a cluster of related rights that together form, create, and protect the liberty

---

[35] Ibid., 67.

of humans to "live out" their faith. Breaking article 18 of the UDHR into its component parts, one may see that four rights work together to define the scope of religious liberty:[36]

1. *Freedom of thought, conscience, and religion,* which protects the right of people to believe or to not believe in a higher power.
2. *Freedom to change one's religion or belief,* which could be construed as a part of the first right. But as will be discussed further below, because this aspect of freedom of religion and belief is so controversial, it is included here separately.
3. *Freedom to manifest one's religion or belief,* either alone or with others, through teaching, practice, worship, and observance. Of course, the devil is in the details on what these four manifestations include and how they may be limited.
4. *Freedom from discrimination* from the state and private actors based on a person's belief or lack of belief.

Americans will immediately notice that article 18 is much more detailed than the First Amendment to the US Constitution. Although the First Amendment has been expanded upon by the courts in a variety of ways, the text itself has two main clauses: the Establishment Clause and the Free Exercise Clause.[37]

A unique element of the American system is the fact that the First Amendment sets up two competing rights that work against and with each other to secure religious freedom. The Establishment Clause prevents the state from taking any action that favors a particular religion or

---

[36] The full text of article 18 is as follows: "Everyone has the right to freedom of thought, conscience and religion: this right includes freedom to change his religion or belief, and freedom, either alone or in community with others and in public or private, to manifest his religion or belief in teaching, practice, worship and observance" (Universal Declaration of Human Rights, G.A. Res. 217 [III] A, U.N. Doc. A/RES/217[III] [December 10, 1948]).

[37] See Amendment I (1791): "Congress shall make no law respecting an establishment of religion, or prohibiting the free exercise thereof; or abridging the freedom of speech, or of the press; or the right of the people peaceably to assemble, and to petition the Government for a redress of grievances" in *The Constitution of the United States,* adapted from S.PUB. 103–21 (1994) and available from http://www.senate.gov/civics/constitution_item/constitution.htm.

denomination in a way that would constitute the establishment of a state religion. On the other hand, the Constitution requires the state to preserve the "free exercise" of religion, which inevitably requires the state to take positive action to protect the expression of religion.

Article 18 does not operate in the same way, in part because the UDHR is an international document, ratified by nearly the entire international community in existence at the time.[38] This international community of course includes theocratic states that would be unwilling to accept a definition of religious freedom that prohibits the establishment of a state religion.

Surveying these rights, one might ask what the difference is between the freedom of religion and the related concepts of freedom of thought, freedom of speech, freedom of assembly, and freedom of conscience. Some have wondered if freedom of religion really ought to be protected *directly*, through a right to religious freedom, or whether it is better to protect the freedom of religion *indirectly* by protecting the freedom of thought, assembly, speech, and freedom from discrimination.

While it is certainly true that there is some overlap between religious freedom and other freedoms, it is important that religious freedom be given its own, intentional protection. First, respecting the freedom to manifest one's religion requires the recognition that a person's faith is of a different character than his ideas or way of life. Faith may lead to ideas and a pattern of life, but faith itself is deeper, more central to the core. To be protected, this core must be respected and understood. To say that a person's religion is merely the sum of a person's ideas, habits, and so on misses something fundamental about what religion actually is.

Second, if religious freedom is protected only indirectly, the risk is that religious freedom will become only a marginal interest among other interests. If we are interested only in protecting the freedom of speech, then religious speech becomes just a category of speech alongside political,

---

[38] Eight members of the United Nations abstained from the vote: the USSR, Ukraine, the BSSR, Yugoslavia, Poland, South Africa, Czechoslovakia, and Saudi Arabia. For a fuller discussion of the reasons for the abstentions, see Johannes Morsink, *The Universal Declaration of Human Rights: Origins, Drafting & Intent* (Philadelphia: University of Pennsylvania Press, 1999), 21.

cultural, and economic speech. If we are only interested in protecting the freedom of assembly, then churches and synagogues are only another type of gathering, alongside political, civic, and cultural gatherings. The importance of articulating a freedom of religion that stands next to the freedom of speech and assembly—rather than underneath those related rights— becomes plain.

In the United States today, secularists are openly questioning whether religious freedom ought to be separately protected or whether it is already protected by other constitutional rights. The debate over the state and federal religious freedom restoration acts is a good example of this dynamic. Just over two years ago, the federal Religious Freedom Restoration Act of 1993 was passed nearly unanimously—only three senators voted against the bill—and signed into law by President Clinton. The bill was introduced by now-Senator Chuck Schumer (D-NY) and the late Senator Ted Kennedy (D-MA). But today, many secularists and liberals wonder whether religious liberty needs protecting at all or, worse, whether religious liberty stands against other agendas they wish to advance.

It is therefore critical that Christians continue to champion the importance of religious liberty, and pointing to the problem of international religious liberty may help remind Americans of all stripes how important it is to protect the right to believe or not believe as each person wishes.

One brief aside must be made regarding the UDHR as international law because the UDHR was never intended to be a source of legal obligation. Within the NGO community, it is common to hear the statement that a country is "violating" article 18 of the UDHR. Such a statement would have been incoherent in 1948 because the purpose of the UDHR was to provide a starting point for defining citizenship, not international charters.[39] It was understood that these rights would be mediated and protected by the relationship between persons and their states, not by the relationship between a state and an international organization.

The drafting and negotiation of the language of article 18 of the UDHR provides deep insight into the international political dynamics at work

---

[39] Moyn, *The Last Utopia*, 13 ("But even then, it was universally agreed that those rights were to be achieved through the construction of spaces of citizenship in which rights were accorded and protected").

when discussing religious liberty even today. During the drafting of article 18, there was significant debate about what the right should encompass. The original draft of article 18 was perfunctory: "There shall be freedom of conscience and belief and of private and public religious worship."[40]

This brief formation was unacceptable to the United Kingdom, which led the charge in offering a more expansive counterproposal.[41] In the subsequent negotiations over the wording of this provision, the UK formulation became the new starting point for what would become the final, ratified article 18.

A number of states challenged this more expansive formulation of what became article 18, notably the Soviet Union and Saudi Arabia. The Soviet alternative stated, "Everyone must be guaranteed freedom of thought and freedom to perform religious services in accordance with the laws of the country concerned and the requirement of public morality."[42] The United States objected to the conditioning of the right of freedom of religion to the "laws of the country concerned," as this conditioning would eviscerate the universality of the right.[43] The Soviet representative claimed to be concerned about limiting extreme expressions of religion like human sacrifice and self-flagellation.[44] But the international community agreed that the Soviet proposal would obviously do much more than this, and it was rejected.

Saudi Arabia also proposed an alternative formulation of article 18, which was to delete everything but the first sentence: "Everyone has the right to freedom of thought, conscience, or religion." In effect, the Saudi proposal would have emptied article 18 of its substance, leaving its interpretation and application up to each individual state. According to Malcolm Evans's review of the proceedings, it was clear from the outset that the real intention of the Saudi proposal was to remove the reference to the right to change one's religion.[45] Ultimately, the Saudi proposal was rejected by the drafting committee by a vote of 22 to 12, with 8 abstentions.

---

[40] Evans, *Religious Liberty and International Law in Europe*, 183.
[41] Ibid., 184.
[42] Ibid., 185.
[43] Ibid., 185–86.
[44] Ibid., 186n66.
[45] Ibid., 187–88.

As Evans points out, however, this shows that nearly half of the drafting committee did not formally endorse a right to change one's religion.

This debate exposed the divide between Muslim states and Western states on the issue of whether a person should be able to change one's religion. For the Muslim states, this issue was rooted in the question of punishment for apostates, which will be discussed in more detail below. Ultimately, the debates held at the UDHR set the stage for future debates on international obligations related to religious liberty, in particular the debate on the ICCPR, to which we now turn.

The International Covenant on Civil and Political Rights

While the Commission on Human Rights created by the UN Charter immediately disavowed any power to oversee human rights abuses within any sovereign state, the CHR did begin a process of drafting an international covenant that would formalize the commitment of states to the rights enumerated in the UDHR. Two international conventions were devised to formalize these commitments, the International Covenant on Civil and Political Rights and the International Covenant on Economic, Social, and Cultural Rights. Drafting of the ICCPR took nearly two decades, and the covenant includes an article that relates to religious liberty, also article 18.[46] The enforcement mechanism created by the ICCPR is the Human Rights Committee, which performs a monitoring and reporting function.

---

[46] The language of article 18 of the ICCPR is: "1. Everyone shall have the right to freedom of thought, conscience and religion. This right shall include freedom to have or to adopt a religion or belief of his choice, and freedom, either individually or in community with others and in public or private, to manifest his religion or belief in worship, observance, practice and teaching. 2. No one shall be subject to coercion which would impair his freedom to have or to adopt a religion or belief of his choice. 3. Freedom to manifest one's religion or beliefs may be subject only to such limitations as are prescribed by law and are necessary to protect public safety, order, health, or morals or the fundamental rights and freedoms of others. 4. The States Parties to the present Covenant undertake to have respect for the liberty of parents and, when applicable, legal guardians to ensure the religious and moral education of their children in conformity with their own convictions." (International Covenant on Civil and Political Rights, December 16, 1966, S. Exec. Rep. 102–23, 999 UNTS 171).

The negotiations over the language of article 18 followed a similar pattern to the UDHR negotiations, and the same issues emerged, although the divisions had ossified since the drafting of the UDHR. The Soviet Union remained concerned about the protection of atheistic and political beliefs, and majority-Muslim states were concerned about the right to change one's religion. Egypt, for instance, proposed that the reference to the right to change one's religion be deleted because it is implied in the very concept of religious freedom.[47]

The end result of two decades of negotiation was a definition of the right of religious liberty that was somewhat less precise than the UDHR: "Everyone shall have the right to freedom of thought, conscience and religion. This right shall include freedom to have or to adopt a religion or belief of his choice. . . ." Part of the reason for this was the need to create and preserve what may be called diplomatic ambiguity. In light of the concerns over the right to change one's religion, language was offered that could be interpreted in both ways: Western nations that believed that the right to change one's religion was a fundamental part of the whole could walk away feeling that article 18 of the ICCPR indeed protected this right, particularly because the article references the adherent's "choice." States on the other side of the debate could also claim victory because the ICCPR's article includes no explicit mention of the right to change one's religion.

In the end, however, the ICCPR as a mechanism for advancing (let alone protecting) religious freedom, particularly in majority-Muslim countries, is a mixed bag. Nine member countries of the Organization of Islamic Cooperation (OIC) did not sign the ICCPR. Saudi Arabia, for instance, which was quite active during the drafting and negotiation of the ICCPR, ultimately did not sign the treaty.

Many of the other countries that did ultimately sign the ICCPR did so conditionally, with a treaty reservation. Also called *understandings* or *declarations*, treaty reservations modify the country's obligations under the treaty by laying out its objections to or interpretations of the treaty when signing. The reservation by the Kingdom of Bahrain was typical: "The Government of the Kingdom of Bahrain interprets the Provisions of Article 3, 18 and 23 as not affecting in any way the prescriptions of the Islamic

---

[47] Evans, *Religious Liberty and International Law in Europe*, 196.

Shariah."[48] Other reservations were more indirect. For instance, the reservation of the Maldives reads, "The application of the principles set out in Article 18 of the Covenant shall be without prejudice to the Constitution of the Republic of Maldives."[49] As the Republic of the Maldives is an Islamic republic that applies Sharia law, this reservation effectively limits article 18 by the Maldivian interpretation and application of Sharia.

In effect, the ICCPR represents a softening of the specificity around what religious liberty is since the UDHR. As we will see with the Declaration on the Elimination of Religious Intolerance and Discrimination, that trend has continued.

The Declaration on the Elimination of Religious Intolerance and Discrimination

No international treaty dealing solely with the issue of freedom of belief has been ratified, although the process for developing one has begun. In 1981, the UN General Assembly issued, without a vote, the Declaration on the Elimination of All Forms of Intolerance and of Discrimination Based on Religion or Belief. This declaration purportedly amplifies article 18 of the UDHR, adding specificity to the right to religious liberty. However, as a practical matter, the declaration dilutes international statements on an important aspect of religious liberty: the right to change one's religion.

The original draft of article 1 of the declaration, which laid out the core of the right, reads, "Everyone has the right to adhere, or to not adhere, to a religion or belief *and to change* in accordance with the dictates of his conscience—without being subjected to any pressure, inducement, or undue influence likely to impair his freedom of choice or decision in this matter."[50] Because of pressure from Egypt, which represented the interests of other countries, the reference to the right to change one's religion was dropped out of the draft. The final text of the declaration reads, "Everyone

---

[48] United Nations, *Multilateral Treaties Deposited with the Secretary-General: Status as at 1 April 2009*, UN Publication E.09.V.3 (New York: United Nations, 2009), chap. 4, pt. 4, p. 4.

[49] 2386 UNTS 288 (December 19, 2006).

[50] Commission on Human Rights, Report on the Twentieth Session, § 294, delivered to the Economic and Social Council, UN Doc. E/CN.4/874 (1964).

shall have the right to freedom of thought, conscience and religion. This right shall include freedom to have a religion or whatever belief *of his choice*, and freedom, either individually or in community with others and in public or private, to manifest his religion or belief in worship, observance, practice and teaching."[51] The declaration removes an important verb: "to adopt," a further softening of the idea of agency over one's religious belief.[52]

As a result, the compromise language in the declaration is the weakest of the three international instruments that deal with religious liberty, representing a trend that is moving in the wrong direction. Because of the difficulties associated with drafting and passing the declaration in the 1980s, work on an international convention was stopped, and it has not been picked up since. Most commentators agree that the divisions are still too deep to tackle an international convention on religious liberty.

One practical example of this is the recent trend within the UN General Assembly toward condemning the "defamation of religion" and focusing on xenophobia. In 2009, for instance, the UN General Assembly adopted a resolution condemning the "use of the print, audio-visual and electronic media, including the Internet, and any other means to incite acts of violence, xenophobia or related intolerance and discrimination against Islam or any other religion, as well as targeting of religious symbols."[53] The resolution in effect legitimizes blasphemy laws, which have been used by dominant religions to oppress minority religions or to suppress religious speech by minorities.

Whether one believes that a specific convention dealing with international religious liberty would be helpful depends on two things: one's view on whether international institutions ought to be reaching into sovereign states in the first place and one's view on whether even the perfect international treaty could actually improve the lives of religious minorities

---

[51] Declaration on the Elimination of All Forms of Intolerance and of Discrimination Based on Religion or Belief, G.A. Res. 36/55 art. 1, para. 1, UN Doc. A/RES/36/55 (November 25, 1981).

[52] Article 18 of the ICCPR reads, in relevant part: "Everyone shall have the right to freedom of thought, conscience and religion. This right shall include freedom to have *or to adopt* a religion or belief of his choice" (International Covenant on Civil and Political Rights, December 16, 1966, S. Exec. Rep. 102–23, 999 UNTS 171 [emphasis added]).

[53] G.A. Res., UN Doc. A/RES/62/154 (March 6, 2008) (Combating defamation of religions). The resolution was adopted by a vote of 108 votes to 51 with 25 abstaining.

in the world today. Regardless, drafting and ratifying an international treaty that provides actual protections for religious minorities is impossible today. There is not a broad enough consensus about how religious liberty should be protected and the manner in which it is appropriate for states to criminalize blasphemy and apostasy.[54] With that idea in mind, let us now examine these two issues in detail.

Case Study: Apostasy Laws in Majority-Muslim Countries

The question of whether a person should have the right to change her religion has been a persistent problem in international debates on religious liberty. Another way to frame the question is whether states should have the right to criminalize apostasy and blasphemy. This is an issue primarily in majority-Muslim states, although throughout history most countries and civilizations have criminalized blasphemy at one point or another.

The discussion above regarding the debate over the freedom to change one's religion opens up a question: Is Islam compatible with religious liberty? Ultimately, this is not an interesting question, nor is it a particularly coherent question, as no religion can be assessed in the abstract. Any discussion of what a religion *is* must be grounded in the current and historical practice of its adherents. More fundamentally, we must recognize the fact that all major religions have texts, teachings, and traditions that may be used to justify violence, as well as mitigating texts, teachings, and traditions that drive back toward principles of peace and pluralism. On the topic of blasphemy, the Christian Bible contains Leviticus 24:15–16 (ESV): "And speak to the people of Israel, saying, Whoever curses his God shall bear his sin. Whoever blasphemes the name of the LORD shall surely be put to death. All the congregation shall stone him. The sojourner as well as the native, when he blasphemes the Name, shall be put to death."

---

[54] This of course raises the question of whether specificity in an international treaty is ultimately necessary. Goodman and Jinks argue that vagueness in a treaty can be positive because it brings states who are otherwise far apart for discussion and coordination (*Socializing States*, 112 [citing Kenneth W. Abbott and Duncan Snidal, "Hard and Soft Law in International Governance," *International Organization* 54 (2000): 421]).

Christians do not believe this law is in force today because of Christian theology of the fulfillment of the Mosaic law. But it is in our Bible, so when amateurs in Islamic theology seek to quote the Qur'an, let us do so with a measure of humility. After all, history did not start in 1776. We of course disagree with sequences of Christian history that came before us, but in the eyes of the global community, we can never fully disavow those events. Our tradition today stands on the shoulders of pogroms and blood libels against Jews in Europe. It stands on the shoulders of the Crusades, the Spanish Inquisition, the Thirty Years' War, the American conception of Manifest Destiny, and the Colonial Era.

Indeed, today Dietrich Bonhoeffer is extolled as a true Christian in the face of Hitler's use of Christianity as a pretext for the Holocaust. But we need to recognize that some of our Jewish friends don't exactly see the situation quite so neatly. Some Jews look at the Nazis the same way non-Muslims look at the Daesh: uneasily, wondering how much of the ideology of the false, deadly heresy is inherent in the mother religion. To put it differently, some Jews wonder even today, is Christianity a religion of peace?

And so while this question may feel absurd to us, let us approach the discussion of blasphemy and apostasy laws with a spirit of humility that acknowledges the fullness of our own history and how that history informs the way the rest of the world views Christianity. With this brief introduction, because freedom to change one's religion forms part of the core of the Christian conception of religious freedom, let us turn our discussion to apostasy laws under Islam.

From the very formative period of Islam, the definition of apostasy and the punishment for apostasy was a subject explored and worked out by Islamic jurists. Since the premodern era, these early interpretations have been built on and revised, and today a spectrum of opinion exists regarding two questions: (1) What is apostasy? and (2) How should it be punished?

According to classical Islamic law, apostasy against Islam may be committed in a number of different ways, including denying the existence of God; denying one or more of the attributes of God; or refusing to accept any one of the fundamental practices of Islam, such as denying the doctrine that there are five obligatory prayers each day, declaring that something which is prohibited (*haram*) is actually permissible (*halal*), or worshipping idols.[55] Indeed Islamic legal scholars have over history dedicated much energy to defining what exactly constitutes apostasy; different Muslim sects and schools of jurisprudence have developed so-called apostasy lists, which enumerate the ways that a Muslim may become an apostate.[56]

The primary problem with apostasy laws is that these laws can become a pretext for the group in power to stifle and punish dissenters. Some schools define apostasy so broadly that even the smallest theological digression is tantamount to the commission of apostasy.[57] It is easy to see how these laws can become a pretext for the group in power to stifle and punish dissenters or those with differing theological interpretations. But of course, all Muslim scholars agree that for a Muslim to convert to another religion constitutes apostasy.

Let us turn now to the second question: How is such a transgression punished and what punishment comes along with apostasy? In classical Islam, there was broad agreement across Islamic legal scholars that the punishment for apostasy is death and, further, that the administration of this punishment is obligatory for Muslims.[58]

In modern Islam, theological views surrounding punishment for apostasy are much more diverse; many Muslims today believe that criminalization of apostasy is abhorrent.[59] But even with that said, twenty-one countries in the world today criminalize apostasy—half of the countries in the Middle East and North Africa region.[60] Even if moderate voices are beginning to speak up to moderate Islam's position on apostasy, horrific

---

[55] Abdullah Saeed, "Pre-modern Islamic Legal Restrictions on Freedom of Religion, with Particular Reference to Apostasy and its Punishment," in Emon, Ellis, and Glahn, *Islamic Law and International Human Rights Law, supra*, 226, 227; Jeroen Temperman, *State–Religion Relationships and Human Rights Law: Towards a Right to Religiously Neutral Governance* (Leiden: Martinus Nijhoff Publishers, 2010), 183.

[56] Saeed, *supra*, 228.

[57] Ibid.

[58] Ibid., 231.

[59] Abdullah Saeed and Hassan Saeed, *Freedom of Religion, Apostasy and Islam* (Hants, UK: Ashgate, 2004), 88, 93; Frank Griffel, Introduction to *Shari'a: Islamic Law in the Contemporary Context*, ed. Abbas Amanat and Frank Griffel (Stanford: Stanford University Press, 2007), 13–14.

[60] Angelina E. Theodorou, "Which Countries Still Outlaw Apostasy and Blasphemy?" Pew Research Center ThinkTank, May 28, 2014, http://www.pewresearch .org/fact-tank/2014/05/28/which-countries-still-outlaw-apostasy-and-blasphemy/.

stories emerge every year. Although she was later released under international pressure, Meriam Ibrahim was sentenced to death in Sudan for apostasy while she was pregnant. She gave birth in jail.[61]

One dynamic that is important for those interested in international religious freedom to grasp is the fact that many Islamic cultures have come to believe that the UDHR is a reflection of Judeo-Christian or rational culture and tradition and is therefore incompatible with Islamic law.[62] For instance, in 1981, the Iranian representative declared to the United Nations that Muslims could not implement the UDHR and that in the event of any conflict between the UDHR and Islamic law Iran would always side with Islamic law.[63] If religious freedom advocates do not fully comprehend—and perhaps even empathize with—this dynamic, we will end up talking past our Muslim friends, even those who agree with us.

Several attempts have been made within the Islamic context to grapple with questions of human rights, and two such instances are worth exploring. The first is the Cairo Declaration on Human Rights, adopted by the Organisation of Islamic Cooperation in 1990.[64] Although a number of rights are enumerated, such as equal protection under the law, the declaration provides no commitment to religious liberty. To the contrary, article 10 of the Cairo Declaration provides, "Islam is the religion of unspoiled nature. It is prohibited to exercise any form of compulsion on man or to exploit his poverty or ignorance in order to convert him to another religion or to atheism."[65] Further, article 24 provides that "all the rights and freedoms stipulated in this Declaration are subject to the Islamic Shari'ah."[66]

---

[61] "Sudanese woman facing death for apostasy gives birth," *BBC*, May 27, 2014, http://www.bbc.com/news/world-africa-27586067.

[62] Muhammad Khalid Massud, "Clearing Ground: Commentary to 'Shari'a and the Modern State,'" in Emon, Ellis, and Glahn, *Islamic Law and International Human Rights Law*, 105.

[63] David G. Littman, "Human Rights and Human Wrongs," *National Review*, January 19, 2003, http://www.nationalreview.com/article/205577/human-rights-and -human-wrongs-david-g-littman.

[64] Organisation of Islamic Cooperation, *The Cairo Declaration of Human Rights in Islam*, Annex to Res. No. 49/19-P (August 5, 1990).

[65] Ibid.

[66] Ibid.

To put it mildly, the Cairo Declaration is, from the perspective of Christians and other religious minorities living in majority-Muslim countries, less than satisfactory. But another way to read the Cairo Declaration is that Islamic scholars do, on the basis of their commitment to Islam, believe that the only valid human rights are those that spring from Islam itself. Evangelical Christians should recognize that line of thinking; after all, we also believe that what is right and wrong springs solely from our revealed Scriptures.

In the past few years, there have been positive trends. In 2014, as a response to the rise of the Islamic State, Muslim scholars from all around the world gathered to denounce the Islamic State in a letter issued directly to the so-called caliph Abu Bakr al-Baghdadi, condemning as un-Islamic the Islamic State's formulation of Islam.[67] In 2016, a diverse group of Muslim scholars gathered to issue the Marrakesh Declaration on the rights of religious minorities living in majority-Muslim countries.[68] The Marrakesh Declaration does not specifically address the right to change one's religion, but the declaration does affirm the UDHR without reservation. Time will tell, but this might demonstrate a softening on the issue since even 1990, when the Cairo Declaration was issued.

Much more must be done, and much more is needed in order for religious minorities living in many majority-Muslim countries to experience true freedom. The question of what can be done is where we now focus our attention.

Conclusion: Where Do We Go from Here?

As the past two years have shown, we must act. Our spiritual brothers and sisters are being slaughtered, persecuted, and harassed around the world every day. But as should be clear at this point in our discussion, international law is not the answer to our problems. Bald references to abusing

---

[67] Open Letter to Ibrahim Awwad Al-Badri, alias "Abu Bakr Al-Baghdadi," http://www.lettertobaghdadi.com.

[68] Forum for Promoting Peace in Muslim Societies, *Marrakesh Declaration on the Rights of Religious Minorities in Predominantly Muslim Majority Communities*, January 27, 2016, http://www.marrakeshdeclaration.org/marrakesh-declaration.html.

states' commitments to international law, the UDHR, or the ICCPR will always fall short of the mark if these are our only solutions. So where do we go from here?

Religious freedom advocates need to do two things at the same time: First, we need to hold Islamic societies accountable, calling attention to wrongs when they are committed against religious minorities, whether the minorities are Christian or not. But second, we must work with leaders in the Islamic community to articulate a vision for religious freedom based on broad, shared values like human dignity. Within these relationships, we must be humble and patient, recognizing that our own history is littered with missteps. But also we must firmly resolve to do all in our power to prevent the atrocities of history—even our own atrocities—from repeating themselves. By engaging, we can begin to tear down the walls that separate our civilizations.[69]

The church also needs to recognize that other points of persuasion exist toward religious liberty. A growing body of research shows that the most open and pluralistic societies are also the most prosperous.[70] Islamic societies may still need to embrace religious freedom in terms of Islam itself, but working through economic systems like venture capital and multinational corporations may also be part of the solution.

We need to be present in the discussions taking place at the United Nations and in other intergovernmental contexts. It is imperative that Baptists are involved in these discussions, building relationships with those who may be able to help, and working to be connected to the global network of advocates for these issues. Out of a fear of the formation of a transnational order, many conservative advocates have retreated from Geneva. We should work against overreaches by the United Nations but use the mechanisms that exist for good as well.

We must leverage the power available to us and work for material inducement where we can. In extreme examples, international pressure

---

[69] Goodman and Jinks, *Socializing States*, 118.

[70] See Brian J. Grim, Greg Clark, and Robert Edward Snyder, "Is Religious Freedom Good for Business? A Conceptual and Empirical Analysis," *Interdisciplinary Journal of Research on Religion*, 10/2014; Brian J. Grim and Roger Finke, *The Price of Freedom Denied: Religious Persecution and Conflict in the 21st Century* (New York: Cambridge University Press, 2011).

through the UN, such as the UN Security Council, may be available. But as a global body of believers, we need to be creative and recognize that there may be other ways to apply pressure: strings attached to humanitarian and military aid, threats to cut off such aid, diplomatic back channels, and so on. God has given us great creativity, and we should apply this whenever we can.

Lastly, the church needs to invest in and build networks of local advocates and lawyers all across the world. Many already exist, and they need more help and more funding. This will mean working with churches, networks, and other religions with whom we may agree on almost nothing else. But in many places where Christians are small minorities, if the church is divided, it will fall.

Let us pray that the global church has learned its lessons from ignoring our brothers and sisters in Christ in the Middle East. Let us pray that one of the ways the Lord is working in and redeeming the rise of Daesh in Iraq and Syria is that this generation of Western believers will not forget the global church and will be their advocates, as we are told to do in Proverbs:

Speak up for those who have no voice,
   for the justice of all who are dispossessed.
Speak up, judge righteously,
   and defend the cause of the oppressed and needy. (Prov 31:8–9)

CONCLUSION

THE END OF
RELIGIOUS LIBERTY

Jason G. Duesing

*About midnight Paul and Silas were praying and singing hymns to
God, and the prisoners were listening to them.*

ACTS 16:25 ESV

The visit to Macedonia had gone well. Paul and company arrived in
Philippi days before and on the Sabbath went to a place of prayer and
met a gathering of women. Among them was Lydia, who listened intently
to the good news they shared about Jesus Christ and was converted. Then,
after they moved on, another woman met them; she was an enslaved
fortune-teller who followed and badgered them because an evil spirit possessed her. After a few days, Paul commanded the spirit, in the name of
Jesus, to come out of her and she was freed, though still not from her physical enslavement. Her owners had profited from her fortune-telling, and,
with that at an end, they turned on Paul and Silas and brought them to the
rulers, charging them with advocating "customs that are not lawful for us."

A crowd attacked as well, and so the rulers had Paul and Silas stripped, beaten, and thrown in jail.

Paul and Silas had merely engaged the Roman culture with the gospel, helping those who would listen and healing those oppressed by spiritual warfare. Because this work overturned an idol of financial profit, they were isolated, misrepresented, and made to suffer unjustly. Now they were wounded and in prison surrounded by other prisoners. And at this time when they should be sleeping or weeping, they sang.

Why did they sing? The verse informs that they were singing to God, and we can infer that the hymns were songs about God and his work. They sang to remind themselves of present and future truths God revealed and to indicate their trust in God regardless of their circumstances. Their hope was in God, not in their might or their friends. They knew, regardless of how this scrape went, their ultimate future was secure and safe in God.

When believers in Christ Jesus think of the future, we are not practicing escapism or avoiding reality. Rather, we are setting our gaze on that which is more real than the present. The Bible talks about our faith having an anchor of hope to the future (see Heb 6:19), and there sits the Son of God, the Founder and Perfecter of our faith (Heb 12:2), on whom we are to set our minds (Col 3:2) and eyes (Heb 12:2). God through his Word has left a storehouse of information and detail about what is to come. Much is mysterious to be sure, but much is revealed.

The question, then, is, why are we told so much about how the world will end?

God, in his kindness, desires for his children to know and be certain about his character and actions. He recorded his activity in history in order to instruct his future children (see 1 Cor 10:11) so they would know of the advent to ascension of his Son, the Messiah. But he also recorded (Col 1:26–27) that which has yet to take place in order to give them assurance and hope (Heb 11:1) so that they would know and expect his return (2 Tim 4:8). This is the ultimate value of studying and having a theology of the end times. As Russell D. Moore writes, "A person's eschatology, then, has everything to do with the way he lives life now—whether one trusts Jesus for a future kingdom, or whether one grasps at the passing securities of this present age."[1] Paul and Silas were able to sing in the face of injustice and the loss of their freedoms because they knew that God is faithful (1 Pet 4:19) and that in the end God would make things right (Rom 12:19).

Our First Freedom

In this revised edition of *First Freedom*, the authors have endeavored, first, to show how Christians have defended religious liberty throughout history. Christians have sought—though not perfectly or consistently[2]—to ensure freedom of all religions in order to adorn the public marketplace of ideas and not to coerce or establish one religion over another.[3] Second, this volume has sought to present the biblical and rational defense for the practice and protection of religious liberty in the United States and abroad.[4] Third, this volume has reviewed the present and future threats to religious liberty as its advocates seek to weather "a movement to drive religious belief, and especially orthodox Christian religious and moral convictions, out of public life."[5]

---

[1] Russell D. Moore, "Personal and Cosmic Eschatology," in *A Theology for the Church*, ed. Daniel L. Akin (Nashville: B&H Academic, 2014), 714.

[2] The 2012 Evangelicals and Catholics Together statement on religious freedom puts it well: "In making this statement, we confess, and we call all Christians to confess, that Christians have often failed to live the truths about freedom that we have preached: by persecuting one another, by persecuting those of other faiths, and by using coercive methods of proselytism. . . . It is this memory of Christian sinfulness that gives us all the more reason to defend the religious freedom of all men and women today." See "In Defense of Religious Freedom (2012)," in *Evangelicals and Catholics Together at Twenty*, ed. Timothy George and Thomas G. Guarino (Ada, MI: Brazos, 2015), 137.

[3] As the late Richard John Neuhaus said, "As long as public space is open to the full range of symbols cherished in [a] community, there is no question of one religion being 'established' over another." Neuhaus, *To Empower People*, cited in Randy Boyagoda, *Richard John Neuhaus: A Life in the Public Square* (New York: Image, 2015), 207.

[4] Even as people disagree on the nature and role a country like the United States has in exporting its views of religious liberty to other nations, as Anna Su notes, the point is that "the slow realization of religious freedom in a society is and should be a profoundly political act, one that is built on continuing deliberation, contestation, and mutual recognition." Su, *Exporting Freedom: Religious Liberty and American Power* (Cambridge: Harvard University Press, 2016), 162.

[5] "In Defense of Religious Freedom (2012)," in George and Guarino, *ECT at Twenty*, 137.

Given this comprehensive (and we hope helpful) examination of the state of religious liberty, one might be tempted to despair, for the future is difficult to predict and the rise of restrictive trends is discouraging. Therefore, in this brief conclusion, much like Paul and Silas singing, I hope to remind and prepare readers for the ultimate reality of the removal of religious liberty from the earth, and why we should trust God concerning when it occurs.

Religious Liberty's True End

When we talk of religious liberty in the United States, we acknowledge its present fragility with words like *threatened* and with calls to "defend" it.[6] While this book exists to aid in this noble task of educating, reminding, and encouraging believers of these truths worth strengthening, should believers find their liberties removed or suppressed in the days ahead, we should also recognize that we will not really reach the end of religious liberty until Jesus' return. On that day, the time of religious freedom will end. Everyone will bow and acknowledge the one true religion and one true God. Until then, in the most important sense, every day is a day of grace and a day of liberty. Thus, even if the future practice of religious liberty in this country is virtually unrecognizable to the generations of men and women who died to preserve the first freedom, grace still exists for a time through a certain future truth. This eternal perspective should provide hope, but it should also serve as a sobering call to action, for the grace God shows by granting any form of religious liberty on earth is finite.

Near the end of his life, when Paul was in prison again, he wrote a letter to the Philippian believers. The church that formed after his time in jail with Silas became his first church in Europe. The church in Philippi was

---

[6] Howard M. Friedman, distinguished university professor and professor of law emeritus at the University of Toledo, is the author of "Religion Clause," cited frequently as one of the one hundred top legal blogs in the nation. In December 2015, he assembled his "Top Ten Religious Liberty and Church-State Developments" for the year, and they included a wide spectrum of issues, ranging from US Supreme Court rulings on same-sex marriage, prisoners' rights issues, Title VII, license plates as government speech, and other topics such as the Affordable Care Act, to RFRA laws, anti-Muslim sentiments and terminology, and transgender rights. See http://religionclause .blogspot.com/2015/12/top-ten-religious-liberty-and-church.html.

one with whom he maintained contact and likely would have visited again as they served as key supporters of his work (see Phil 4:15). He wrote to encourage them to pursue unity and joy even in suffering, and, to that end, at the center of his letter (2:5–11) he gave them a hymn. It is as if he knew they would need encouragement in singing.

The hymn in Philippians 2 tells of the humbling, sacrifice, and exaltation of Jesus Christ. In the verses describing the exaltation, Paul references a statement from Isaiah and shows why, in the last day, religious liberty will come to an end. He writes, "God has highly exalted him and bestowed on him the name that is above every name, so that at the name of Jesus every knee should bow, in heaven and on earth and under the earth, and every tongue confess that Jesus Christ is Lord, to the glory of God the Father" (Phil 2:9–11 ESV). Here Paul is communicating truths that are both *already* and *not yet* manifest. God has already exalted Christ Jesus and given him the name "Lord." He has already handed all things over to him (see Matt 11:27), put all things under his feet (Eph 1:22), and given him all authority (Matt 28:18). Yet Paul reveals that a future day is coming when the name of Jesus will go forth and all creatures will bow and confess him as Lord. At this time, which Paul in 1 Corinthians 15:24 calls "the end," Jesus will finally destroy death and see the complete fulfillment of Psalm 8:6, when all things are put in subjection under his feet (1 Cor 15:23–28).

Paul's use of Isaiah 45:23 in Philippians 2 ties his hymn to the larger and weightier biblical story. This reference to God the Father saying "to me every knee shall bow, every tongue shall swear allegiance" (ESV) is part of a larger passage (Isa 45:18–25) that, as Bible scholar Moises Silva explains, "constitutes one of the most powerful OT affirmations of the uniqueness of the God of Israel in the context of his redeeming work."[7] There, Isaiah is crusading against idolatry by vigorously defending the sole uniqueness of the God of Israel. By ascribing this text to Jesus, Paul is making a profound trinitarian statement that shows that the divinity of God the Son is not a challenge to the monotheistic God of the Bible.[8]

---

[7] Moises Silva, "Philippians," *Commentary on the New Testament Use of the Old Testament*, ed. G. K. Beale and D. A. Carson (Grand Rapids: Baker Academic, 2007), 837.
[8] Ibid., 838. Silva states, "Although not an explicit or precise quotation, this use of Isaiah is especially significant because of its profound implications for Paul's

Yet Philippians 2:10–11 is not the only time Paul refers to Isaiah 45:23. In Romans 14:10–11, Paul points to the last day and says, "For we will all stand before the judgment seat of God; for it is written, 'As I live, says the Lord, every knee shall bow to me, and every tongue shall confess to God'" (ESV). As New Testament scholar Thomas Schreiner notes, here Paul is ascribing to God the Father the day of widespread allegiance, but this only furthers Paul's point in Philippians 2 of exalting Christ. Schreiner explains, "The fact that Paul can apply the same OT text to God in Romans and to Christ in Philippians reveals the high stature of Christ."[9] Yet clearly this exaltation and subjection are both already true and not yet complete. As John Calvin reminds us, "the kingdom of Christ is on such a footing, that it is every day growing and making improvement, while at the same time perfection is not yet attained, nor will it be until the final day of reckoning."[10] Thus, we live in the times *in between*, and we bear the burden and joy of knowing that the end of religious liberty is coming. What else then is there for us to learn from this future end that can help us to know how to live between the times?

First, these passages depicting the future day of judgment give readers both a word of warning and a promise of hope. The warning comes in

conception of Christ. . . . [I]t patently expresses his own conviction that the worship of Jesus Christ does not compromise Israel's monotheistic faith. On the contrary, Jesus Christ the righteous Savior bears the name of the one Lord, Yahweh, 'to the glory of God the Father.'" See also Thomas R. Schreiner, *New Testament Theology: Magnifying God in Christ* (Grand Rapids: Baker Academic, 2008), 326–27: "The text in Isaiah engages in a polemic against idolatry, insisting emphatically that the God of Israel is the only true God. . . . If we gather together the themes assembled, we see something astonishing. Paul confessed along with Isaiah that there is only one God. Yet, he applies to Jesus what Isaiah attributes to Yahweh—every knee bending and every tongue confessing. Clearly, Paul teaches that Jesus shares in the same divine nature as Yahweh himself, but Paul does this without denying monotheism or the distinctions between the Father and the Son."

[9] Schreiner, *New Testament Theology*, 330. See also Mark A. Seifrid, "Romans," in Beale and Carson, *Commentary*, 685.

[10] John Calvin, "Commentary on the Epistle to the Philippians" in *Calvin's Commentaries*, vol. 21 (Grand Rapids: Baker, 2003), 62. See also Peter T. O'Brien, *The Epistle to the Philippians*, NIGTC (Grand Rapids: Eerdmans, 2013), 243: "The exaltation of Jesus has *already* taken place and God has graciously given him his own all-surpassing name of the Lord (vs. 9); yet the bowing of *every* knee does not occur, at least on earth, until the final day."

the realization that there is a clock winding down, and one day the triune God will no longer exercise patience with those who do not worship him alone. At that time all will bow and confess that God is supreme, true, and Lord. The bowing especially conveys this acknowledgment, as the Bible regularly identifies this posture with concession that the one to whom one bows is superior. Hence Elijah is told to track the faithful by those who have not "bowed the knee to Baal" (1 Kgs 19:18). When one bows and confesses, this is submitting, conceding, and openly declaring what is true about the One who is superior and exalted.[11]

Further, this day of acknowledgment is universal but not universalism. No one will escape participation, whether repentant or not. John Piper explains, "Believers and unbelievers will acknowledge in that day that Jesus has triumphed over every enemy—believers, to their everlasting joy, and unbelievers, to their everlasting shame."[12] This day will serve as a reversal of sorts of Nebuchadnezzar's golden image in Daniel 3. Then, the king demanded and coerced that all "fall down and worship," lest they face judgment by fire (v. 5). Nebuchadnezzar sought a universalism of worship solely for himself. However, the three Jews rightly refused, acknowledging that there was One more worthy of their devotion. Whereas Nebuchadnezzar demanded and attempted to coerce a universalistic worship, the true God does not coerce[13] or universally redeem; but he still will receive, in the end, universal concession and acknowledgment from all creatures. Jesus Christ will reign in triumph over even those who do not worship him but acknowledge their defeat by bowing and confessing.[14]

---

[11] O'Brien, NIGTC, 243, 250, states, "one ought to understand the bowing of the knee as an act of submission to one whose power they cannot resist."

[12] John Piper, "And All the Earth Shall Own Him Lord," October 24, 1982, http://www.desiringgod.org/messages/and-all-the-earth-shall-own-him-lord.

[13] As the helpful ECT statement puts it, "The New Testament . . . never depicts Jesus the Lord as coercing faith. Quite the contrary: Jesus reasoned with his listeners, instructed them in parables, called them to repent, and invited them to believe the good news of God's kingdom," in "In Defense of Religious Freedom (2012)," in George and Guarino, *ECT at Twenty*, 139–40.

[14] In the history of Christianity, some have sought to read Philippians 2:10–11 as implying universal redemption. Steven R. Harmon in his *Every Knee Should Bow: Biblical Rationales for Universal Salvation in Early Christian Thought* (Lanham, MD: University Press of America, 2003), presents early patristic interpretations of Philippians 2:10 (and other passages) that draw those conclusions. Harmon himself

Yet these passages also provide an ongoing word of hope. One of the lowest points in Charles Spurgeon's ministry came just as he was preparing to preach to more than ten thousand people gathered at the new concert hall in the Royal Surrey Gardens. After he concluded his prayer, someone in the crowd yelled "Fire!" and that the balcony was collapsing, when nothing of the sort was happening. Panic set in and the crowds pushed to exit, while those assembled outside attempted to enter. Seven people were trampled to death and many more injured. Spurgeon was devastated by the loss of precious human life, to the extent that he considered leaving the ministry. When he returned to the pulpit weeks later, he preached "The Exaltation of Christ" from Philippians 2:9–11. It was a way to encourage his congregation and his own soul. He said, "This text afforded sweet consolation to every heir of heaven,"[15] and continued,

> In the midst of calamities, whether they be the wreck of nations, the crash of empires, the heaving of revolutions, or the scourge of war, the great question which [a Christian] asks himself, and asks of others too, is this—Is Christ's kingdom safe? . . . He finds it sufficient consolation, in the midst of all the breaking in pieces which he endures, to think that Christ's throne stands fast and firm, and that though the earth hath rocked beneath *his* feet, yet Christ standeth on a rock which never can be moved. . . . Oh! my soul anticipates that blessed day, when this whole earth shall bend

---

does not offer his own assessment other than relegating the matter to "a mystery of divine and human freedom," 133n7. However, as I have attempted to show here, the text and context of Philippians 2, Romans 14, and Isaiah 45 clearly do not conclude or portray universalism. See O'Brien, NIGTC, 239; Richard R. Melick Jr., *Philippians, Colossians, Philemon*, NAC (Nashville: Holman Reference, 1991), 108; and Moore, "Personal and Cosmic Eschatology," in Akin, *A Theology for the Church*, 702: "Jesus does indeed triumph over all things, making peace through the blood of his cross (Col 1:20), but this peace does not mean the redemption of each individual. Instead, Jesus triumphs over his enemies—as they are all consigned to damnation beneath the feet of his sovereign kingship. Yes, every tongue confesses Jesus as Lord eschatologically— even Satan himself (Phil 2:9–11). This does not mean that every tongue calls out to him for salvation. Instead there is universal recognition that Jesus has triumphed over every rival to his throne. The redeemed will love this truth; the impenitent will lament it."

[15] Charles Spurgeon, "The Exaltation of Christ," November 2, 1856, in *The New Park Street Pulpit*, vol. 2 (1856), http://www.spurgeon.org/sermons/0101.php.

its knee before its God willingly! I do believe there is a happy era coming, when there shall not be one knee unbent before my Lord and Master. . . . But even now, while waiting for that era, my soul rejoices in the fact, that every knee does virtually bow, though not willingly, yet really.[16]

Thus, as those living in an era of religious liberty between the time of Christ's ascension and his certain return, the knowledge of what awaits us on the last day should serve as a warning to all outside of Christ that the freedom to worship other gods without the judgment of the one true God will come to end. For those in Christ, the knowledge of the last day should provide hope that, no matter what trials come or earthly freedoms are diminished, God will make all things new. He will put all things under his feet and declare himself finally triumphant.

Second, these passages remind all that, until that day of judgment comes, each day is a day of grace, and thus it is not too late to repent and believe in Jesus Christ. Russell Moore puts it this way: "Christian eschatology maintains that the 'day of salvation' is *now* (2 Cor 6:2), during this lifetime's temporary suspension of doom. After this the grace of God is not extended—only his justice, and that with severity."[17] Indeed, God kindly tolerates a world that worships things created by humans and other futile systems or philosophies in order that many may come to repentance (Rom 2:4). He is patient, "not wishing that any should perish" (2 Pet 3:9 ESV), and reminds us that "now is the day of salvation" (2 Cor 6:2) because no one knows the day or the hour when he will return (Mark 13:32). Thus, whoever confesses with their tongue and bows in their heart now (Rom 10:9–10) that Jesus is Lord will not perish but have eternal life (John 3:16). As Spurgeon preached,

And now, lastly, beloved, if it be true, as it is, that Christ is so exalted that he is to have a name above every name, and every knee is to bow to him, will we not bow our knees this morning before his Majesty? You must, whether you will or no, one day bow your knee. . . . O that now those that are on earth might willingly

---

[16] Ibid.

[17] Moore, "Personal and Cosmic Eschatology," in Akin, *A Theology for the Church*, 702.

bend their knees lest in hell it should be fulfilled, "Things under the earth shall bow the knee before him."[18]

Whatever happens to the state of religious liberty in the United States and other nations, a final end to religious liberty for all will come with the return of Christ. At that time, there will be no more hope for the lost. Thus, we pursue religious freedom in the present for the sake of others to be saved before the end.

Religious Liberty's End Goal

When thinking of the end of religious liberty, therefore, we should consider not only the warning and hope that comes with the knowledge that one day freedom to worship any god will end but also the purpose of religious freedom in the here and now. That is, what is the *end* goal of religious liberty?

In Philippians 2:11, Paul says that the universal submission of humanity to the lordship of Christ at the end of time takes place "to the glory of God the Father." Bible scholar James Hamilton explains, "Every knee will bow to him (2:10), every tongue confess him Lord, and this is to the glory of the Father (2:11). The life that Paul calls the Philippians to live is based on the glory of God in salvation through judgment accomplished in Christ's death on the cross."[19] The reigning King who made the heavens and the earth should receive honor and glory forever and ever (see 1 Tim 1:17). To the one who put forward his Son as a propitiation so that God the Father might be just and the justifier of all those who fall short of the glory of God (Rom 3:21–26) belongs glory and dominion forever and ever (1 Pet 4:11). The one who gave his Spirit as a Helper to teach, convict (John 14:26; 16:8), and send his children as witnesses to the nations (Acts 1:8), to him be glory in the church, throughout all generations, forever and ever (Eph 3:21). The glory of God in salvation through judgment is the *end* goal of religious liberty on earth.

With that glorious end in mind, we can return to where this conclusion began, with Paul and Silas singing in the Philippian jail: "Then he brought them out and said, 'Sirs, what must I do to be saved?' And they

---

[18] Spurgeon, "The Exaltation of Christ."

[19] James M. Hamilton, *God's Glory in Salvation through Judgment: A Biblical Theology* (Wheaton: Crossway, 2010), 486.

said, 'Believe in the Lord Jesus, and you will be saved, you and your household'" (Acts 16:30–31 ESV). In the middle of their singing, an earthquake interrupted, and the upheaval released Paul and Silas from their chains and confines. Yet instead of running for safety, they remained for the safety of their captor. Knowing that the jailer would receive the death penalty should they escape, they assured him they had not left, and, shaken and afraid, the jailer came to see for himself. Their steadfastness in their punishment, even when given the opportunity for freedom, prompted the jailer to ask how he might escape his own spiritual captivity: "Sirs, what must I do to be saved?"

Paul and Silas were misrepresented, imprisoned unjustly, and robbed of their freedoms, but they did not despair. Instead, entrusting themselves to their faithful Creator, they looked and sang to God, knowing their captivity was temporary, even if it should lead to death. Why did they sing? They sang to God about God to find strength in God.

But their singing also had another purpose: to help those listening learn of the coming judgment of God. Following the earthquake, more important than their freedom was the life of another. So they stayed, because the jailer's eternal destiny was at risk. After the upheaval, they stayed so at least one who heard the good news could repent and believe.

Hope. Warning. Good news that Jesus is Lord shared while there still is time even at the risk of one's security, safety, and rights—all for the glory of God.

This is the true end of religious liberty.

APPENDIX

Baptist Faith and Message 2000
Article XVII: Religious Liberty

God alone is Lord of the conscience, and He has left it free from the doctrines and commandments of men which are contrary to His Word or not contained in it. Church and state should be separate. The state owes to every church protection and full freedom in the pursuit of its spiritual ends. In providing for such freedom no ecclesiastical group or denomination should be favored by the state more than others. Civil government being ordained of God, it is the duty of Christians to render loyal obedience thereto in all things not contrary to the revealed will of God. The church should not resort to the civil power to carry on its work. The gospel of Christ contemplates spiritual means alone for the pursuit of its ends. The state has no right to impose penalties for religious opinions of any kind. The state has no right to impose taxes for the support of any form of religion. A free church in a free state is the Christian ideal, and this implies the right of free and unhindered access to God on the part of all men, and the right to form and propagate opinions in the sphere of religion without interference by the civil power.

Genesis 1:27; 2:7; Matthew 6:6–7,24; 16:26; 22:21; John 8:36; Acts 4:19–20; Romans 6:1–2; 13:1–7; Galatians 5:1,13; Philippians 3:20; 1 Timothy 2:1–2; James 4:12; 1 Peter 2:12–17; 3:11–17; 4:12–19.

"Here We Stand:
An Evangelical Declaration on Marriage"[1]
(June 26, 2015)

As evangelical Christians, we dissent from the court's ruling that redefines marriage. The state did not create the family, and should not try to recreate the family in its own image. We will not capitulate on marriage because biblical authority requires that we cannot. The outcome of the Supreme Court's ruling to redefine marriage represents what seems like the result of a half-century of witnessing marriage's decline through divorce, cohabitation, and a worldview of almost limitless sexual freedom. The Supreme Court's actions pose incalculable risks to an already volatile social fabric by alienating those whose beliefs about marriage are motivated by deep biblical convictions and concern for the common good.

The Bible clearly teaches the enduring truth that marriage consists of one man and one woman. From Genesis to Revelation, the authority of Scripture witnesses to the nature of biblical marriage as uniquely bound to the complementarity of man and woman. This truth is not negotiable. The Lord Jesus himself said that marriage is from the beginning (Matt. 19:4–6), so no human institution has the authority to redefine marriage any more than a human institution has the authority to redefine the gospel, which marriage mysteriously reflects (Eph. 5:32). The Supreme Court's ruling to redefine marriage demonstrates mistaken judgment by disregarding what history and countless civilizations have passed on to us, but it also represents an aftermath that evangelicals themselves, sadly, are not guiltless in contributing to. Too often, professing evangelicals have failed to model the ideals we so dearly cherish and believe are central to gospel proclamation.

Evangelical churches must be faithful to the biblical witness on marriage regardless of the cultural shift. Evangelical churches in America now find themselves in a new moral landscape that calls us to minister in

---

[1] On June 26, 2015, a coalition of evangelical leaders assembled by the Ethics and Religious Liberty Commission released this statement in response to the decision by the Supreme Court to legalize same-sex marriage. See "Here We Stand: An Evangelical Declaration on Marriage," in *Christianity Today*, June 26, 2105, http://www.christianity today.com/ct/2015/june-web-only/here-we-stand-evangelical-declaration-on -marriage.html.

a context growing more hostile to a biblical sexual ethic. This is not new in the history of the church. From its earliest beginnings, whether on the margins of society or in a place of influence, the church is defined by the gospel. We insist that the gospel brings good news to all people, regardless of whether the culture considers the news good or not.

The gospel must inform our approach to public witness. As evangelicals animated by the good news that God offers reconciliation through the life, death, and resurrection of His Son, Jesus, we commit to:

- Respect and pray for our governing authorities even as we work through the democratic process to rebuild a culture of marriage (Rom. 13:1–7);
- teach the truth about biblical marriage in a way that brings healing to a sexually broken culture;
- affirm the biblical mandate that all persons, including LGBT persons, are created in the image of God and deserve dignity and respect;
- love our neighbors regardless of whatever disagreements arise as a result of conflicting beliefs about marriage;
- live respectfully and civilly alongside those who may disagree with us for the sake of the common good;
- cultivate a common culture of religious liberty that allows the freedom to live and believe differently to prosper.

The redefinition of marriage should not entail the erosion of religious liberty. In the coming years, evangelical institutions could be pressed to sacrifice their sacred beliefs about marriage and sexuality in order to accommodate whatever demands the culture and law require. We do not have the option to meet those demands without violating our consciences and surrendering the gospel. We will not allow the government to coerce or infringe upon the rights of institutions to live by the sacred belief that only men and women can enter into marriage.

The gospel of Jesus Christ determines the shape and tone of our ministry. Christian theology considers its teachings about marriage both timeless and unchanging, and therefore we must stand firm in this belief. Outrage and panic are not the responses of those confident in the promises of a reigning Christ Jesus. While we believe the Supreme Court has erred in its ruling, we pledge to stand steadfastly, faithfully witnessing to the biblical teaching that marriage is the chief cornerstone of society, designed to unite men, women, and children. We promise to proclaim and live this truth at all costs, with convictions that are communicated with kindness and love.

Resolution on Religious Liberty
Southern Baptist Convention Annual Meeting
Russellville, Kentucky (1866)

We solemnly resolve, in the face of the world, and in the fear of God—

1. That we believe civil government to be of divine appointment, and that magistrates should be prayed for, and obeyed, in all things, not contrary to the rights of conscience and the revealed will of Christ.

2. That Christ is the Supreme Ruler, of the Church—that it is his prerogative to put men into the gospel ministry, and that they are amenable only to him for the discharge of its functions—that all interference with these functions [is] on the part of conscience; and that when the claims of civil rulers come in conflict with those of Christ, it is our duty to "obey God rather than men," and endure the consequences.

3. That we express our sincere sympathy and high regard for those ministers, who, in following the dictates of their consciences, and maintaining the authority of their Supreme Lawgiver, have cheerfully submitted to fines, imprisonments, and other "pains and penalties," and that we will earnestly pray that rulers may be so considerate and just, and that Christian ministers may be so discreet and upright, that the cause of Christ may not be hindered, and the name of God [may not be] blasphemed.

4. That in adoption [of] these resolutions, the Convention expressly disavow any disposition to interfere with political affairs, and have regard solely to the question of religious liberty.

Resolution Concerning Freedom of Religion
Southern Baptist Convention Annual Meeting
Memphis, Tennessee (1935)

1. That we hereby reaffirm our devotion to the fundamental New Testament doctrine and fundamental principle of the American government, the separation of church and state; religion must be kept free from

all entangling alliances with government and government must not assume patronage, sponsorship or control over religion in any form.

2. That we also declare it to be our abiding conviction that this fundamental doctrine of the New Testament and sacred principle of government cannot be maintained if and when the government becomes the financial sponsor for churches, provides financial subsidies for churches or other religious institutions, or appropriates money out of the public treasury to sectarian institutions.

3. That we would call the attention of Southern Baptist pastors and churches to these matters and would urge them with all diligence to maintain this doctrine in all of their activities and relationships and at all costs to abstain from borrowing money from the government, receiving the financial endorsement of the government and receiving appropriations of funds from the public treasury, whether national or state.

4. That we would enter our earnest protest against the violation of this principle by any Baptist church or Baptist Institution or by others, and especially against the appropriation or application of public funds to sectarian institutions of whatever name or order.

Resolution on Religious Liberty
Southern Baptist Convention Annual Meeting
Atlantic City, New Jersey (1964)

In this anniversary year we are grateful for the witness which our Baptist movement has been privileged to bear. The discernment of the call of God in Christ has led us to a glorious experience of evangelism and missionary outreach through the power of the Holy Spirit.

Our leaders and our people have firmly rejected the use of the coercive powers of government in the realm of religion. Baptists had much to do with writing the First Amendment into the Constitution of the United States and have been in the forefront in preserving the religious liberty that our nation has enjoyed. We have unflinchingly declared our desire for separation of church and state in resolutions, in sermons and in policies and practices. "In applying this principle to the field of public education, we affirm the historic right of our schools to full academic freedom for the pursuit of all knowledge, religious or otherwise." Motion carried.

1. We, the messengers of the Convention hereby affirm our support for the concepts and the vocabulary of the First Amendment, including both its prohibition upon government roles in religious programs and its protection of free exercise of religion for the people.

2. We enunciate our concern that public officials and public servants of all types shall have the same free exercise of religion as other citizens, but that this freedom does not entitle them to use public or official powers for the advancement of religious commitments or ideas. In applying this principle to the field of public education, we affirm the historic right of our schools to full academic freedom for the pursuit of all knowledge, religious or otherwise.

3. We appeal to the Congress of the United States to allow the First Amendment of the Constitution of the United States to stand as our guarantee of religious liberty, and we oppose the adoption of any further amendment to that Constitution respecting establishment of religion of free exercise thereof.

4. We urge all our channels, leaders, and churches to involve themselves thoroughly in study of the biblical, the historical, and the contemporary issues related to religious liberty to the end that our heritage of freedom and responsibility under God may be clearly understood and appreciated by the next generation and by ever larger proportions of the world's peoples.

On Religious Liberty
Southern Baptist Convention Annual Meeting
Phoenix, Arizona (2003)

WHEREAS, We, as Southern Baptists, hold that the Scripture is the inspired and inerrant Word of God and the supreme standard by which all human conduct, creeds, and religious opinions should be tried; and

WHEREAS, We join millions of other evangelicals in affirming the exclusive claims of Jesus Christ as God and the only Savior and in affirming the necessity of personal faith in Him (John 14:6), truths which are at the very heart of the Christian faith; and

WHEREAS, Genuine faith, by definition, cannot be coerced or legislated; and

WHEREAS, Southern Baptists and other evangelicals have been subject to intense criticism for our insistence that a faith, which engenders or encourages religious persecution or interferes with free exercise of religion, is not consistent with the revelation of God; and

WHEREAS, Southern Baptists and other evangelical Christians have in recent months been increasingly portrayed by the media and by international government sources as intolerant and even dangerous because of our commitment to Christ as the only way of salvation; and

WHEREAS, The basic human right of religious liberty was formulated in America originally by freedom-loving activists, many of whom also cherished the confidence that only in Jesus could one know God; and

WHEREAS, It has become apparent that many in government and media have forgotten or willingly misrepresented the long history of Baptists as determined advocates of freedom, especially religious liberty; and

WHEREAS, There is a growing movement to label the preaching of the Christian gospel a "hate crime"; now, therefore, be it

RESOLVED, That the messengers to the Southern Baptist Convention meeting in Phoenix, Arizona, June 17–18, 2003, call upon the media, government, and society at large to recognize that Baptists have been and continue to be ardent advocates of religious liberty; and be it further

RESOLVED, That we call on all social orders professing to desire the best for their citizens to embrace absolute religious liberty as a basic and essential human right; and be it further

RESOLVED, That we remind the international community that religious liberty is not merely the right to remain in the religion of one's birth, but includes the right of anyone to change his religious loyalties without fear of persecution; and be it finally

RESOLVED, That we call on the government of the United States of America not only to continue the most vigorous support of the First Amendment to the United States Constitution at home, but also to protect this most basic and essential liberty of people around the world by openly advocating this freedom for all and by considering candidates for government assistance on the basis of their willingness to protect their citizens against all forms of religious discrimination and persecution.

On Protecting Religious Liberty
Southern Baptist Convention Annual Meeting
New Orleans, Louisiana (2012)

WHEREAS, God has made the human conscience inviolable (Romans 2:14–15; 1 Corinthians 4:3–5; 8:12; 10:29); and

WHEREAS, God has granted to all human beings the freedom to worship or not to worship according to the dictates of their consciences (Matthew 23:37; Revelation 3:20); and

WHEREAS, History is replete with examples of the disastrous results of governmental efforts to interfere with individual conscience and religious belief; and

WHEREAS, Our Baptist forebears suffered great persecution from civil authorities, including beatings, imprisonment, and death because of their commitment to the inviolable nature of conscience and faith; and

WHEREAS, The First Amendment to the United States Constitution protects United States citizens from any interference by the Federal Government in their "free exercise" of religion; and

WHEREAS, The Department of Health and Human Services has determined that all health care plans under the Patient Protection and Affordable Care Act (PPACA) must provide free of charge contraceptives and abortion causing drugs and devices, even if such provisions violate the faith convictions of religious employers, health plan providers, and participants; and

WHEREAS, President Obama and his administration is requiring health plans under PPACA to maintain a separate abortion fund supported by a premium surcharge on health plan participants regardless of their religiously-informed convictions about abortion; and

WHEREAS, The Justice Department (Hosanna-Tabor Evangelical Lutheran Church and School v. EEOC, 2012) has asserted that government has the authority to determine which ministries of a church qualify for First Amendment staffing protections, in clear violation of the biblical teaching that churches are unique institutions by virtue of their divine origin (Matthew 16:18); and

WHEREAS, The United States military is currently engaged in efforts to normalize homosexual behavior in the armed services, threatening the ability of chaplains to perform ministry according to the dictates of their consciences and the teachings of their faith; and

WHEREAS, The Justice Department has argued that the federal definition of marriage as the union of one man and one woman is unconstitutional, threatening the ability of religious business owners and religious organizations to offer their services to those only who share their faith convictions about marriage; now, therefore, be it

RESOLVED, That the messengers to the Southern Baptist Convention meeting in New Orleans, Louisiana, June 19–20, 2012, steadfastly object to the administration's efforts to undermine the religious liberty of American citizens; and be it further

RESOLVED, That we call on President Obama to instruct the Department of Health and Human Services to withdraw its insistence that health care plans provide contraceptives and abortion causing drugs and devices and instead exempt from this requirement all religious organizations and people of faith, whether in their private capacity or as employers, who declare a religious objection to such coverage; and be it further

RESOLVED, That we deplore the provision in the PPACA that sets up a separate abortion fund in health care plans as well as the administration's efforts to require United States citizens to pay for abortion through their health care premiums contrary to the dictates of their faith; and be it further

RESOLVED, That we declare our support for the Constitution's recognition of the unique nature of the church and insist that the Justice Department retract its offensive, unconstitutional attitude toward the church; and be it further

RESOLVED, That we wholeheartedly support the ministry of chaplains in the United States military and call on the Obama administration to instruct our military leaders to ensure the freedom of chaplains to minister to members of the armed services according to the dictates of the chaplains' consciences without fear or coercion; and be it further

RESOLVED, That we express our deepest appreciation for every person who serves in the armed services of our nation and call on the Obama administration to guarantee the right of those who have volunteered to serve to express their religious convictions about homosexual behavior without fear of reprisal; and be it further

RESOLVED, That we call on the Justice Department to cease its efforts to overturn the Defense of Marriage Act and instead engage in a vigorous effort to defend this law of the land from every challenge; and be it finally

RESOLVED, That we pledge to defend the God-given and constitutionally guaranteed right of every American citizen to worship God freely in thought, word, and action, according to the dictates of his or her conscience.

CONTRIBUTORS

Jason G. Duesing, provost and associate professor of historical theology, Midwestern Baptist Theological Seminary

Barrett Duke, vice president for public policy and research and director of the Research Institute, the Ethics and Religious Liberty Commission of the Southern Baptist Convention

Evan Lenow, assistant professor of ethics, Bobby L. and Janis Eklund Chair of Stewardship, director of the Richard Land Center for Cultural Engagement, director of the Center for Biblical Stewardship, and chair of the ethics department, The Southwestern Baptist Theological Seminary

R. Albert Mohler Jr., president and Joseph Emerson Brown Professor of Christian Theology, The Southern Baptist Theological Seminary

Russell D. Moore, president, the Ethics and Religious Liberty Commission of the Southern Baptist Convention

Paige Patterson, president and professor of theology, Southwestern Baptist Theological Seminary

Andrew T. Walker, director of policy studies, the Ethics and Religious Liberty Commission of the Southern Baptist Convention

Thomas White, president and professor of systematic theology, Cedarville University

Travis Wussow, director of international justice and religious liberty and general counsel, the Ethics and Religious Liberty Commission of the Southern Baptist Convention

Malcolm B. Yarnell III, professor of systematic theology, director of the Oxford study program, director of the Center for Theological Research, and chair of the systematic theology department, Southwestern Baptist Theological Seminary

INDEX